Corporate Politics for IT Managers

Corporate Politics for IT Managers

How to get streetwise

Keith Patching and Robina Chatham

OXFORD AUCKLAND BOSTON JOHANNESBURG MELBOURNE NEW DELHI

Butterworth-Heinemann
Linacre House, Jordan Hill, Oxford OX2 8DP
225 Wildwood Avenue, Woburn, MA 01801-2041
A division of Reed Educational and Professional Publishing Ltd

A member of the Reed Elsevier plc group

First published 2000

British Library Cataloguing in Publication Data
Patching, Keith
Corporate politics for IT managers
1. Executives – Promotion 2. Success in business
3. Information for technology – Management
I. Title II. Chatham, Robina
658.4'09

ISBN 0 7506 4792 2

Library of Congress Cataloguing in Publication Data
Patching, Keith.
Corporate politics for IT managers: how to get streetwise/Keith Patching and Robina Chatham.
p. cm – (Butterworth-Heinemann/Computer Weekly Professional series)
Includes Index.
ISBN 0 7506 4792 2
1. Information technology – Management. 2. Office politics. 2. I. Chatham, Robina. II. Title. III. Computer weekly professional series
HD30.37.P375
650.1'3'0880904–dc21 00–036052

Typeset by Avocet Typeset, Brill, Aylesbury, Bucks
Printed and bound in Great Britain by Martins the Printers, Scotland

Contents

About the authors vii
Butterworth-Heinemann/*Computer Weekly* Professional Series ix
Foreword xiii
Preface xv
Acknowledgements xvii
The cartoons – notes on the characters xix
Introduction – the IT tribe xxvii

Part One What's the problem? 1
1 The IT stereotype and organizational politics 3

Part Two I'm just trying to do my job! 11
2 Coping with the stereotype 13
3 The phantom IT strategy 16
4 Projects – the illusion of being managed 22
5 Staying alive 45
6 Writes of passage 55
7 Meetings (of minds?) 65
8 Reinventing the wheel 79
9 Firefighting and rework 87
10 Shattering the illusion 93

Part Three Why won't other people let me do my job? 97
11 Leading, managing and abdicating 99
12 Recruiting into the tribe 111
13 Talk to me 122
14 Where are you when we want you? 128
15 Lock horns and push 139
16 Business priorities and culture – the unspoken agenda 143
17 Breaking the taboo – marketing IT services 152
18 Suppliers and consultants – the wolves at the door 163

19 Let someone else do it for a change 170

Part Four Becoming streetwise 177

20 Shades of grey 179
21 Say hello to the rest of your brain 188
22 Blowing the whistle 203
23 All stressed out and nowhere to go 208
24 Lighten up a little 218
25 IQ is not everything 224
26 The road to Damascus 237
27 You lead; I'll follow 258
28 The front row of the grid 278
29 Where am I going? 284

Part Five Riding off into the sunset 293

30 You are not alone 295

Appendix: Leadership questionnaire 305
Index 311

About the authors

Keith Patching uses his background in psychology and social anthropology to understand how people learn, and what makes one manager different from another. He specializes in management development through writing, teaching and one-to-one coaching and counselling, developing strategies that are geared to the psyche and style of each individual. Having been the manager of ICL's Management Centre, he has significant experience of the particular problems and issues facing IT people.

Robina Chatham has 14 years' experience in IT management, culminating in the position of European IT Director for a leading merchant bank. She started her career as a mechanical engineer within the shipbuilding industry, where she pioneered the introduction of computing onto the shopfloor. This sparked off an early interest in the people issues associated with IT. Now turned an academic and psychologist, she uses her real world experience to help senior IT managers improve their personal impact and influence within a business context.

Butterworth-Heinemann/ *Computer Weekly* Professional Series

John Riley, Managing Editor, *Computer Weekly*
David Taylor, CERTUS
Terry White, AIS, Johannesburg

There are few professions which require as much continuous updating as that of the IT executive. Not only does the hardware and software scene change relentlessly, but also ideas about the actual management of the IT function are being continuously modified, updated and changed. Thus keeping abreast of what is going on is really a major task.

The Butterworth Heinemann/*Computer Weekly* Professional Series has been created to assist IT executives keep up-to-date with the management ideas and issues of which they need to be aware.

Aims and objectives

One of the key objectives of the series is to reduce the time it takes for leading edge management ideas to move from the academic and consulting environments into the hands of the IT practitioner. Thus, this series employs appropriate technology to speed up the publishing process. Where appropriate some books are supported by CD-ROM or by additional information or templates located on the publisher's web site (http://www.bh.com).

This series provides IT professionals with an opportunity to build up a bookcase of easily accessible but detailed information on the important issues that they need to be aware of to successfully perform their jobs as they move into the new millennium.

Would you like to be part of this series?

Aspiring or already established authors are invited to get in touch with me if they would like to be published in this series:

Dr Dan Remenyi, Series Editor (Remenyi@compuserve.com)

Series titles

IT investment – Making a business case
Effective measurement and management of IT – Costs and benefits
Stop IT project failures through risk management
Subnet design for efficient networks
Understand the Internet
How to manage the IT help desk
Delivering business value from IT
How to become a successful IT consultant
Prince version 2: A practical handbook
Considering computer contracting?
A hackers guide to project management
Inside track: provocative insights into the world of IT in business
Revitalising the IT department
Delivering IT strategies
Information warfare
Strategic planning for an e-business
Knowledge management for IT professionals

Foreword

This book is a must if you are already an IT manager or aspire to be one. It is a breath of fresh air – a serious message presented with both insight and humour.

The quality of IT management is crucial to the strategic success of the knowledge economy. Organizations need IT managers who are skilful at navigating organizational politics while delivering technical projects of high quality. IT managers need a career which is both rewarding and fun. Here is a book which will help bridge the gulf where IT managers all too often find themselves stranded.

This is a book which will help you deal with the challenges. It offers practical advice on how to grow and market your personal and managerial talents. For those with an eye on the boardroom, it provides insight on how to gain the necessary recognition.

It is up to each individual to choose what they wish to do about the issues raised. If a fraction of those who read the book do something positive with the ideas presented here the state of UK plc will be for ever enriched. There will also be an important and influential group of IT managers whose careers are fulfilled and are shaping future business organizations.

Judith Scott
Chief Executive
British Computer Society

Preface

This book is about becoming streetwise in the boardroom. It is dedicated to the many IT managers we have known and worked with who have, year after year, complained that no one will listen to them.

It is a serious book, but with a humorous slant. Our 'hero' is Martin, the archetypal IT manager, supported by Terminal One, his only true friend. Martin is not, by nature, streetwise. Our hope is that, by the time we get to the end of the book, he will become so. He appears throughout in cartoon form. He tackles the kinds of challenges that IT managers throughout the world tackle, and he suffers their frustrations.

There is a bit of Martin in all of us; there is a bit more in all of us who are IT managers, including you, if that's your job. And one bit of Martin that many of us share is a sensitivity to criticism, both direct and implied. Well, there's a lot of implied criticism in this book, but all of us, from time to time, have to accept some painful truths if we are serious about changing our behaviour for the better.

We are in the business of management development. This book is the fruits of our experience in helping real IT managers become more politically astute and to 'reinvent' themselves. Our work forces IT managers to take it on the chin. It isn't everyone else's fault. You must deal with the frustrations yourself. Many of them are of your own making.

If you're still reading this, welcome on board. It's a bumpy ride, but if you hang on in there, you may, like some of our protégés, be able to say that, taking this route, users who have always been political assassins in the past are now 'putty in my hands'.

Keith Patching and Robina Chatham
k.patching@cranfield.ac.uk
r.chatham@cranfield.ac.uk

Acknowledgements

This book has been significantly helped along by the following, who we'd like to thank. Firstly, vineyards in France, especially those producing excellent Chablis. Our thanks also go greatly to John and Alison for putting up with partners often more distracted by writing than focused on domesticity.

Colleagues at Cranfield have helped in a variety of ways, although we have shied away from showing them too much of what we have written, in case it shocks them. And clearly, we owe a debt of gratitude to the ever increasing number of friends and colleagues who have chosen to spend time with us, either at Cranfield or elsewhere, sharing in the learning about organizational politics and IT management. Many of their stories live on in our text or cartoons.

Vital work has been done by Robina's mum in helping with the proofreading, and by Sox and Freeway for their purr…fect encouragement. And we'd also like to thank our publishers for their courage in publishing a book which may irritate a number of readers.

Thoughts on anthropology
With essence of philosophy
Will lift life in technology
If seasoned with psychology.

Margaret Chatham, September 1999

Acknowledgements

The cartoons – notes on the characters

Introduction – why not human characters?

The characters in the cartoons are not human. This is deliberate. First, we are dealing with a number of stereotypes. As our research indicates, the way many people view IT professionals (and many others, such as estate agents and accountants) is through stereotypical images. Non-human characters emphasise these stereotypes and make the point better.

Secondly, we are trying at all times to entertain and educate. IT people, the majority of the potential readers of the cartoons, may take a little longer to latch onto the symbolism of non-human characters. But by forcing them to make the extra intuitive leap, we shall be engaging the parts of the brain which they often let lie dormant. The more we can help them work with imagination and metaphor, the better they ought to become in dealing with ambiguity and complexity.

The key characters themselves

Martin, the IT manager – a sound-activated tin can

Martin is our hero. Intelligent, dedicated, devoted, hard-working, he is the stereotypical IT manager. He really does want the best for everyone, and is convinced that IT can change the world – if only people would listen. But Martin is often disappointed by the 'luddites'. People often seem to misunderstand him; they fail to listen and to learn. They may even treat him with a degree of contempt.

Martin has a tendency to withdraw when people are unkind to him. He feels that many of his most senior colleagues are selfish – putting their own interests before those of the organization. They play political games which Martin does not approve of. He knows that, if he tried to play the same games, he would not win.

Martin is a tin can; computer salespeople talk of 'selling tin'. Martin is very closely associated with the computers he manages. He wears headphones to listen to music while he programs the computers; he wears dark glasses to ward off the bright lights of political reality. The world is often a bit much for Martin, who suppresses his senses to make life just that bit more bearable. As a sound-activated tin can, he may sometimes be seen to be dancing to the tunes of his masters.

Terminal One – Martin's intelligent terminal

Terminal One is Martin's best friend. This is because Term (his pet name) is not complicated with political intrigue or ambiguity. Martin knows where he is with Term.

Terminal One is logical, intelligent, predictable, persistent and totally naïve: a good foil for Martin. Unfortunately, Term is often too logical even for Martin, whose human frailties can be exposed by his best friend's complete honesty.

The sheep – Martin's staff

Sheep are innocent, harmless, naïve and vulnerable. But they have fun as lambs, and as they grow older, can become very light on their feet, climbing over rocks and pathways which humans find too slippery and dangerous.

Martin's staff have a very wry sense of humour. They know that Martin is the boss, but they are not averse to having the occasional sarcastic dig at him. They do not want the trappings of management, delighting in the simple life of grazing on their programs, and being protected from the foxes by Martin and the other senior folks.

The finance director – Martin's boss

Martin's boss is even more logical than Martin; but he is also much harder. He hovers menacingly over the organization shrieking 'downsize, downsize!' and 'rip out costs!'

The finance director (FD) has very little patience with Martin, whom he sees as a wimp. Martin is always getting technical with him; Martin is too soft on the users, and has trouble saying 'no'. Martin is terrified of his boss – with very good reason.

The marketing director – Martin's most important internal customer

The sporty marketing director is in complete contrast to Martin. This director is sharp, fast, and likes the good life. He dines out at expensive restaurants, and has a very laid back attitude to life in general. He is cynical and streetwise. He plays the political game like a world champion.

The marketing director has very little time for IT in general, and for Martin in particular. He does not dislike Martin, but pities his naïve view of the world. However, as IT becomes increasingly important to the business, the marketing director is beginning to get frustrated with Martin's slowness and his pedantic ways. There could be some difficult times ahead for Martin's relationship with this slippery customer.

Derek Meadows – works for a school of management

Martin has realized that it be a good idea for him to undergo some management development. He attends courses at Derek Meadows Management Development.

The tutor, Derek Meadows himself, is a caring and experienced management developer who has a particularly soft spot for IT people. His approach is based upon the need for IT people (and other managers) to understand themselves as much as it is to understanding management theory. Derek constantly tries to help Martin to develop himself through gaining greater access to the less intellectual side of his personality.

The chairman – Martin's role model

The company chairman does not have a lot to do with Martin. He is rarely to be seen, but is a powerful figurehead. Martin is in awe of him, even though at times, Martin thinks the chairman is a bit out of touch with the technological realities of modern business.

The chairman likes to take the global view, and will occasionally be prepared to attend presentations on IT. He generally understands nothing of what he hears, but in good avuncular fashion, will feign interest, and will congratulate when he can.

The computer salesman – a fox

Martin hates having to deal with suppliers. The fox-like salesman always seems to be able to smooth-talk his way to deals which Martin later regrets – or is unsure about. There's nothing obviously wrong with the salesman – he is suave, sophisticated, apparently friendly and always good for a laugh. But somehow he is not to be trusted. To him, IT people are sheep to be fleeced. After shearing they are cold and naked. But their fleece grows back after a while – ready for another round of negotiations.

The salesman is a frequent visitor. He says that it is to make sure that Martin and his colleagues are kept right up to date with the latest developments. Martin suspects that the fox's motives are not so altruistic. The more often he visits, the more he is likely to sell.

The personnel director – a frog

The frog lives on the edge of the pond – neither in nor out. He is pedantically correct, and knows the rules inside out. He has big eyes with which to see everything which goes on in the organization, but he keeps most of it to himself

Martin does not like the personnel director. He thinks he is unfair in his dealings with the IT department, treating them with less respect than they deserve. Unfortunately, Martin's knowledge of employment law, and of the company's policies is woefully small. The frog can leap over him with a single bound.

However, as time passes, Martin recognizes that the personnel director holds a great deal of promise. As Martin recognizes the potential value of personal and management development, he may come to strike a deal with the frog. Will Martin be the princess who kisses the potential prince?

The consultant – a magnifying glass

Consultants are frequent visitors to Martin's shop, often called in by Martin's boss rather than Martin himself. Martin has a healthy scepticism about consultants, who he feels often work against him rather than for him. He is cautious of their slick use of words, and their questionable motives.

But Martin has to admit (when he is feeling strong) that many of the consultants he works with do have a disarming ability to magnify situations strongly

enough to bring them into the kind of focus needed to understand them. But time and again, that clearly viewed situation is uncomfortable for Martin. His frailties are so often exposed. And Martin feels that, perhaps, the consultant could be a little more supportive, a little less brutal, in the ways in which otherwise hidden truths come into view.

Martin's wife – a mystery to Martin

Martin is happily married. He is a home-loving man, and likes to think that he is a devoted husband. But like many married men, he is not always as well in tune with this wife's needs as she would like him to be. He can be insensitive and clumsy, even though he has absolutely no desire to hurt her.

Martin is just a little frightened of his wife's almost witch-like ability to read him (and other people). Somehow she seems able to know things about him and others which Martin cannot see even about himself. He calls it 'women's intuition', but secretly knows that her empathy is something which he ought to know how to develop in himself.

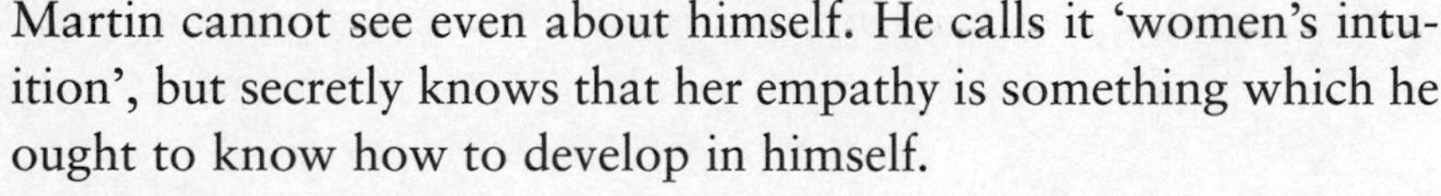

Introduction – the IT tribe

This introduction is written for the benefit of non-IT readers. It sets the scene and introduces some of the challenges IT managers face from a non-technical perspective.

The IT revolution – like, when?

As we become increasingly aware of the human side of progress, we in the western world are turning to non-technical disciplines to help answer some of our more difficult questions. We are surrounded by 'gurus' who jostle with each other to foretell ever stranger stories of the technological futures which await us, as we harness the microchip with greater and greater proficiency. But so many of the predictions which have been made over the past thirty or more years about the kind of society which technical progress can offer have failed to materialize.

Do we really want, for example, a 'paperless office'? If so, why have we singularly failed to achieve it, given how many years it has apparently been within our grasp.

Just because something is possible it may not be desirable. It is possible to run all our businesses electronically these days. Despite the complaints of IT providers that, in the phrase 'paperless office'

what they really meant was 'less paper' and not 'no paper', the vision which they often presented was paper free. Yet it hasn't happened, and is unlikely to happen – at least for quite some time. Adaptable though we humans are, there are some aspects of who we are which seem to resist the lure of technology-induced change. Human societies have been evolving for millions of years; the microchip has been with us for less than a generation. Maybe we ought to look beyond technology for some clues as to how we may adapt technology to ourselves, rather than the other way round.

Anthropology and society

The subject matter of anthropology is society in all its various forms. One of the tasks of anthropology during the past century or so has been to record the multiplicity of ways in which the human spirit has manifested itself in culture after culture, from South Africa to New Guinea, from Brazil to Greece. Its role has changed with the advent of the 'global village'. No longer are there 'lost tribes of the Amazon'; the question is, are there 'lost tribes' hidden within our own societies?

But anthropology has not only been concerned with recording difference. It has also noted 'similarities'. Many anthropologists have observed that, despite differences of language and expression, there are a number of patterns of human culture which recur in every recorded society: the use of language; some form of pair-bonding; the telling of stories and myths to pass on the important truths, and so on.

It may be, therefore, that anthropology has a role to play in helping us to identify how we may respond to the opportunities of IT. Will IT transform us into yet more strange and new forms of society? Or will it simply have to fit into the universal patterns of culture which human evolution has established indelibly upon us?

IT people – a different kind of tribe?

One way of exploring these questions is to turn the anthropological lens onto those people directly responsible for delivering IT to the rest of us: the IT professionals. Are they a tribe apart from the rest of us, or are they simply a sub-culture, or caste, within the broader 'tribe' of organizational and business life?

One of the ways of distinguishing different tribes from each other is by language. By this yardstick, IT people almost definitely form a different tribe. Their language is hard to penetrate, and they seem to have very little inclination to learn our own language. This makes communication between us very difficult. And the anthropological record shows that poor communication is often associated with tribal warfare. According to this observation, there should be frequent hostilities between business people and IT people. The evidence is unarguable – the skirmishes which take place at every opportunity can sometimes spill over into full-scale war in the offices of our organizations.

Like most 'aliens' IT people have a number of characteristics which make them different from the rest of us; like many aliens, many of these differences are based upon stereotypes rather than direct observation. What we know about the French, the Australian Aborigines, and the native North Americans is rarely based upon painstaking personal research. It is based upon the limited amount of data anyone needs before feeling sufficiently confident that they can pass judgements upon them.

Stereotyping is morally unwelcome in today's politically correct Western culture; but it is the same mental phenomenon which allowed our forebears to recognize danger in an instant and live long enough to breed. Taking time to check the validity of first impressions could be fatal in the wild. And the mental equipment which kept us in the evolutionary race for millions of years is not going to roll over and die just because it is not considered politically correct to jump to hasty conclusions these days.

The human mind thrives on generalizations. The study of almost any subject (be it mathematics or sociology, history or biology) depends upon generalizations. So when we study the possibility of there being a 'tribe' of IT people, we focus upon those generalizations. Calling them stereotypes is challenging but accurate.

The IT stereotype

The IT stereotype, then, is a generalized description of 'your average IT person'. Like any generalization, it may actually describe no one individual at all. But its strength lies in its generalizability; it allows non-IT people to be prepared to 'know' in advance what to expect. Unfortunately, as we know only too well, this tends to create a filter through which the actual IT person is viewed. Self-fulfilling prophecies are created in this way. It is a shame; but it is human nature.

In preparing for this book, and for much of the work we do professionally with IT people, we undertook some research. We wanted to answer the age-old question:

'Why hasn't IT delivered on its promises?'

But instead of seeking the answers in the technology or the structures of organizations, or in economics, or any other of those areas which had been thoroughly excavated before, we asked about people.

We interviewed hundreds of senior managers. Some were IT managers, but most were not. Most were the business managers who use IT rather than supply it. We asked these managers about the people who deliver IT services to them. We asked them to describe these people – to characterize them. As more and more descriptions were recorded, it became more and more apparent that many if not most business managers have a set of similar views about IT people in general. They may vary these views as they describe each individual IT person, but these variations are just that – variations on a theme. That theme is the IT stereotype.

In some ways it is like the stereotype of the estate agent, the accountant, or the second-hand car dealer. It is a shorthand caricature. It may not apply in fact to any individual, but it prepares us for 'the worst'. Moreover, it colours how business managers *expect* IT people to behave. Expectations are often fulfilled (they become self-fulfilling prophecies) as business people interpret the language and behaviour of IT people through the filters of the stereotype; constantly, largely unconsciously, looking for behaviours which confirm their view, and dismissing behaviours which do not fit in with the paradigm. Not surprisingly, each encounter is both an example of the stereotype and a reinforcement of it.

So the following description is not our view – it is the collective (partly unconscious) view which many business managers hold about IT people in general. If it offends, don't blame us, blame the collective unconscious of the business community.

Among the characteristics of the stereotypical IT person are comfort with logic, facts and data, but a significant lack of comfort with ambiguity and unpredictability. Their world is black and white, and one in which shades of grey are avoided. According to the stereotype, IT people are unimaginative, and do not think laterally or creatively. They are poor at dealing with moral and ethical dilemmas, and avoid making decisions where there are no 'provable' right or wrong answers, preferring to follow clear and unambiguous rules.

IT people are also perceived to be lacking in interpersonal skills. Particularly weak areas include:

- Relationship building, and working as a team within a business context.
- Influencing positively and constructively.
- Dealing with conflict.
- Saying 'no'.
- Communicating in business language.
- Networking among their peers and external business contacts.
- Leadership.

What is more, they do not always create the right image; their dress and posture do not engender business confidence. This reputation is often reinforced by IT professionals' behaviour such as:

- Flippancy and off-handedness.
- Poorly timed campaigns.
- Politically naive remarks.
- Fighting the 'wrong' battles.
- Not knowing when to back down.
- Using inappropriate judgements – intellectual rather than moral or ethical.
- Failing to canvass opinion, and to build relationships and partnerships.
- Not knowing the difference between ownership of ideas and possessiveness.

- Lack of sensitivity to and empathy for others' feelings or needs.

Many IT managers know they have an image problem, but are unable or unwilling to confront the issue. Some literally go into hiding to avoid hearing painful comments about themselves, and some escape into other professions (such as academia and contracting). Many live out the self-fulfilling prophecy, 'I can't win, so there's no point in trying'.

As a consequence, IT managers are often politically naive. They perceive political behaviour as manipulative and unscrupulous, and many therefore engage in avoidance tactics. IT managers have little business knowledge, acumen, or in some cases, interest. They see themselves almost exclusively as IT people, rather than as business managers within their organizations' industry. Their loyalties are to the IT profession rather than to their organization. The business often does not choose to develop general business skills in its IT people, and they themselves often do not seek such development.

It is small wonder that we have not been swept away by the IT tribe. Technologically advanced they may be, but they seem to lack the persuasive powers to lure us into their vision of the future. Viewed as a tribe, they seem doomed to extinction. For many, the letters CIO stand for 'Career Is Over'.

Yet the technological revolution is agreed by almost everyone to be a reality. If we are not to be overrun by the IT tribe, how can they maintain their hold over our imagination as they do?

Tribe or shamans?

Although there is a good deal to be said for studying IT people as a tribe, there seems to be even more value in studying them as 'shamans'.

In many cultures (but less overtly so now that 'magic' has been

'replaced' by science), the mystical 'truths' have been the preserve of groups or individuals within society who do not form a separate 'tribe' but have a special role or roles. These are generically referred to as 'shamans'.

Characterized as having access to powers most ordinary folk cannot get hold of, shamans have often had their own cult status within their respective societies. They learn strange, often incomprehensible dialects, and are treated with a mix of awe for their powers, and contempt for their often 'anti-social' behaviours. Many are not allowed to marry or enjoy the normal pleasures of acceptance within society. They maintain their self-worth by becoming ever more distant and incoherent, locking themselves away until called on to cure some ailment, or deal with some natural disaster. When they do emerge, their behaviour is often unpredictable, so people not directly involved with the immediate situation often steer well clear.

As Western 'civilization' 'takes over' many indigenous cultures, shamans tend either to reintegrate themselves into the mainstream, or to set themselves even further apart, setting up exclusive cults which are open only to the minority who reject the ordinariness of the evolving culture.

Integrating IT into the mainstream

The circumstances which allowed IT people to develop shamanistic roles within our organizations are fading away with the onset of 'chips with everything'. IT is no longer associated with the 'computer'; it lives in our cars, our video recorders, our cameras, and our washing machines. Increasingly we are adopting technologies in which 'fuzzy logic' operates.

'Fuzzy logic' has its roots in Eastern philosophy, rather than in the essentially black and white logic which has dominated Western thinking since the time of the ancient Greek philosophers. Consequently, while we in the West have struggled unsuccessfully for years to create 'artificial intelligence' machines based upon the binary notation which lies at the heart of our computers, Eastern technologists have been able to create cost-effective intelligences which break through the barriers of binary thinking.

The mainframe computer, like almost all Western computers, was built on binary logic. Because of its size and complexity, it became the archetypal religious artefact of the shamanistic IT person; the mystical manifestation of the IT shaman's power. The supporting myths (the mainframe is down) and rituals (the Friday payroll run) have begun to lose their sway. Ordinary folk have now learnt the arts of the IT shaman; we are (or can be, if we want) all shamans now.

So if we can make anything happen that we want, what are we likely to want?

The internet, virtual worlds, global positioning, instant communications with anyone anywhere are all available right now. As we sit next to people at dinner, we can choose to talk to them, or by our mobile phones to people we would prefer to talk to. Co-location is now no longer a determinant of who we deal with, communicate with, or even (I suspect in the near future) procreate with.

For a while these opportunities will present us with a number of 'moral imperatives'. As an example of a 'moral imperative' consider travel. It is perfectly feasible for many people of our generation to travel for their holidays anywhere in the world. No longer are people constrained by distance or expense; people do not have to be millionaires to go on safari to Africa, to visit the Taj Mahal, to go walkabout in the Australian outback, or to live the nomadic life in Mongolia. The fact that one can means that, at least for the 'chattering classes' you must. To say that you would rather not bother is to commit a new sin of omission.

Virtual reality and all the other manifestations of IT will soon create a similar 'moral imperative'. Not to surf the net will be a 'terrible waste of opportunity'.

But this wave of technophilia cannot suppress the underlying human spirit, the patterns of culture laid down over thousands of generations. Technology can give us almost limitless freedom to have anything we want. So what do humans really want? What will the anthropology of the twenty-first century look like?

Reforming the tribes – back to virtual nature

The clues are already there. The internet is allowing clumps of like-minded people to form new tribes. At present, these tribes suffer from terrible shortcomings. Members often cannot even see each other ...

But take all the IT-related capabilities of the twenty-first century; take the long history of human evolution, in which living in small-scale societies, characterized by shared values and beliefs (often confused with 'primitive religion'); take the spirit of freedom; and take the persistent need for a sense of identity in a world bent on making everything the same; and you soon realize that the anthropology of the twenty-first century is one of a re-emergence of difference.

Gaining their identity from shared interests (such as the 'worship' of Jennifer Aniston, or a lifelong commitment to Star Trek), small 'tribes', physically distributed across the globe, but brought into tribehood by the virtual reality of twenty-first century IT, are already starting to form. In the early days, they will be indistinguishable from each other. But as they provide for more and more of the members' sense of belonging, they will begin to drift apart from each other in language, values and comprehension.

IT has the power to overcome physical limitations and barriers. It is unlikely, however, radically to change human beings. For a while, a generation or so, individuals will have the unique ability to choose which 'tribe' they belong to. But after a while, it will be as hard for a Trekkie to marry a Wagnerian as it was for a Capulet to get together with a Montacute.

The IT, which threatened to eradicate forever small-scale societies, will, ironically, be the means by which small-scale (virtual) societies are rediscovered. And yet another phase of human history, which, like all the rest, threatened to change our ways forever, will have come and gone. The means will have changed, for sure; but the ends will be the same as they always were – to belong, to identify with, to have meaning for others, and not for technology.

Conclusions – a message to the IT community

Meanwhile, let's get back to the main theme of the book – our IT people. This introduction has been largely about IT and society. But IT, for the foreseeable future, will still need IT people to look after it. It is for their sake that the rest of the book is written. Let's turn, therefore, from the third person ('they') to the second ('you').

The rest of the book is written for you, the IT manager. It deals directly with the IT stereotype. It does not deny its existence, nor even lament its existence. That would be pointless. But it does offer advice on how to survive, and then to thrive despite the odds being stacked against you.

The first, brief part of the book places the stereotype in context. The second part of the book challenges some of the ways in which your habitual behaviours of the past linger on, and adds fuel to the fire of criticism. In Part Three, we look at some ways to rethink IT services, while in Part Four, we explore the finer arts of becoming streetwise in today's organizational community. If you're prepared to be honest and self-critical, you should find in here many ways of tackling the burden of the IT stereotype and, if you wish, removing the barriers to being considered an equal partner with the other senior business people, including (in some cases) the CEO.

Part One
What's the problem?

1 The IT stereotype and organizational politics

In the many years we have been working in and for IT management, we have come across hundreds of books and courses telling IT managers how to construct IT and IS strategies. We have found even more books on how to 'run' an IT department or function. Many of these books and courses are worthy and helpful. Yet, in our experience, few of them deal with what we believe is the hardest part of being a successful IT manager. That is dealing with the politics in organizations.

All managers, especially those senior enough to be responsible for entire sections of an organization's activities, have to deal with organizational politics. Organizations, being made up of people, are essentially political institutions. But we have found that IT managers are often among the least well equipped to cope successfully in the political arena.

IT has a lot to offer organizations. Yet many organizations fail to take full advantage of IT. One very significant reason for this is that IT managers and their senior peers in other functions do not have mutual respect for one another, nor can they talk to each other in a common language. The quality of their dialogue is relatively poor.

This is no-one's fault in particular. But we do believe it is up to IT managers to take greater responsibility for resolving this problem. In many cases, this means that IT managers, to be able to work effectively in the political arenas of the boardrooms of today's businesses, will need to 'unlearn' many of the lessons they have learnt in becoming lifelong technical experts.

This book will help IT managers think about that unlearning, and provide the bedrock for developing new skills.

For example, organizational politics is not like computer programming – there is no one right answer. We provide no answers, but we do provide the insights, ideas and concepts for IT managers to develop their own style of 'political awareness':

Virtually all the training (both explicit and tacit) which IT people receive throughout their IT lives works on the principle that there is a 'right' answer to everything. Many people go into IT (more or less consciously) because it is somewhere where they can deal with certainties. The profession attracts those for whom getting things right and being precise is important.

But organizational life outside the computer room is not like this. Decisions have to be made on other criteria than the 'purely rational'. This causes many IT people a great deal of unease. Asked to venture away from their anchors of certainty, they cannot determine absolutely where right and wrong exist. More dangerously, they cannot be sure whether other people's motives are 'pure'. In the absence of certainty, many withdraw from the battles, comforting themselves in the belief that organizational politics is no different from self-servingness – another phrase to describe the self-interested squabbles of people for whom organizations are merely convenient places to grub around for personal gain.

We have worked with and talked to many hundreds of IT people at all levels of seniority. One of the authors of this book has many years' experience of doing the job of IT management herself. We have also undertaken research into how non-IT people in organizations view their IT colleagues. Amongst the most frequent issue we have been confronted with among IT managers is that of 'leadership'.

As we shall describe in more detail later in the book, leadership is a crucial aspect of modern management; this holds for IT management as well as other functions. But time and again, we have been told that IT managers do not often make good leaders. This is because leadership is not something which can be done 'by the book'. Leadership is intrinsically political. To be a good leader, you have to get involved, and take responsibility for policy – to play the political game.

What organizational politics is not

Many IT people are highly suspicious of the whole idea of organizational politics. They equate it with dirty dealing, underhandedness and getting one over on one's fellows. They see politics as

a competitive game which, because they have dedicated their time to doing good for the organization through professional devotion to IT service and project delivery, they have not accepted as inevitable nor had the chance to develop skills in this area. This puts them at an unfair disadvantage.

The 'political game' is not like chess (a game which many IT people are good at, incidentally). Chess is rational, logical, and absolutely competitive. Computers have now learnt to be better at chess than even Gary Kasparov. But because some IT managers interpret the 'political game' as though it were like chess, they bring to organizational politics some dangerous assumptions. Amongst the most dangerous assumption is that organizational politics is competitive in the same way as chess is competitive:

- There are only two sides.
- There are a number of well-rehearsed and proven strategies.
- You should never reveal your strategy to your opponent.
- It is the purpose of the game to beat the opposition (or they will beat you).
- Whatever you do to enhance your own position naturally weakens that of your opponent.
- Cool, logical, clever, unemotional people are best at the game.

For some IT managers, many of whom cannot bear to lose, the preferred option is not to play, for fear of losing a game whose strategies they do not understand.

But none of these features of games like chess apply to organizational politics – except in dysfunctional organizations. Many very successful 'players' of organizational politics are successful because they know that, unlike chess:

- There are many 'sides' – or shades of opinion.
- There is nothing well-rehearsed or proven at the leading edge of organizational change.
- You should always discuss and share your views with those who may see things differently.

- The purpose of the game is for everyone to win.
- Whatever you do to enhance your position can also enhance the positions of others.
- Cool, logical, clever, unemotional people are often worst at the game; the political game requires intuition and feeling as well as logic.
- It is about building relationships so that people will want to deal with you again.

This book will explore many of these contradictions. We believe that IT managers need to embrace the challenges of organizational politics. Whilst they hold back, they will not have the levels of influence necessary to realize their own or their IT function's potential, and to form partnerships with other functions within their organizations. It is partnerships such as these which maximize the ways in which IT can create and sustain competitive advantage. Where the most senior IT managers are 'back-room boys', they will rarely be welcomed into the 'inner sanctum'.

In our research few IT managers succeed in achieving the role of CEO; many say that, realistically, they could not aspire to the position. Those who have reflected seriously about this often admit that it is their political ineptitude which holds them back.

Consequences of the stereotype

One of the most significant outcomes from the research we have undertaken into perceptions of IT management is the discovery of a 'stereotype'. In the minds of many non-IT people (including a significant number of very senior non-IT managers), there is a stereotypical picture of 'the IT manager', which we described in the Introduction. Many business people appear to be working with this stereotype, or mental model, of the 'typical' IT person. It is upon this stereotype that the reputation of many actual IT people has been built. And it is against this reputation that many IT people have to fight.

The repercussions of the stereotype are serious:

- IT has little influence on business decisions or the formulation of business strategy.
- IT is often unrepresented at board level, and takes the status of a service function and cost centre.
- IT is held in low regard and has little credibility.

We recognize that most actual IT managers are much more complex and rounded people than the stereotype suggests. However, we also know that organizational life – political life – works far more with stereotypes than with the richness of data

and experience which is available. We are not trying to condone stereotyping, nor even to explain it at this stage. We are, however, aware that, unless the stereotype is accepted and confronted, many of the political challenges faced by IT managers will remain unresolved.

This book will not provide all the answers. Those lie within the psyches of the individual IT managers themselves. But we shall provide some guidelines which IT managers can use to start the process of becoming 'streetwise'.

Part Two
I'm just trying to do my job!

2 Coping with the stereotype

In Part Two of the book, we look at some ways in which IT managers cope with the stereotype we described in the introduction. We use the word 'cope' deliberately, because these approaches often serve to reinforce rather than resolve the implicit negatives of the stereotype.

Broadly, we suggest that many of the 'coping strategies' adopted by IT professionals reinforce the negatives because, in their attempts to feel good about themselves, many of them rely more and more heavily upon those 'unique' strengths which have gained them success in the past.

For example, a very large number of IT people are, in a traditional sense, highly intelligent. Their skills in writing computer programs demonstrate capabilities which many business managers could not emulate. IT people often have developed the ability to manipulate significant amounts of data in complex logical sequences. Many have had their finest moments putting together the 'perfect' set of program modules. There is elegance and satisfaction in well-written programs.

Many IT people become so attracted to this notion of elegance and technical perfection that they fail to take into account (or even see at all) the ultimate purpose of what they are doing – to achieve some business benefit. For some, business benefits are the responsibility of someone else; their own job is bounded by the program or module itself. So long as their bit is OK no-one can accuse them of not pulling their weight.

But as they become increasingly aware of the negative nature of the IT stereotype, IT people (often unconsciously) attempt to redress this implicit attack on their self-esteem by relying more and more upon the intelligence and skills which give them success. They become even more logical, even more data-oriented. Many become stars of their local pub quiz teams. Others take to competitive intellectual games such as chess, mah-jong, and war games.

Many take refuge by surfing the internet, often urging others to join them in this curious mix of community and loneliness. In many cases, the first thing they log onto is the day's Dilbert cartoon. Thereafter, they may settle down to their work; many cut themselves off from the intrusions of the real world by wearing headphones to listen to music (often 'heavy metal', yet another 'rebellious' rejection of the 'stuffiness' of the business world). Many take pride in their self-sufficiency; they do not need anyone else; they can do it all themselves; they know best.

In the eyes of the business world, however, these coping strategies only serve to confirm the stereotype. Names such as 'propeller-head' and 'nerd' are coined to harden the divide between the IT professional and 'ordinary human being'. The vicious cycle continues to denigrate IT people.

In the remaining chapters of Part Two, we shall look more closely at some more structured ways in which IT professionals attempt to cope with the negativity of the stereotype. We shall also point out how, well intentioned though they are, such strategies often serve further to reinforce the very stereotype which the strategies have been developed to counter.

3 The phantom IT strategy

What could be wrong with developing an IT strategy? Surely, everyone knows that one of the most important roles of the most senior IT person is the production of an IT strategy. And everyone also knows that the IT strategy has to be 'aligned with' the business strategy.

It may be true that many IT departments do not produce completed IT strategies which directly support the business strategy. But whose fault is that? Obviously, it has to be the business, failing as they so often do to produce their part of the bargain – a clear business strategy to align to.

There are two main kinds of reason why IT managers try to write an IT strategy. One set of reasons is that they have been told to – by the business, by business schools, by IT gurus, and by their IT suppliers. Indeed, there are few more certain things in life than the need to respond to this call for a document on the technical way forward. We believe that the other set of reasons for developing an IT strategy are, in practice, more influential. But we'll look at those at the end of this chapter.

Aligning with the business strategy

Despite ten years or more of being told that IT strategies must align with the business strategy, few such alignments happen. Business strategies remain, in many cases, elusive and ambiguous. Many remain unwritten, residing in the heads of senior business managers, or in the actions and decisions of the business. Many contain apparent contradictions and uncertainties. Many fail to be written as clear, linear, logical documents which can be used as a check-list to identify what are the IT needs implicit within them.

In the absence of such clarity, many IT managers take it upon themselves to develop their own IT strategies. Unable to wait for clarity, they pioneer – and decide to take the lead.

On the face of it, this seems a good idea. But in many cases, the pioneering spirit lets IT managers down.

Innovation – what does this mean?

Strategies are about the future. Most people recognize that the future is not going to look like the past. Innovation is the name of the game. Therefore, the IT strategy which cannot be directly driven by the business strategy must be driven by technical innovation. It does not take many steps from here to recognize that 'inevitably', the future has to be the internet, or data mining, or some other such technological breakthrough.

But business managers are not impressed by IT-oriented strategies. Many will point to IT 'strategies' of the past, such as the 'paperless office' and ask 'So why are we now inundated with more paper than ever before?' And why, given that the technology has been available for so long, are the airlines not crippled by the massive take-over of video conferencing? And why don't we all have video phones? And why has e-mail made my life a misery instead of solving all my communication problems?

Unfortunately, just because it *can*, it does not mean technology *will* deliver brave new worlds. Yet, without the guidance of a business strategy, what more can the poor IT manager do but make guesses, and go for those technical opportunities which they believe (in their innocence) will shape the future?

Writing the definitive document

Beliefs and uncertainties are not the traditional stock-in-trade of an IT strategy. They are not the traditional ways of thinking within IT at all, which, as we suggested in the Introduction, works best with certainties and accuracy. So, given the technically-oriented guesswork of the stereotypical IT strategy of this chapter, how does the IT manager cope?

In many cases, they cope by writing the definitive work: the 'War and Peace' of the IT community. Rather than an aid to working, the strategy becomes a project in its own right, often occupying the full time devotion of tens of consultants brought in at great expense from the outside. It becomes a document written by and for technical people. To deal with the technical people's ability to pick holes in any uncertainty and ambiguity, the document goes into detail on almost every front. It takes on a life of its own.

But during its gestation period, it remains under wraps. Until the wrinkles have been ironed out, and the questions all answered, it cannot be seen. This would expose any frailties. Whatever the good intentions at the outset, the document by this stage has taken so much energy and time that its successful birth, with no defects, becomes infinitely more important than the business which it was meant to support in the first place.

There is, in many such documents, an attempt at perfection. Ruminating upon what has made life bad in the past, IT people (and their consultant accomplices) often recognize that, with this document, they have the best chance of all to get rid of those legacy systems which hold the business back. All it will take is the complete and comprehensive rewriting of all the systems which give IT a bad name. And all it will take is a good enough business case to support the infrastructure investments needed to deliver such perfection.

The business won't stand still

In the meantime, the business has the audacity to move on from the already uncertain situation which existed when the IT strategy project started. Each shift in the business puts back the release of the strategy; every shift has to be taken into account and all its implications woven into the fabric of the document.

This flies in the face of the inherent tidiness which is driving the IT strategy. More or less consciously, many IT managers use their IT strategies as attempts to tidy up the messy world of business. Many IT strategies could have been written by Mary Poppins.

IT managers want to do things right, to meet the needs of the business. But the business managers won't play the game. Not only do they keep changing their minds, they also berate the efforts of the IT community, often replaying the IT stereotype at their IT people to remind them how ineptly they are seen. This is just not fair. The business people do not see the value of what the IT people are trying to do. Moreover, they are always complaining about 'value for money', and questioning whether they are getting it. One CEO of a telecommunications company admitted that the only thing which kept him awake at night was that he was never sure whether his IT manager was doing a good job or not.

Why write an IT strategy?

Which brings us to the second set of reasons for writing an IT strategy: as a means of getting one's own back. Many IT strategies are thinly-disguised battle-plans, designed once and for all to put those users in their place. Replete with standards and controls, they map out a future in which users do as they are told, follow the rules, tell IT exactly what they want for the next five years, and rejoice in all manifestations of new technology, instead of making fun of the whole idea of technical innovation. IT knows what is best for the business because the business cannot decide when it doesn't understand IT.

In fact, many very successful businesses get by quite nicely without an IT strategy. The problem with IT strategies is that they often lead to portfolios of applications which attempt to do everything for everyone. Yet research continues to show that companies which make the most effective use of IT are often those who constantly realign their IT efforts with the key issues of the day – issues which will change and evolve over relatively short periods of time. The key is simply to focus activities on a few critical things.

We believe that the IT strategy is far more a means of coping for the IT manager than it is a genuine contribution to the business. Our advice is to stop, and to get out there amongst the business people. Not so that you can gather data for squirrelling away in your IT office, or to document in the perfect 'strategy'. But to build relationships with your colleagues, and to take your place amongst them as a business manager rather than as a writer of 'science' fiction.

Formal statements of business goals and strategies are inadequate inputs to IS activity. Such statements can never be rich enough to capture the full essence of critical business needs as they emerge. It is only through dialogue with fellow executives that the IT manager can tease out the motivations, meanings, and priorities; know the mind of the business; sense the impending changes; and maintain the relevance and timeliness of IT effort. Without such insight, IT is more likely to be seen as an expensive liability than a company asset. And an IT strategy won't alter that perception.

4 Projects – the illusion of being managed

The stereotype of the IT *person* is not the only one you have to deal with. Just as important is the stereotype of the IT *project*. We all know that IT projects are always late and over budget, and never deliver what they promised. We all know as well that it is not our fault. So why do IT projects keep reinforcing this stereotype. Why can't people in the business learn not to impose upon us unrealistic demands and expectations which condemn IT projects to failure even before they have started? Are they doing it just to get at us?

This chapter will provide one answer to this set of questions. You may not like the answer; it may not be the only or even the best answer. But it will be compatible with what we are suggesting throughout the book:

> 'it' is not your fault, but that if you want 'it' to change, then you have to do something different

In the spirit of the book as a whole, this is not a chapter on how to do project management. It is about the *impact* of project management, and its pitfalls and risks, on your standing as a senior contributor to the business – how project management helps or hinders your route to becoming 'streetwise'.

What the business wants

IT projects are a response to something which is wanted by the business. But in many cases, what the business wants is practically impossible. Senior business managers discuss a new product, a new service, a new approach to customers, or some other grand scheme. They set targets, measures, deadlines. Essentially, they sketch out a broad project plan.

And then they ask IT to deliver its part.

Dates have already been committed to; the launch campaign has been scheduled; there is a huge dependency upon everything coming together at the right time, often to an immovable and published deadline. The problem is that you have just been asked to perform the impossible.

You try to manage their unrealistic expectations. You tell them that what they have asked for would need all your people working overtime, with total disregard for all the other ongoing projects and support activities; and with nothing left for contingency. And all you get is aggression, or patronizing smiles and a reinforcement of the importance of the project. You are told simply and forcefully to stop whinging and find a way to make it happen. All it takes is a bit of imagination ...

So you are left with a 'plan' which contains the seeds of its own destruction, and a significant amount of the responsibility, and all of the accountability, to make it happen; and from past experience you know who the convenient scapegoat will be when it all goes wrong.

Starting to fight your corner

You present to your team the expectations and wait for the howls of protest. You absorb their bad feelings in your own style (see Chapter 11 for more on your management style), and agree that the users are a pain in the neck. (In a survey of 760 IT managers, they said that the most serious difficulty they faced was with user specifications. In other words, projects would be so much easier if it were not for the users! But maybe the survey was unfair; it's a bit like interviewing 760 zebras about their attitude to lions.)

So, siding with your team against the lions (users) you ask for their help to put together a response: the detailed IT project plan. Or project plans.

Because by now, you have learnt that it pays to offer the business some options. You are 'streetwise' enough to know that users like to feel as though they are in control, even though they hand over all the responsibility to you. You offer them 'choices'; although you know that there is only one 'right' choice (which is the best technical solution for the business), you know this will not be the 'acceptable' choice.

Usually your offer looks a bit like this:

- Plan 1: The 'ideal' option, but this would have to be delivered late.

- Plan 2: What can be realistically delivered to the deadline (but far short of the spec).
- Plan 3: The bare minimum requirement for Day 1 operation, which is only achievable with a following wind, and with absolutely no contingency for anything to go wrong.

Although Plan 3 is the one which is almost guaranteed to get *you* into trouble, it's what they always choose!

The other challenge is when, because of the speed of change in the business, you have several big projects on your hands at the same time. Whatever you call a big project, don't take on more than one at a time; if you really have to, you may need to take on two. But, for heaven's sake, be realistic and stop at that. You may think you can deal with more by artful juggling, but the chances are you can't. And you may be pressured by some really important users to take on just one more big project. But be bold, and remember how many big projects fail.

Oh, yes, many such projects are packaged up as successes. The cracks are papered over, and the holes plugged for the sake of face. But one of the main reasons why so many projects are, under the surface, so horribly short of the ambitious goals which were set for them is that they are just too big, and there were just too many distractions and changes to the initial spec.

You see, you're just too prone to say yes. And this leads you into the challenge of trying to 'manage the impossible'. You use your estimating activities as much to provide you with room to negotiate as to 'tell it like it is'. You already know that, when it comes to estimating costs and timescales, the users are in your hands. During this unique phase of a project, you may have a bit of power (so long as the users are IT illiterate, and you have gathered sufficient historical data on how long things actually took on previous occasions). You know that, at this stage, you are laying the foundations for the pressures and stresses which will be placed upon you. You don't want your estimates to commit you to even more pressure than you can help. Estimating, clearly, is a serious business.

Estimating

One aspect of the stereotype of the IT person is their unwillingness to give off the cuff estimates. As some of the business managers in our research asked, 'Why do IT people have to be so damned slow and pedantic with their estimating? Why can't they give us a rough estimate? Why do they take two weeks even to come up with estimated project costs and timescales? We don't want detail; we just want a ballpark figure. Why are they so reluctant to do this?'.

Your answer is probably along lines like this, 'The problem with

off the cuff estimates is that the business holds us to them. They promise that they will only use them as guidelines. But time after time, our "guidelines" become treated as fixed-in-concrete "guarantees"; which they later use to beat us over the head with. Making such promises is like signing our own death warrants, even if we use such caveats as "very, very soft estimates only" and "order of magnitude only". We've learnt the hard way not to make these "promises", and to take care before being held to any kind of budget'.

Of course you have to defend yourself from being held to unrealistic budget constraints and deadlines. But this should not deter you from drawing up some rule of thumb guidelines to provide the business with some 'ballpark' figures. You should use these rules of thumb to provide estimates quickly, which are unlikely to be so far off the mark that they will get you into trouble. It is far better to use such rough estimating tools than to refuse to provide rough estimates altogether.

There are two reasons for this. The first is that your reluctance to respond reinforces the stereotype. The good you may do yourself in avoiding commitments which you may not be able to meet is often outweighed by the harm you do to your own and others' reputations for uncooperative behaviour. Each time you are seen to be obstructive, uncooperative, stubborn, unimaginative, and just plain bloody-minded, you confirm yet again some of the

reasons why so many senior IT people are kept out of the 'inner sanctum'. Take some calculated risks.

The second is that it is possible to draw up a set of guidelines which you can use to provide rough estimates within a few minutes. These guidelines may lack precision, accuracy and technical elegance, but they will not be so far off the mark that they will commit you to substantially any more effort than estimates which you may spend two weeks on.

As an example, here's a set of project estimating guidelines or 'rules of thumb' which have been successfully used in an insurance company for many years. They are dated, we realize, but the principles remain good, even after all these years.

1 *User confirmation*
The following figures were derived from examination of specific projects classed according to their functional complexity:
- full system development (e.g. Motor Accounts) – 24 days;
- medium (e.g. Covernote automated update) – 5 days;
- simple (e.g. Temporary Motor Stats interface) – 2 days.

2 *Conversion*
The following times per program are based upon previous VSE to MVS conversions:
- COBOL on-line – 4 hours;
- COBOL batch – 6 hours;
- Assembler – 4 hours;
- Easytrieve Plus – 2 hours.

The total program conversion time should be increased by 60 per cent to allow for planning and testing.

3 *Development*
The figures below assume the use of debugging and abend aid tools. The absence of such tools would increase development timescales.
Programming (coding and unit testing, per program):

Batch	difficult	– 15 days
	medium	– 10 days
	simple	– 5 days
On-line	difficult	– 15 days
	medium	– 7 days
	simple	– 3 days

The following ratios were applied to programming time:

Figure 4.1 Estimating guidelines and estimates

Detailed design	= Programming/2.5
Functional and technical design	= Detailed design
System test	= Programming/2
Data Conversion; a straight file copy	= 2 days
Contingency on normal projects	= 10 per cent
Contingency on projects with many unknowns	= 20 per cent

4 *User training*

User training may range from simple modification of a minor change to a system to full-scale training in the use of a newly developed system. Training requirements, including preparation time, have been estimated on the basis of the anticipated extent and complexity of the changes to systems and procedures:

full systems development	– 24 days
difficult	– 10 days
medium	– 5 days
simple	– 2 days
no change to procedures	– 0 days

5 *Working time*

A seven-hour working day is assumed.

To allow for holidays, training and sickness, a four-day week, sixteen-day month has been assumed.

6 *Scaling other phases*

Basic concept

The 'hard' estimate for the next stage (a phase or group of phases) plus the actual effort for previous phases is used as a base from which all other phase estimates can be derived by means of scaling.

The table below shows the percentage breakdown of the total project effort over the development phases:

Phase	*Percentage of total effort*
Preliminary survey	1 (maximum 5 days)
Feasibility study	5–7
Systems analysis	12–14
Logical design	4–6
Physical design	10–12
Construction	36–44
–Program design	6–8
–Coding and testing	18–20
–System testing	12–16
Acceptance testing	9–11
Implementation	12–14
Post implementation review	1

These percentages can be used to give an estimate for any phase from any other phase. For example, if systems analysis is estimated at (or actually took) sixty days, the 'scaled' estimate for programming would be:

60 x 36/12 man days = 180 man days

Figure 4.1 (*continued*)

The actual estimating guidelines you may want to use are likely to be different from these, which are offered simply as an example set which have been used very successfully in one organization. It is a set of ideas to copy and modify.

As time goes by

You've jostled for position, and taken away with you a set of broad requirements which you already have deep misgivings about. You know things will get worse …

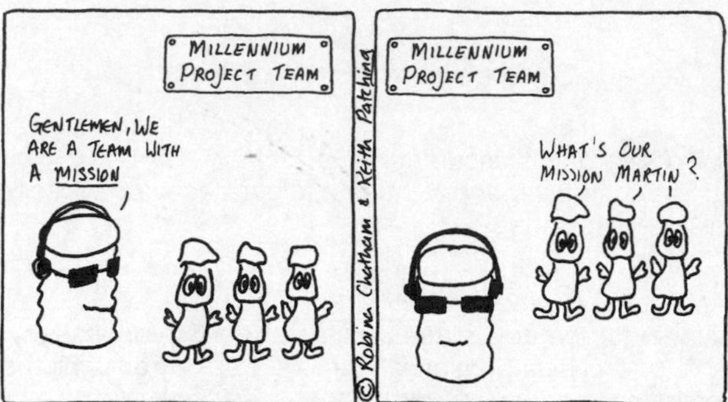

The next phase is to pin down the user requirements. Members of your team are allocated their own tasks, and they set off to try to negotiate with these overly demanding users. You have, however, been able to achieve one of the most important goals at this stage – and that is to get the users to agree collectively to the 80:20 rule.

By this we mean the rule that says that 80 per cent of the final functionality is probably all that can be achieved within the timescales and budgets. It has been agreed that, because of the importance of the project, those 20 per cent of 'nice to have' features will be ditched in exchange for the 80 per cent 'must have' elements. You have been able to make the users realize that the effort expended in bringing to fruition that 20 per cent extra amounts, in total, to 80 per cent of the effort. The numbers have been agreed, and you have a clear road ahead.

In principle.

The problem is that each user believes that it is not they who have to give up the extra 'nice to haves', but someone else. Your team members are told that the principle of 'bending' the business round the system is fine in other areas, but *here* we really cannot be expected to change our procedures and practices 'just to fit in'. Your team members are faced with the task of negotiating, and they may not have the necessary skills ('streetwise skills') to deal with this negotiating process as well as they might.

Little by little the project gets even bigger than it was when it started. Projects come in various sizes. What constitutes a big project, and what a small one will depend upon what happens in your organization. But, in the context of your own organization, you can feel the equivalent of a London Ambulance or Torus coming on. This is called 'scope creep'; it is when, as time goes by, everyone in the business mulls over the project, and sees yet more ways in which it can be enhanced. After all, the business is not standing still while project planning takes place. And users often have very fertile imaginations.

You grit your teeth. It's not going to happen this time.

As you tell the users how much the project is going to cost, and how long it is going to take, they will always tell you to shave bits off here and there (as well as 'change this bit or the other' and 'please could you add this thing in, too?') so that the project has some chance of achieving benefits before they become obsolete. Business managers come and tell you that the original plan has to be cut down, so could you see your way to reducing the overall cost or time schedule? And, so you don't appear to be uncooperative, and because you are a 'nice guy', you agree. And you end up wondering what is left of your original, beautiful project plan.

You know that, once the pressure is on, you'll be asked to cut this and cut that. You want to say yes, so you start to cut your own

As time goes by

plans to accommodate. Updating the project plan goes out of the window. Documentation and reconciliation go next, if they have indeed survived thus far, quickly followed by annual and then monthly reporting. And as for the post-implementation review that was always going to be a casualty, because, you know that your knowledgeable staff will be tied up with bug-fixing for some time post implementation. Anyway, post-implementation review is always a painful experience which is easily lived without. (The problem which results, of course, is that we never learn from our mistakes, because they are too uncomfortable to face.)

Hard on the heels of this project comes the next. This time, you're determined to dig in your heels and do it properly. But ... since the last one had a few holes in it (not your fault, of course), there's some damage limitation to do on your image. Yet another project has come in late and over budget, and your job's on the line. So, although in the ideal world you'd do this project absolutely according to the book, you can't afford to upset anyone else, so, once again you compromise your ideals and you're back in the same old trap. You'll let slip those inessentials, and you're back where you were before.

Not this time, you tell yourself. By now the message has been loud and clear for long enough. All the business schools, gurus and the consultants agree that IT projects are as much the responsibility of business users as they are of IT. Joint project teams are the order of the day, along with 'the business' taking responsibility for project leadership, for providing team members, and for taking accountability. If you believe what you read in the trade press, everyone else seems to be doing it, so ...

....this time the users are really going to have to take their share of the job.

Sharing the tasks – sharing the responsibilities

It's time to educate the users. To help you do this, you set up a time log. The purpose of this is to show users just how much time they are causing you to spend on rework and other low value activities. You issue project team members with a weekly time log sheet which asks them to account for their time in the manner shown in Figure 4.2.

> During the coming week, keep a log of your activities to the nearest half hour using the forms on the following pages. Note the time taken by each activity, and mark each with one of the codes below:
>
> RW (REWORK) – Time spent in redoing work that you or another did and which did not meet requirements, or wasn't done right.
>
> PN (PREVENTION) – Time spent preventing potential problems or errors from taking place.
>
> PL (PLANNING) – Time spent thinking about work to be done in the future, and figuring out how it needs to be done, and who and what will be needed to do it effectively.
>
> FF (FIREFIGHTING) – Time spent repairing systems or relationships damaged by the actions of yourself or others.
>
> CO (COMMUNICATIONS) – Letting others know, or finding out from others, information which is important to get the work done.
>
> W (WORK) – Actually doing work that does not fall into any of the above categories.
>
> A (ADMINISTRATION)

Figure 4.2 Time log

You already know that too much time is being spent firefighting and reworking. This is costing the organization a lot of time and money. It can only be prevented if the whole project team – users and your people, can work together to the plan, and not keep changing their minds and requirements.

The key to all this is your knowledge that the cost of correcting software errors is many times more expensive at the live stage than at the requirements stage. Estimates from a whole variety of research activities suggest that the relative cost of correction of software errors follows an exponential curve, with the cost at the live stage escalating to over 100 times that of a correction at the requirements stage. Changes even at the design and programming stages are still relatively low cost; so keep on the lookout for changes to the specification as early as possible.

It is often uncomfortable to be on the lookout so early in a project for modifications. At this stage, people are excited and forward-looking. They do not want to slow down progress by looking for problems. You need to be that much more vigilant early in the project, to overcome the naive enthusiasm which so often obscures the hidden dangers.

So you remind the users of their responsibilities. You show them diagrams and tables which reinforce the shared responsibilities and risks of the project.

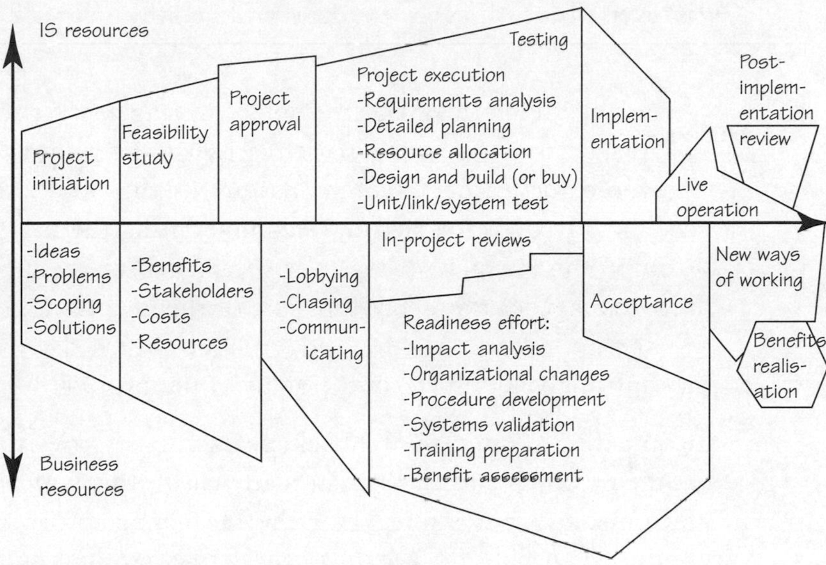

Figure 4.3 Project 'iceberg' diagram

You make it as easy as possible for users to play the game with change requests. You keep reminding them of their role in the project. You keep reiterating that this is a business project with an IT core element. But somehow you know that, in their hearts, the users are passing the total responsibility to you.

Confronting problems – when and how?

So you watch and wait. Like the boiled frog, you cannot be sure just when the water is too hot for comfort, since each little niggle, by itself, is hardly cause for major panic. But by the time the water is really too hot, your energies have been sapped too far to enable you to jump out.

Project meetings raise more and more problems and challenges. Niggles creep in, and however much people try to avoid it, blame starts to be apportioned. Under stress you or your staff may find it even more difficult to deal with conflict in a constructive manner.

Avoidance (often a favourite conflict management strategy of IT people, according to our research) ceases to be an option. There is no room for further accommodation, as the project parameters are already overstretched by accommodating the users' requests. Compromise (which for many projects has been the favoured conflict management strategy for most of the negotiations) begins to wear thin – there are few trade-offs left which do not look like complete abandonment of the goals of the project.

Competing is often the fallback, as each party tries to save face, and emerge unscathed. But, in many cases, this is the worst conflict management strategy for the IT manager to adopt. Many senior IT people do not have the 'streetfighting' skills of their

senior colleagues. Competing means 'win-lose', and it is often an uneven fight. It can also lead, once again, to further damage to the reputation of the senior IT person; and by the same token, to further reinforcement of the stereotype.

Getting it right – what does this mean?

IT projects can cause senior IT people deep stress. The suicide of at least one senior IT manager has been blamed on the stresses of failing projects; at the very least 'heads will roll' more than often means the senior IT people will be the scapegoats for project shortfalls.

One big question has to be answered here: If everyone knows that IT projects are always late and over budget, why do people keep giving such high levels of responsibility to the very IT people who seem to be to blame for this repeated phenomenon? In other words, why don't users take over IT project management and run the projects themselves? After all, that's what everyone keeps asking them to do.

Part of the answer lies in the 'mystery' surrounding project management. After all, IT project management is not very different from the management of other, 'ordinary' projects. The 'mystery' centres upon the role of IT within the project. Over the years, the peculiarities of managing IT (in other words, the technology itself), have seeped into IT project management. It is often as though IT projects had no people in them, just systems and procedures.

IT project management is just another aspect of the overall problem of the IT stereotype. IT project management has emerged out of *IT management* rather than *organizational* or *people management*. And it has brought with it a terrifying need for certainty. It often works on the tacit assumption that there is a right way of doing things, even though each project is unique – it has not been done before. This assumption seems to drive people in search of that one (often elusive) right way. And it blinds them to the essentially ambiguous and uncertain nature of organizational life. After all, projects happen in organizations, and they involve people.

But please do not deal with this by separating the roles of 'task manager' and 'people manager'. Some organizations have tried this ridiculous idea in the hope that they can isolate the task from the people who perform that task. For goodness sake confront the situation head on. Projects involve people, and you can't get round that one by pretending that the task issues are different from the people issues.

Ambiguity and uncertainty in projects

Some projects take on almost religious connotations – there is a heaven (the completed project), there are commandments (thou shalt report progress at 0900 every Monday morning), and there are sins, both of omission (failing to complete the change control sheet according to the rules) and of commission (dropping a module without express permission from the Steering Committee). The long history of failures of IT projects reinforce the need for vigilance – see what happens when you don't follow the true path. Each project failure makes the need for certainty more obvious.

Like many vicious circles, this search for the certainties will provide defence from failure and its consequence is almost invisible to those who fan its flames. Rather than using the evidence to recognize the need for greater alignment with the principles of good 'ordinary' management, they see it as a reminder of the need for absolute certainty, and for complete obedience to the rules.

Projects are and will always be ambiguous and uncertain. The best way to deal with this realization is to encourage different perspectives, to try out many different avenues, and to be prepared to rethink when things begin to show signs of going off track. This means regularly admitting 'failure'. We believe that pulling out of avenues which are not going to lead to success is better than stubbornly pursuing lost causes.

So what will become of the IT manager who keeps saying, 'This idea is not going to work'? Surely they will soon gain the reputation of a quitter? We suggest not. There are some organizations in which the 'whistleblowers' are cast out into the wilderness, whether they be staff or managers. These are the kinds of organizations in which projects are doomed to failure anyway, so you can't do anything about that, short of changing the organization's culture.

But in organizations where senior managers are mature enough to receive bad news without shooting the messenger, confronting problems head on will be a sign of effective management, not of failure.

More ideas have to be abandoned early at senior levels in organizations than at lower levels. This is because there are no right *strategic* answers. Senior managers learn that pulling out of doomed projects and ideas is a sign of flexibility, and not of quitting. It is evidence of a willingness to experiment, to explore, and to learn. It is far easier to learn from mistakes which have not been compounded by layer after layer of compromise, and which are still simple, than from the enormous disasters which many IT projects become.

The reputation of the senior IT manager will be better served by this kind of willingness to admit error – to be flexible – over many little activities, than to be forced by circumstance to accept responsibility for the massive failures which are the inevitable result of trying to cover up evidence, and of a lack of courage to say – earlier rather than later – 'I've screwed this one up; can we work together to salvage it before it sinks completely?'.

Bring me solutions, not problems

However, there is an issue here concerning dealing with problems. As many IT managers know, confronting the problems is not enough. Many senior business managers say, 'Bring me solutions, not problems'. And you may feel upset by this, since you may feel that it is their problem which they do not want to deal with. You may feel that the problem is just too complex to let you bring them solutions. You just can't find the solutions.

Most IT project managers, and most senior IT managers grew up as programmers. Programming was attractive to them because of their innate style of dealing with life. The job of a computer programmer is 90 per cent technical. It will come as 'second nature' to people with this background to seek technical solutions to problems. You may be like this yourself. Like many, you may have recognized in yourself a desire to pursue the largely impersonal, certain world of IT, and been happy in those good old days when you were given a programming task to get on with, by yourself, with no one to tell you how to do it, and with scope to compile the most elegant – the best – solution.

For many IT people, their 'natural' love of technical solutions has been set in concrete by their early experiences of work. The downside to this reinforcement is often a lack of imagination and creativity when it comes to complex human or organizational problems. We have worked with many IT people who, when faced with this kind of challenge, simply have no idea of how to think round the problem, or to come up with innovative ways of dealing with the problem.

The strengths of technical approaches to problems lie in the step-by-step, logical, linear, search for 'the best' solution. For truly technical challenges, such as building 747s, bridges, and computer programs, this approach has proven its worth millions of times. But applying this technical approach to IT projects builds into those projects their own seeds of destruction. Because this approach builds into projects, which are about people more than technology, assumptions about certainty which will inevitably be proved incorrect. It will constrain people sufficiently to make conflict and problems inevitable. And it will create a project culture of linear thinking which will make problem solving, during the inevitable crises, unimaginative and ineffective.

For the stereotypical IT manager (and for many 'real' IT managers as well), when logic fails to find a solution, there is little imagination to help out.

Users, many of whom may have the non-technical imagination to find radical solutions to such problems, will often not want to play by now. In many cases, they will have been turned off the whole enterprise by the very 'religious' nature of the IT project. From your team's perspective, their constant demands for changes and additions will mean that, by now, they are to be avoided as dangerously undisciplined. Although your team will complain that users do not take their share of responsibility, many of them

(secretly or even unconsciously) will prefer to keep these 'impure' users out of the frame.

Why IT projects fail

When we said that IT projects seem to take on almost religious connotations, we were referring to the consequences of this kind of linear, and certain thinking. One reason why users feel uncomfortable involving themselves in IT projects is that they cannot or will not be held in check by these kinds of rules and restrictions. IT projects die by their own hand. The more they are bound by lists, rules, checks, restrictions, regulations, and so on, the more they drive out the human spirit of creativity, of innovation, of dealing with ambiguity, and of fun.

People brought up in technical environments may not see the horror of this kind of approach. Many business users see it all too clearly. And they keep well away.

It may seem a little daunting at this stage, but try this:

Throw away the rule book

For your next project, think about breaking each and every rule you have held dear in the past. Think of a project as being about people and behaviour, rather than about plans, technology and reports. Be radical, revolutionary, and bold. Be human.

Being invited to the party earlier

One problem with this radical approach is that it may not kick in early enough to avert the major danger – the establishment of unrealistic goals – which is said to cause most of the project failures anyway. What is the point of being flexible and adaptable if the project as a whole is doomed to failure whatever the senior IT person does?

None at all. It merely becomes an exercise in damage limitation.

The point is not to be flexible to try to save doomed failures, but to establish a different approach altogether so that you will be invited earlier. One main reason why many senior IT people are not invited to contribute to the early discussions about major projects is because their colleagues know that they will demand certainty when none can be guaranteed. The stereotype is to blame. And it is therefore the stereotype which needs to be attacked, rather than the symptoms.

This is of little comfort in the short term. But if the problems of IT projects were simple, they would have been solved long ago. The problem of IT projects, like so many of the problems discussed in this book, and besetting many senior IT managers, is one requiring long-term investment in a thorough rebuilding of reputation. If you want to be invited to the table early, you have to demonstrate that you, as an individual, are not typical of the stereotype. And to do this you will have to adopt behaviours which will not solve the short-term problems of today's IT projects.

These new behaviours may not even solve the problems of the IT projects of tomorrow. But they are almost certain to have a positive influence on the IT projects which follow, because they will address the causes of IT project failures rather than their symptoms. And these causes, we believe, lie in the ways of the stereotypical IT managers. Change those behaviours (and thereby change the stereotype), and IT projects will be different kinds of activity.

Rebuilding the stereotype

The approach we have taken in this chapter is both inconclusive and counter-intuitive for many IT managers. It is inconclusive because it will be only in Part Four of the book that we can start to provide practical ways of dealing with the big issue of the stereotype. The little advice we have given in practical terms here is counter-intuitive because we are suggesting flying in the face of almost everything which IT people have been taught about project management.

But this is no different from other heresies we have and shall continue to promote, such as advising against writing an IT strategy. Desperate times such as these, when IT Directors are advised not to put too many pictures on the wall, as they'll soon have to take them down again, demand desperate measures. Scrub that project manager's workbench and get out and talk to people. Forget the project plan and start throwing out the silly projects. Get used to going back time and time again and saying, 'This just won't work, let's go at it another way'.

And get used to taking ten minutes to provide a rough estimate. It will only be when IT managers unwind a little, and start being imaginative, adventurous, and a bit more carefree that they'll become a bit more streetwise and a bit more likely to be asked, way before a major project starts, 'What do you reckon; can we do it in the time available? Do you have any other thoughts?'. And when that happens, please do not say, 'Give me a couple of weeks, and I'll get back to you'.

5 Staying alive

Everyone agrees (and we do too) that you have to provide a good IT service. The bad news is, however, you don't get any brownie points for getting it 'right'; in the eyes of the users this is a taken-for-granted – it is your job, part of your purpose in life. You will only get recognition when you get it 'wrong', and then in a form you would rather not receive. If you are perceived as providing a poor service (most users/customers would probably use a stronger epithet than 'poor') you are unlikely to be long for this world, with hostile outsourcing as one of the most likely alternative solutions.

Providing a good service is like buying a ticket for the lottery. Fate determines that you're unlikely to win anything, but if you don't join the game, you're not even meeting fate halfway.

So this chapter is not going to go into lengthy details about providing a good service – there are hundreds of books on this subject already. But we will play with a few important ideas about service management which we think are important for you to take on board on your way to success.

The legacy

Books and films, like the myths and stories of the past, often focus on the conflict between two warring factions. Many add a twist to the tale by showing how, within one of the opposing camps, there is internal conflict going on as well.

Internal conflict has been the experience of many within IS – development and operations have often been at loggerheads. Some of the battles have evolved into lifelong feuds, as grudges are

developed and carefully nurtured. Listening to members of each side talking about the other is entertaining as well as educational.

It's not surprising. Like many of the classic conflicts of literature and mythology, operations and development represent two universal forces – that for conservation and stability on the one hand, and that for change and evolution on the other. As operations work with every fibre to create certainty, regularity, and predictability for the service provided to users, development keep upsetting the equilibrium by asking for new programmes, new modules, new procedures and new schedules. In the eyes of many of those from operations, users are not the enemy – development is.

But this brings into the frame one of the important ironies in life. Becoming streetwise depends on gaining an appreciation and understanding of these ironies, and being mature and robust enough to work with them (as later parts of the book will describe).

The irony here is that the IS development process is both flexible and rigid at the same time. Developers work to rules and principles of good coding and systems design, often citing standards of various kinds to let users know why they can't have what they want in exactly the way they want it. Many developers may work as hard as they can to be flexible, but, in the end, there are constraints – often those which have an impact on operations. Try as they might, they can't satisfy all the users all the time. The perception from the users can often be that developers are rigid and inflexible.

And then the system goes to operations. It upsets the status quo – it needs special attention and will not fit neatly into schedules. In the eyes of operations the developers are profligate wasters of precious resources – space and time. They do not appreciate the intricacies of writing good JCL, and as a result are often at the root of much wasted precious machine resource. They are always running late, are too soft on the users, and are squeezing 'just this one amendment' into tonight's change schedule, despite knowing full well that the procedure demands a three-day hand-over period. Developers are piggies in the middle, damned for being too rigid and too flexible at the same time.

Of course, with the advent of client-server technology and so on, the conflict has changed. In the early years of the twenty-first century, it is anachronistic to spend time on a conflict which must surely have gone away. But the legacy is one of the conflict between stability and change, not only one of conflict between the operations and development functions. The forces remain, even if the roles and functions have altered.

Habits don't have to be old to be hard to break

The adage 'old habits are hard to break' seems to imply that new habits are easy. We don't believe this – unless you are prepared to take a very liberal view of what is meant by 'old'.

The computer operations 'business' is, in organizational terms, pretty new – but not too new to have had the chance to adopt habits which are hard to break. The significant differences in operations support required from client-server technology demand a 'mindset' change – which doesn't always happen. In our experience, many operations functions are still trying to run client-server technology like they ran the mainframes of old. The old ways worked, so it is hard for them to break the old ways and adapt to the new.

Mainframes were big and powerful. But from an operational point of view they were simple. There were relatively few variables to juggle with. But with client-server technology, there are too many possibilities to legislate for. The rules and procedures which used to cover every eventuality and provide instructions as to what to do in the event of failure just can't cover all that can now go wrong.

The command and control, rule-governed environment of the mainframe regime was perfect for the time. Allowing discretion to operations staff was too risky. Consequently, operations became the place where thinking was not encouraged. Operators with brains would satisfy their intellectual needs by playing games – chess, bridge, and so on, and not on the challenges of the business. Similarly, users who wanted to know about the constraints and challenges of computer operations could be told in a sentence or two exactly what they needed to know. Life was simple. Dialogue never needed to be sophisticated.

The complexities of the client-server environment cannot fully be tested. There are just too many permutations.

Think of the analogy of the holiday trade. The mainframe environment is like the package holiday. High volume, low cost and low flexibility add up to a highly regulated business in which almost every eventuality can be anticipated, tested and dealt with before anything goes wrong. (Anyone reading this who has had a poor experience on such a package holiday ought to have sued the holiday company for every penny they could – there is no excuse.)

However, holidaymakers who want to break free from these constraints may choose an adventure holiday – breaking new ground, and benefiting from the uncertainties inherent in this different kind of experience. Now the numbers of things which can go wrong are exponentially multiplied. It would be harsh on the holiday company to be blamed for many of the unexpected turns of event which may befall these adventurers, and many of holiday insurance policies reflect this. The holiday company representatives on adventure holidays need very different skills from the reps on the package holiday. Like the package holiday reps, they do need to take responsibility, but they cannot work to a script; there are just not enough scripts written.

Therefore, when things do go wrong, there is a greater need for clarity of explanation – for effective dialogue between tour operators and holidaymakers. The same is true between computer operators and users. Operators now need intellect, flexibility, and the interpersonal skills to deal with the unexpected and its impact on users who may fail to realize the risks they have been led into by adopting client-server technology. And the ability to manage expectations wouldn't go amiss either.

The users break into the fortress

There has been a steady growth over the past fifteen years or so of 'end-user computing'. The users have broken through the fortifications and fighting is now hand-to-hand, within the fortress itself. 'Expert' users realize that, using proprietary office packages which combine spreadsheets, databases and graphics, they can

simulate in a few days what has traditionally taken months or even years for the IT people to produce. A great deal of the mystique has gone, and along with it much of the 'take it or leave it' relationship.

Expectatations have been raised. Local computer or even consumer electronics stores in every high street enable users to be IT people in their own right; glossy airline magazines and fox-like computer salesmen promise systems in minutes with no effort; and suddenly the IT department's estimate of nine months for a solution which could be delivered by the user's fourteen-year-old son in three evenings looks shaky. The fact that he can't build multiuser systems processing millions of transactions does not prevent proud fathers from taking a fresh and somewhat cynical look at the productivity they get from their IT department.

Those high street stores create in the minds of users (in some cases possibly unconsciously) a consumer mindset which cries out for a market-led response from IT. Chapter 17 explores this response. It is in contrast with the 'I'm only trying to do my job!' approach which we are looking at in this part of the book.

Measuring up

As the users swarm over the ramparts, brandishing their demands for better service, IT managers pick up their protective armour and attempt to ward them off. The favourite piece of armour seems to be the 'measure'. If we can show how good we are, the thinking goes, then they will like us and stop attacking.

Many such defences are formalized into service level agreements (SLAs), probably the clumsiest weapon since the blunderbuss, renowned for killing almost as many people who used it as people they used it against. SLAs share this uncanny ability to shoot the wrong people.

SLAs are clumsy because they miss the point. IT is a service business, and as such, needs to recognize that service quality is measured by the overall experience of the service user, and not by the proximity to perfection of the component parts – especially when these parts are expected to be perfect anyway. Imagine an airline which advertised itself as shown in Figure 5.1.

Figure 5.1 Is this how to advertise airlines?

The fact that no airline uses this kind of measure is due to basic psychology – you don't want to get the customer's mind focused on something which could go wrong. Yet think of the number of times SLAs and other less formal 'agreements' measure similar things: over 98 per cent up time; less than 2 per cent

systems failure, and so on. The fact that such things are easy to measure is often the only real excuse IT people can give for this kind of focus. For whose benefit are these things really being measured?

Small wonder, then, that so many SLAs are sources of conflict. Tying each other hand and foot to levels of service which are largely irrelevant is pointless, and removes flexibility. And even when the measures are pertinent, the very nature of the relationship is under question from the start.

Consider the couple entering into the sanctity of marriage who feel it necessary to document who gets what in the event that they part company. We suspect that these kinds of prenuptial contracts in personal relationships (in which the contract is predicated upon the breakdown of that relationship) are a primary cause of relationship breakdowns themselves. SLAs are simply prenuptial contracts between IT and the business. And just like those in personal relationships, they are based upon a basic lack of trust and mutual respect for the other party.

Time and psychic energy are wasted upon close scrutiny of the key measures in many SLAs. Instead of the actual service itself, contracts become the focus of the relationship. They therefore shackle IT managers to the ground floor of the relationship, rather than enable them to turn their backs on this basic stuff and start to climb up the hierarchy of user needs.

This hierarchy is illustrated in Figure 5.2. It shows how different kinds of focus deliver different kinds of benefit. The lowest level – the subject of this chapter – has to be delivered effectively for the IT function to have the right to exist. Good service delivery provides the platform for the more strategic influencing which takes place higher up the figure, which serves both as a reminder of the importance of service delivery, and also as a signpost towards greater value added, and thereby, greater acceptance of IT into the 'inner sanctum'.

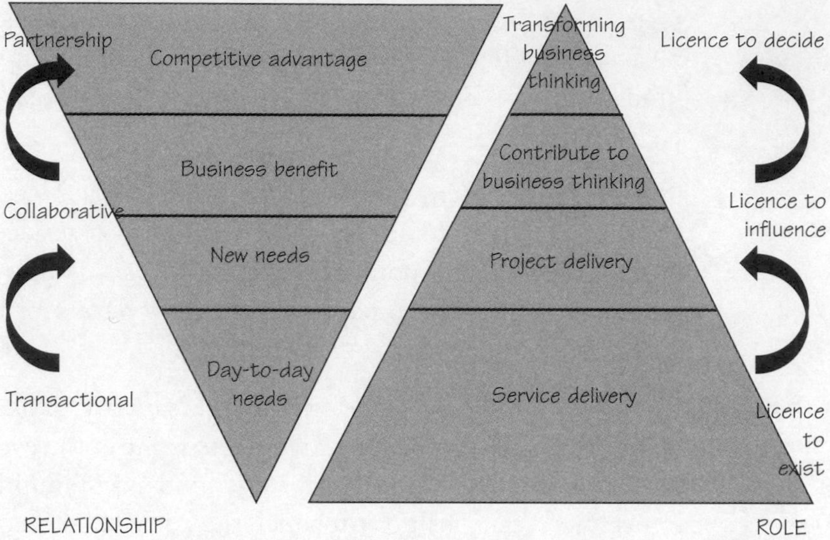

Figure 5.2 Twin-triangles model

Conclusions

We called this chapter 'staying alive' because we wanted to reinforce the key point:

> You don't get brownie points from providing a good service; but if you don't provide one, you should be shot.

The twin-triangles model helps to map out the route upwards towards becoming streetwise. IT managers who spend any but the most fleeting moments dealing with matters on the lowest level of this model are doomed never to get onto the streets – let alone get wise on the streets. This activity needs to be delegated – but effectively.

6 Writes of passage

For many IT managers, reading and, moreover, writing, form a major part of their daily activities. When the Finance Director says, 'they report to me', they mean more than a simple reference to an organization chart – 'reporting to' often means just that for IT – lots and lots of report writing.

It is embedded in the nature of IT that a lot of writing gets done. Most development methodologies are riddled with reports:

- Feasibility studies.
- Project initiation documents.
- Systems specifications.
- Technical specifications.
- Project plans.
- Weekly/monthly progress reporting.
- Phase end reports.
- Systems documentation.
- User documentation.
- Operations documentation.
- Post implementation reviews, etc.

There are hundreds of reports inherent in all sorts of IT activities. And IT managers get very used to the idea of putting pen to paper – or finger to keyboard these days. It has become so 'natural' to the task that many IT managers do not stop to question what they are doing and why. Reporting is an apparently necessary part of the job.

Some IT managers get carried away with this writing stuff. Reports are important, and therefore being engrossed in report writing is similarly important.

Writing also meets several of the stereotypical IT manager's needs. It can provide the opportunity to create lists of facts; it can be a very data-intensive activity. A great deal of the documentation which goes with IT is factual, logical and unemotional. It wraps the IT manager in the comfortable blanket of information. If in doubt, add more facts.

Writing is an essentially introverted activity – to be done alone and behind closed doors. It puts up barriers to intrusion from the outside world.

It is intellectually challenging, and has no place for the messy, emotional world of people and politics.

Reports need to be orderly, tidy, organized, structured and obedient. Reports do not answer back, they are never insolent and they are attended to (or apparently so). They are a great place for expressing things in your own way, and in your own language. IT managers writing reports are often composers or literati *manqué* – here in their creations, they can be performers. They can write for hours on end, using their own style, and putting across their points of view with no fear (until the report may actually be read) of interruption, contradiction or criticism.

Consequently, most reports written by IT managers are impenetrable, lengthy, jargon-filled, and pointless. And, in some cases, dangerous.

It is central to the IT stereotype that IT people talk a different language. They also write it. When written documentation is a crucial part of the business interaction between IT and users, jargon and obscure, lengthy, and confusing text can lead users to signing off things which, in an ideal situation, they would never agree to. Faced with the prospect of wading through page after page of material which they know they'll never understand, many users put their flimsy trust in the discussions they have had previously with IT, and hope that those discussions have been faithfully documented. But for the black and white world of the IT stereotype, a signature is an absolute and unconditional surrender. What has been signed for has been agreed.

You will be very familiar with this complaint. You are probably smiling (or grimacing) to yourself, because you have cracked this one at least. It has been years since you first were told that IT needs to communicate in non-jargon. So you are now adept at speaking and writing in plain English. But before you move on, don't forget to check your self-confidence against both 'fog indexes' and your most critical customers. They may be good at spotting jargon, because they may use their own version of it too.

The fact is that it is not only IT which uses jargon. The business does, too. IT jargon may even have arisen partially as a defence against the jargons of others. But two wrongs don't make a right.

As an exercise in appreciating how users may feel when presented by a stereotypical IT report, monitor how you feel as you read the following extract. It's real:

> *The move from a structuralist account in which capital is understood to structure social relations in relatively homologous ways to a view of hegemony in which power relations are subject to repetition, convergence, and rearticulation brought the question of temporality into the thinking of structure, and marked a shift from a form of Althusserian theory that takes structural totalities as theoretical objects to one in which the insights into the contingent possibility of structure inaugurate a renewed conception of hegemony as bound up*

with the contingent sites and strategies of the rearticulation of power.

(This wonderful piece was noted in *The Guardian*, Editor section, 23 January 1999. It won first prize in the annual 'bad writing' contest held by the academic journal *Philosophy and Literature*. Its origin was an article entitled 'Further Reflections on the Conversations of Our Time', published in the scholarly journal *Diacritics*. Its author is Judith Butler, professor of rhetoric and comparative literature at the University of California at Berkeley.)

Somewhere in this weird and wonderful world there must be a group of people for whom this kind of language makes sense, and is clear as a bell (well, let's be generous and assume there is). But to those of us outside the clique, reading such stuff brings on:

- An immediate sense that, will and tenacity permitting, by working at it, this will make sense.
- A glazed expression.
- A deep breath as we try again.
- A sense of frustration.
- Deep despair.
- Loss of the will to live.
- Insanity.

But not necessarily in that order. This is how most non-IT people feel as they grapple with the RAMs, ROMs, and extranets IT people serve up as 'received wisdom'. If you don't like it, why inflict it on others?

Perhaps the answer lies not in the information reports are meant to convey, but in the protection the written word appears to provide.

In this politically naive world, written documents have an almost religious significance. A signature forms a hard and fast contract – it puts up fences and boundaries which are inviolate. The user's signature is, in this respect, like the internal memo, the minutes of a meeting, the terms of reference of a committee. Putting it in writing is to pass from uncertainty and ambiguity and into certainty. By putting it in writing, the stereotypical IT manager moves from vulnerability to full protection. Putting it in writing protects your back. Writing is a rite of passage from naked exposure to cover, defence and comfort.

These are the writes of passage.

The problem is that, like many of the suits of armour of the middle ages, the protection is largely in the mind. The little victories provided by sign-offs become long-term defeats, as the stereotype is reinforced again and again – and with it, alienation from your customers.

Writing is for readers

One of the most important things many IT managers get to realize (eventually, for some) is that language is not just a means of communication. People 'do things' with words. When we make a promise, this is an act of doing, not just communicating; when we make a vow, this says more than 'let me inform you of my intentions.' And when we say 'I love you', we are not simply conveying a more or less 'true' description of our feelings about someone. These kinds of uses of words change things, they don't simply report things.

By the same token, written language changes things. Despite the deeper wishes of many IT people, there is no such thing as a 'value-free', totally objective document in organizational life. Anyone who writes about any activity in organizations with the assumption that they are not making value-judgements, stating opinions and risking upsetting readers is naive in the extreme. Writing is for readers, not for the writer. It is vital, therefore, that as you write, you are thinking about and feeling for your readers more than you are thinking about and feeling for yourself.

This advice is not simply motivated by a warm and fuzzy notion of being kind to your readers. It makes good practical sense. It is about understanding how we human beings actually work.

In Part Four of the book, we'll delve deeper into these essential human characteristics. For now, let's just focus on the practical implications for effective written communications.

One of the key reasons for putting things in writing is to persuade someone to do something. You may want someone to:

- Accept your ideas for changing something.
- Choose an option you are recommending.
- Stop pestering you for something you can't deliver.
- Give you a raise in salary.
- Pat you on the head and say you're wonderful.
- Maintain the internal IT function rather than outsourcing it.

Or to do any of a whole host of other things. The essence of your written word is that it helps achieve that outcome. Wouldn't it be nice if you could open your standard 'persuade the boss to give me a raise' file and print it off whenever you wanted? But, because writing is an act of changing things, its effectiveness differs depending upon circumstances. When we write that one plus one equals two, we know that we don't have to reframe that each time we want to convey that piece of information. But, since writing within organizations is not just about communicating facts, we have to write differently each time to achieve the changes we set out to effect.

Consider, for example, the following four statements about computers:

- Computers are electronic devices which provide a means of processing a great deal of data, fast, accurately, and tirelessly.
- Computers are the technology of tomorrow.
- Computers have the capacity to serve the world, or to destroy it.
- Computers get in the way of face-to-face relationships.

They are miniature representations of very different ways of expressing thoughts and feelings about what is apparently the same subject. They are not just different bits of data – they appeal in different ways to different kinds of people. They are miniature examples of the ways in which, if you want to persuade different kinds of people, you have to make radical changes to the style and feel of what you write. We'll develop this particular idea further in Chapters 11 and 13.

For now, let's look at a few simple rules.

Writing for effect – the basics

Know your readers and what you want them to do about what you are writing

Each reader is a unique individual. In business, we have the luxury which writers for the public do not have, of knowing the very individual for whom a document is written. The more you can get inside their head and appreciate how they are going to feel about what you have written, the more likely you are to write persuasively. This takes empathy as well as writing skills.

Assume ignorance – assume intelligence

This now classic piece of advice remains important. Distinguish between ignorance – which is a reasonable state of not knowing facts or information – from unintelligence. For years people have made and reinforced this mistake – radio and television quiz shows with titles like *Brain of Britain* and *Mastermind* encourage us to think that knowing lots of facts means being intelligent. Your readership is likely to be intelligent, but not in possession of the facts you wish to convey. Don't treat them as stupid.

Keep it short and simple

Most documents you, as an IT manager, will need to write can be ten pages or less in length. Any more detailed information should be relegated to an appendix. Remember, the main purpose of your document is to persuade, not just to inform and that your readership are busy people. The longer a document gets, the more information you can pack in, but the less persuasive it becomes. Remember the law of diminishing returns.

Tell the reader which bits to read

If you write a document which has a number of different potential readers (and you can't write separate documents for each), indicate clearly which sections are of relevance to each reader. Guide them; don't let them wade through irrelevancies in search of the few paragraphs they need to deal with.

Choose your medium

Ask yourself honestly, am I writing this because it suits me? Is an e-mail (or whatever medium you have chosen) the best way for my readers? Maybe you are writing when you should be getting out and talking. Are you absolutely sure that you aren't hiding behind your keyboard? If you have any doubts at all, stop writing, and go out and meet real people.

7 Meetings (of minds?)

Meetings in Melanesia

When people from Europe were first in contact with the indigenous peoples of highland New Guinea in Melanesia, they assumed that, although there were differences in language, culture, technology and so on, they had come across people with fundamentally the same drives and ambitions. It was puzzling to them, therefore, when they introduced football to the people known as the Gahuku-Gama.

The problem was not with teaching the Gahuku-Gama the skills or rules of football – these were a piece of cake. The difficulty arose when the referee blew the whistle after ninety minutes and the teams played on. For the Gahuku-Gama players there was no way the game could end at that time, since one team was leading.

It would have been a serious loss of face for the leading team to stop playing to the best of their ability to let the other side catch up. But the game could not end with one side being superior to the other. It was very late at night when the teams arrived at the necessary draw.

The rules of the game for the indigenous peoples of highland New Guinea are fundamentally different from the rules of many of the games we play. Throughout Melanesia 'reciprocity' is the name of the game – everyone strives to maintain a healthy balance. Clearly, not everyone is equal in strength, wit, and so on. But it is vital to the way of life that inequalities (such as winning or losing at things) are things to be worked through and eliminated.

Among many of these peoples, the traditional ways of working things out was through meetings of all interested parties gathering for lengthy debates. During these debates it was important that one's own point of view was put across strongly and clearly. But also that, in putting this point of view, no one else would be made to appear to lose face or position. The debates were emotional and noisy. People would stride up and down the centre of the village shouting and gesticulating, thwacking their buttocks for effect. One's whole self was thrown into the complicated game of getting a positive result for everyone.

For most of us in the Western world, this seems crazy. Apart from anything else, it is so time-consuming. This is true. All our technology in the West has successfully made time the scarcest of resources. For the indigenous peoples, time was plentiful. And if it was spent in achieving win-win, it was time well spent. Meetings in Melanesia worked to a very different set of rules.

Why don't the French do meetings properly?

Even in the West, the underlying assumptions of what we mean by 'meeting' vary widely. Even our nearest neighbours across the Channel have a very different mindset when it comes to meetings. British managers when first exposed to the 'French' way of meetings are often bewildered or even incensed by what goes on.

People turn up late (and I mean late – often by half a day, not just a few minutes). They chat among themselves when someone is speaking to the group. They walk out to conduct other affairs while the meeting is still going on. They scream and shout at each other in a most unseemly manner. And finally, they fail to implement what appears to have been decided at the meeting, explaining that the session was for airing views rather than coming to any conclusions. The decision had already been taken anyway!

Many of the 'rules' of meetings are unwritten. Most managers learn how to conduct themselves at meetings by watching and doing. Like the Gahuku-Gama and the French, we learn about meetings by a process of acculturation. The 'right' way of doing meetings is simply the way we have (mostly unconsciously) learnt by long (and often painful and tedious) examples. This chapter looks at the ways in which meetings have become part of the IT management culture, and suggests some simple ways of getting out of some of the more painful traps we fall into.

Some sample areas of conflict

What are meetings for? At the superficial level, they are for exploring options and taking decisions. They involve lots of people, because, theory has it, 'two heads are better than one'.

If the textbooks are to be believed, the way to succeed at meetings is by planning the event as a task. The keys seem to be:

- Getting the right people together for the task.
- Setting clear terms of reference for the meeting.
- Articulating clear objectives.
- Setting an agreed and manageable agenda.
- Appointing a good chairperson who keeps the participants on the straight and narrow.
- Pausing for frequent summaries to confirm agreement and progress.

These are all good and fine, and we do not want to argue with their appropriateness. But alone, they miss a number of tricks.

Divergent and convergent thinking

One area in which many actual meetings fail is in the 'disentanglement' of divergent and convergent thinking. Divergent thinking happens when ideas are produced, often rapidly, and without critical examination. Often used in the first stages of brainstorming, this is a means of tapping into the creativity of the human mind. The broad aim of divergent thinking is to 'hitchhike' on other people's ideas, and, by accumulating a huge number of ideas, bring into consciousness the one great idea which would otherwise go unnoticed or unthought.

Convergent thinking is the process of whittling down ideas – of combining and editing them towards a decision. It is through convergent thinking that people arrive at the way forward. It uses critical rather than creative principles, and analyses rather than imagines.

Everyone 'knows' that the 'right' approach to these useful approaches is to allow each its own space, with divergent thinking coming first, and convergent thinking bringing it all together.

When meetings are set up specifically for these purposes, they often follow the rules. Participants are first of all made familiar with the rules of brainstorming, for example, and away goes the group. This can be highly constructive, especially if methods are used to maintain the flow for long enough. Research shows that ideas seem to peak and decline, and then spring back to life again.

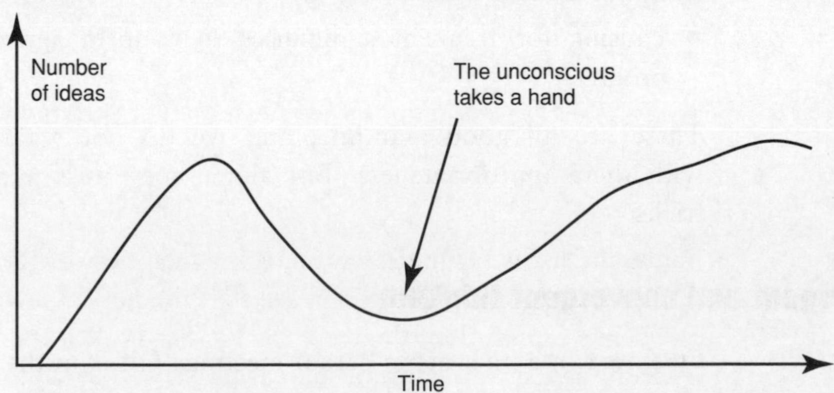

Figure 7.1 Ideas timeline

However, there is often a difference between 'meetings' (as a general description), and specific events set up to follow the brainstorming process. Once a meeting takes on its 'normal' function, divergent and convergent thinking begin to get tangled up. Unless they are carefully managed, people at meetings do not normally follow these simple rules – because a 'meeting' is perceived to be a different process from a brainstorm.

Meetings often obscure the presence of divergent and convergent thinking. Here's an example of how it may work.

A meeting is called to work on a strategy. All the right people are there, and they share an excitement and enthusiasm for developing the way forward. The mood is good, and each participant is determined – this time – that the group will work constructively together. Each is on their best behaviour.

The agenda and ground rules are agreed. Everyone knows the objective. So someone kicks the meeting into life. They pick up a pen and, standing at the flip chart or white board, suggest the kind of things that must be taken into account at the outset:

- Our current product and services portfolio.
- Profitability ratios for the various products and services.
- What the competition are doing.
- Data on customer satisfaction.
- A SWOT (Strengths, Weaknesses, Opportunities, Threats) analysis.

and so on.

While the list is being drawn up, some members of the group are nodding in approval. They can see that the key areas for analysis are being captured and agreed. As the list builds, they add their own thoughts, and gain an increasing sense of comfort that the job they are planning to do will be thorough and effective. Some people like this approach.

But as time passes, there are others in the group who are getting increasingly agitated. Already, for them, the meeting is going horribly wrong, because their 'natural' approach to strategy setting (and to many other things in life) is very different from this. People are different, even though they appear the same on the surface, and they have been 'socialized' in similar ways. In this case, we are witnessing realists versus innovators.

Suddenly one of the innovators can stand the 'realists' way no longer, and they leap up, grab the pen and say that all this is pointless. Facing a mix of ruffled feathers and silent approval, the interrupter turns over the page of the flip chart, or ring-fences a space on the white board and says: 'The way you develop a strategy is not by looking at where we are today, but at where we want to be. We should be defining our vision – our goal. All we are doing here is constraining our thinking. We'll never move forward if we are always looking backward.'

Murmurs of agreement come from some quarters, but the realists fight back. They've seen this kind of 'blue skies' idea before. They know that a strategy has to be rooted in where we are now, not in some airy-fairy future. Visions and missions are just fine words which fail to deal with the day-to-day realities of running a successful business in real life. The debate breaks out into a free-for-all, and the good intentions begin to sink under the waves of disagreement. (We shall have much more to say about these kinds of differences between people later in the book.)

Setting agendas – if you can do that, you don't need the meeting

The example we have just used is not unique. And it does not only apply to meetings which have been set up specifically to deal with 'strategy'. The fact is that many meetings fail to achieve their stated intention simply because what the agenda says means different things to different people.

Setting agendas – if you can do that, you don't need the meeting

This is why sometimes it takes almost the whole meeting time to agree on how to tackle the items on the agenda. We try simply to agree which items we shall discuss, and in which order, but end up discussing the items there and then. We find it hard simply to talk about issues for an agenda, and seem to be drawn into the discussion, despite agreeing that we should follow the rules and the agenda. What is it that makes a discussion one about the agenda, as opposed to one about the item itself?

The answer to this is very easy to put into words, but often very difficult to put into practice. We tend to put it into words through such documents as the 'terms of reference' for a group or meeting. But things don't always work as smoothly as the terms of reference or the ground rules would suggest.

Clearly, something happens at meetings which means that good intentions and rational plans go awry. As rational, sensible, well-

educated people, we ought to be able to get on with the agenda, clear the decks, and get back to work without having to sit through hours of frustration and argument. What stops us?

Let's start with the whole idea of 'having a meeting'. A meeting so defined has invisible but powerful boundaries round it. By 'having a meeting' we enter a psychological space where different rules apply. Sometimes people ask, 'Has the meeting started yet?' as though there is some kind of threshold over which we all have to step for the meeting to start. The reply is sometimes, 'No, but shall we start?' and then the meeting becomes a psychological reality, living through the language and behaviour of the participants until the meeting is 'declared' closed.

Why do we need these invisible boundaries? What is different within them?

People talk differently at meetings. 'Meeting-speak' is more formal and more structured than the way we speak outside those boundaries. When we're not in meetings, we'll tend to allow a more free-flowing approach to what we say. Many people change the way they speak at meetings so much that they sound like bad actors in a soap opera. There's a self-consciousness about their delivery – a measured care which appears as though they're delivering a script.

Some of the ways in which over-simplistic 'management training' is delivered reinforces this self-conscious 'role playing'. Take, for example, the ways in which some trainers take respectable research, such as that of Meredith Belbin, and imply to managers that meetings and other 'teamwork' demand that we take on such simplified roles. 'Profiling' questionnaires are handed out with minimal explanation and managers 'learn' that they are 'Shapers' or 'Plants'. Not surprisingly, those managers start to live out the roles, becoming caricatures of themselves, and hiding behind tragicomic masks. It's a bit of a drama.

The 'dramatic' character of meetings is reinforced by the setting. Like a stage-set, the furniture for meetings is arranged to suit the story; like a play, there's usually only one speaker at a time – something a good chair tries to ensure at all times. And like a play, there's a start and a finish. In most drama, even if we know the actors personally, we know not to interrupt the drama to ask if they'd like to come to dinner after the show. While the show is on, we all pretend – actors and audience. We follow the script and the rules. And when it's all over, we can resume normal behaviour. We wait until after the meeting to invite people for a drink.

We started the chapter by referring to the peoples of New Guinea. You may have found some of what we said about them strange. What a silly way to go about a game of football. Now turn the tables on yourself. Imagine one of those tribespeople watching one of your meetings. Explain to them what is going on and why. Explain the tables and chairs, the agenda, the chair, the language, the dynamics and the outcomes. To the outsider, there's something almost supernatural about our faith in meetings and the liturgy of the agenda.

Given the enormous number of people who, when asked if they like meetings, would say that they don't. And given the enormous number of people who, if asked, would say that meetings are frustrating and inefficient, why do they keep happening? Are meetings part of our religion? Must we keep attending them, as others attend religious services?

Meetings and 'reality'

Hang on a minute. Aren't meetings a bit more down to earth than this? 'In reality' meetings may have their inefficiencies, and they may follow different rules. But this may simply be because meetings are places where people bring their different values and perceptions and look for ways of resolving them, at least in so far as decisions can be taken, and those differences put aside in the inter-

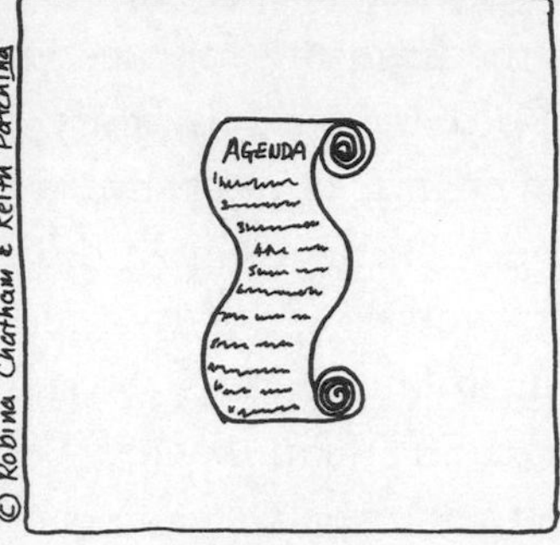

ests of progress. To reconcile these differences you have to have rules, surely. And if those rules produce behaviour which may look strange to outsiders, then so be it. In the end, we may argue, things get done. Meetings make things happen.

But what do they make happen? Try a little experiment. After a meeting you did not attend, ask each individual who was there to tell you briefly what happened. You may have tried this before, and come away with the suspicion that they were at different meetings. Differences may be reconciled in one sense at meetings. But in another sense, these differences are reinforced. Because where people come into meetings with different perceptions, they also go through those meetings with different perceptions – about what went on during the meeting itself.

People take minutes of meetings to deal precisely with this problem. Like history books, these minutes can record only some of the 'truth'. Despite the 'fact' that what happened in history cannot be changed – what's done is done – historians continue to write more books about the past. What they are doing is offering different interpretations of what has happened. What they are saying is that there is no such thing as the definitive version of the past. Even minutes of meetings are a form of interpretation. They can record every word spoken, but they may still miss the most important things which take place.

In the last chapter on writing, we suggested that IT managers may like to consider the impact of what they write more than the content. This is because persuasiveness is not the same as being factually correct. Meeting minutes, like reports, may be accurate records of the 'literal truth', but they rarely do more than record the superficial.

'Task' and 'process' – a crude but significant distinction

Being 'right' is not enough.

Organizational politics operate in the zones where there are no right answers. In other words, there are, in every human endeavour, a number of different ways of defining the 'right way'.

For many IT managers, the 'right way' is defined by technical efficiency or effectiveness. But every IT manager also knows that if the ends are suspect, technical 'rightness' does not define the 'right way'. Genocide can be done with increasing efficiency through advances in 'defence' technology. But political debates have to be about the 'why' as well as the 'how'.

Meetings are the primary arena for organizational politics. Superficially, debates in meetings are about finding the 'right way'. Under the surface they are about exploring each others' values, visions, characters, desires, emotions and 'political' leanings. This is one reason why, although many of the relatively technical issues which are often debated at meetings could easily be resolved by fewer people than actually attend, it is unproductive in the long run to exclude those with a legitimate interest in the debate.

Many meetings which fail to achieve the 'task' outcomes set for them are nevertheless highly effective in 'process' terms. Through airing differing views people become more human – less one-dimensional. Caricatures and stereotypes begin to break down when people get to know each other. If you take with you into a meeting as your primary outcome that you want to understand more about your colleagues, you want to find out more about their own ideas, you want to treat them as people rather than as more or less efficient cogs in the decision-making machine, you may begin to recognize why meetings persist despite their apparent inefficiency.

Many of the frustrations felt by people about meetings stem from an unconscious belief that meetings are about technical outcomes – about getting things done. Also (often unconsciously) people recognize that one person sitting alone at a workstation could accomplish much more than these 'committees' which take forever to make progress. The mistake being made by people who think like this is that technical outcomes are what meetings are all about. This is the naivety which continues to believe that the story of Little Red Riding Hood is about an innocent little girl and a wolf (read *The Uses of Enchantment* by Bruno Bettelheim, Penguin Books, London, 1976 if you're puzzled by this one), or that *West Side Story* is just about gangs in New York.

Do not ignore the task

So even if Little Red Riding Hood is about 'other stuff', it's still a good story on the surface. It does none of us any good to try to work solely at the undercurrents. Bettleheim makes a good point about fairy tales, but you wouldn't read Bettelheim to your children at night. And just because most of the impact of meetings takes place under the surface, don't stop trying to get the 'story' right.

This means that the work you do to ensure that the right people are involved, that the right time is set aside, the right agenda is drawn up, and a tight rein is maintained over the discussion is all to the good. However, try in addition the following ideas as a starter:

- Limit your meetings to one hour maximum.
- Try having meetings in rooms with no chairs.
- Deal with as many items as you can informally, maybe even over a drink instead of in a meeting.
- Spend more time asking about other people's ideas and feelings, and using their answers to appreciate them as people.
- Present your thoughts more as things to play with rather than as precious jewels – try thanking people for pointing out alternative suggestions.
- Set up more meetings with people other than your staff and suppliers (e.g. your customers and your peers in other organizations) – think less of the 'task' outcomes and more of the 'process' – meetings are the main vehicle for getting to grips with the politics in your organization – so meet with the people who matter.
- Stop looking only on the surface – consider what is happening beyond the agenda – learn to read people and body language.

The fact is that successful people do not spend as much time 'in meetings' as unsuccessful people do. Time and again in our researches with the most senior people in business, we find them in control, with time to spare to discuss with us the more far-reaching issues, rather than the operational issues which tend to dominate meetings in our culture. They just don't get bogged down with these things. They are not 'busy' and self-important like many IT managers we have met, who seem incapable of managing their way out of the never-ending cycle of interminable and ineffective meetings. The most successful senior managers do attend meetings, but selectively and effectively.

Later, we'll delve deeper into ways in which the 'streetwise' IT manager can go further in making 'meetings' more effective. But that has to wait until we have had time to build stronger foundations in Part Three.

8 Reinventing the wheel

One day you decide you need a washing machine for your home. So what do you do? You have a number of options, one of which is to build one yourself. There are very good reasons for this. Your washing needs are not exactly the same as anyone else's. Besides, you are sure that you could come up with a more elegant solution than all these professional washing machine builders could. So you could gather together a team of people who, collectively, and under your management, could design and build you your customized washing machine.

Of course, you're not tempted by this route. It's easier and quicker to buy one. After all, you're not in the washing machine business. You're no longer a programmer, either. But at times you're tempted to put together a team of programmers to write that system which cannot possibly be bought from the 'shop'. There are times when this is a good idea, for example, if your organization wants to 'gain competitive advantage from IT'; and there are times when it is not.

Gaining competitive advantage from IT

A few years ago, everyone in and around IT was talking about the ways in which IT had revolutionized some industries. There was a good reason for this, because there were some really good stories.

American Airlines, for example, gained an enormous (and lasting) competitive advantage from their on-line reservations system, Sabre. By inviting competitors to use Sabre for a small fee for each booking, American Airlines earned more revenue in one year from the system than they did from flying aeroplanes. And they gained a great deal of information about their competitors at the same time.

Thompsons Holidays, here in the UK, gained fame from their TOPS system. Like Sabre, this was a reservations system. It provided a platform from which Thompsons could gain market leadership in each of their target markets.

Merrill Lynch, American Hospital Supplies, and many others seemed to foretell of significant changes built upon IT. And in some industries this has happened.

For the companies that got there first, there have been some spectacular gains. This has always been the result of 'doing it yourself'. Other revolutions, for example, have not really given much advantage to those who got there first. For banks and other financial services organizations, for example, putting automatic cash dispensers outside branches and in places like motorway service stations and in shopping malls is so easily copied that it becomes standard rather than unique. Given that the manufacturers of ATMs (automatic telling machines) are going to maximize their return on their investments, they will be selling ATMs to everyone else as well. And the same is true of consultancies who help companies develop software solutions that are (temporarily) unique.

The lesson seems to be: 'If you want to gain and sustain competitive advantage from IT, build your own solutions'.

This is perfectly true, but it may tempt some IT managers to see everything they do as potentially providing competitive advantage. And therefore feeling obliged to develop every application the organization needs. This is a mistake. Not all (indeed very few) applications are going to be like this. Some will be about saving money through increased efficiency; others will be about doing core business more effectively.

The applications portfolio – defining what not to reinvent

Our colleagues at Cranfield have for some years worked with a simple but effective tool for classifying applications. Known as the 'applications portfolio', it is shown in Figure 8.1.

Briefly, the idea behind the model is that different kinds of system needs demand different kinds of applications. Those applications classified at the top of the portfolio are about gaining competitive advantage. 'High potential' applications are the laboratory in which 'Strategic' applications are born. They contrast with those at the bottom, which use the power of IT to reduce costs by creating efficiencies ('Support' applications), usually for individuals or for a work-group, or improving effectiveness by providing ways of automating your core business ('Key operational' applications).

The differences between these kinds of applications are often highly significant.

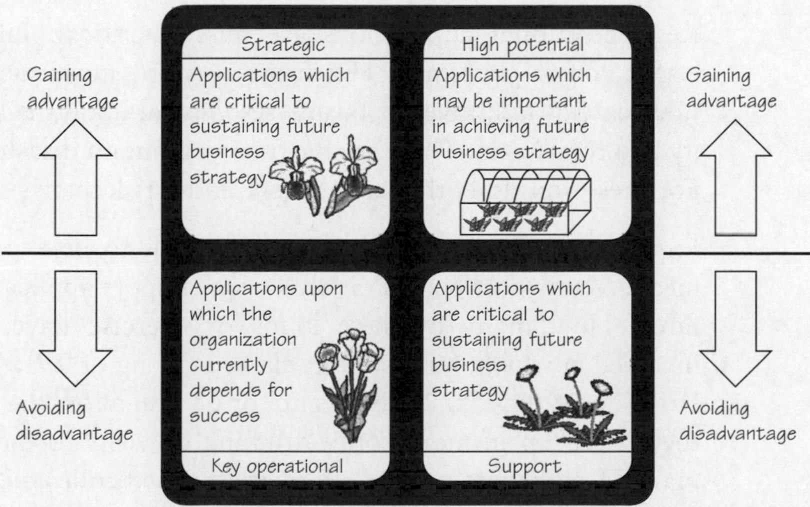

Figure 8.1 Applications portfolio

How you fund them

High potential applications need to be allowed freedom to develop whatever potential they may have – like most R&D projects, these applications may come to naught. But every groundbreaking 'strategic' application we know of started life as a germ of an idea. Many of them start life through the dabbling of amateurs – business managers playing with an idea. If you starve them of all funds, they will never come to light (with all the potential benefits they may bring with them). For these kinds of activity, you can't realistically do a cost-benefit analysis; you simply need to box time or expenditure, just as with any other R&D activity

Strategic applications demand venture funding. Just like any other project which the company is betting its future on, a strategic application may absorb more funds than were originally intended. But the stakes will be high. American Airlines would never have made their fortune with Sabre if they had backed away from the project because it was 'costing too much'.

Key operational applications are mission-critical. Like the air traffic control system at Heathrow Airport, most such applications cannot fail. Lives or businesses depend upon their availability and robustness. These are the ones you put on disaster standby. For these you do both a cost benefit and a risk analysis.

Expenditure on Support applications needs to be kept lean and mean. Many 'cost-benefit' analyses for Support applications are a farce. How many of these kinds of exercise have you been involved in which, for example, claim a saving of 0.2 of a person? Do you add these '0.2' savings up, or do you allow the extra time to be used up in more coffee-drinking or visits to the loo? Too many IT managers, along with their esteemed colleagues throughout the business, pretend they are doing serious grown-up work in building spreadsheet analyses which do very little more than a quick and dirty 'hunch' would achieve. Stop wasting time. You must also be wary of succumbing to the wishes of users who want the latest in PCs, with internal cache, quad speed, soundblaster audio cards, etc. You don't always succumb to your children's demands for the latest trainers, computer games, and so on, so why succumb to users' demands for the latest toys?

You also need to know how to source them

Packages are the most likely solution to your needs for Key operational and Support applications. Unless you are in a very specialized industry, most of your core processes will be similar to those of many other companies. You may need to modify some aspects of the packages you choose. But if the application is truly supporting your core processes, you are unlikely to gain a great deal by re-inventing what is already being used by others. This is even more true in the case of Support applications. If you develop

them yourself, you will be missing the point. If you are found developing your own payroll, personnel, invoicing, or other bog-standard kind of application for your company, you should be shot.

Understand the business you are in, and focus your developmental creativity on delivering IT benefits to activities that are genuinely about the future, and that no one else is doing, by which we mean Strategic and High potential applications. For these, you will not find packages available, since they will not have been invented yet. And if they have, then these will not be Strategic or High potential. You'll be playing catch-up.

Here's a thought: If your IT investments all followed the appropriate approaches for each kind of application, you would truly be seen as adding value to the business, and you would be a hero.

So why are so few organizations able to make these alignments?

It's the users' fault

The problem lies with the users' unwillingness to adjust their basic activities to suit those packages. And not only are they unwilling to adapt themselves to how standard packages operate, but they are also unwilling to adapt themselves to a consistent set of ways of working within the company. Marketing want 'customers' to be defined in one way, while accounts want 'customers' to mean something very different. If we are truly to help such disparate departments to work together, they are going to have to stop seeing the world exclusively through their own lenses.

But here we are back to the central problem of the book. We know, don't we, that our job of helping our organizations exploit IT to the full depends upon users listening to the kinds of cogent arguments which this chapter is presenting. It makes perfect sense to:

- Identify and define the core processes of the business, so that investment criteria can be agreed and applied rigorously.

- Classify IT applications both in accordance to their contribution to those classified processes, and in terms of the management strategies best applied to each kind of application, as defined by the portfolio.

But knowing all this is not the same as getting the business to listen and learn. And as we have been saying all along, having the right argument is not enough.

Our users may be partially to blame, but if we are to make a difference, we will have to apply the 'streetwise' approach. This means starting with an honest confrontation with the stereotype and the ways in which we might inadvertently be reinforcing it.

Perhaps it's our fault, too

In the period when IT was becoming established, the world looked different. NCR used to manufacture its own screws for its cash machines; Cadbury's used to make all its own boxes to package its chocolates. People still had the 'self-sufficiency' mindset. For IT this was fine, since, in those days, there were no packages. Systems development was a pioneering place to be. People went into IT because it enabled them both to map and to populate uncharted territory. A great deal of job satisfaction came from the elegance of design and construction of our COBOL modules.

We learnt (unconsciously in most cases) that it was 'boring' to reuse previously written code; that no one else could code application software which so accurately matched how Doris dealt with enquiries from customers and performed so elegantly. We knew that next time we had to write code for what looked like the 'same' process, we could do it better – practice makes perfect. It became part of the 'IT psyche'. It manifests itself in a variety of ways.

Many IT managers are poor at delegating, for example. Admitting that a package can do a better job is also hard – that's delegating to someone else, too. Many IT managers are going through a crisis of identity. Growing up in pioneering territory, they have learnt skills and approaches that often suit their innate personalities.

They are self-sufficient, independent and proud. They often like to work alone. They are intellectually clever, and like the challenge of a new problem to solve. Deep down, many IT managers don't want to stop tinkering, pioneering and reinventing wheels. They may not admit it – even to themselves. It may not even be 'true'. But it is part of the IT stereotype. And as we suggested at the start of the book, your job is not only to deal with your own skills and behaviours. It is also to deal with the stereotypical image which goes before you.

Moving on

There's a lot of work that can usefully be done with users around the models we have presented here. But our suggestion is that, for many readers, it may not be productive to rush straight into a series of meetings designed to get everyone – business and IT – to agree on the best ways of classifying and managing your processes and applications.

This would be to adopt the naïve approach. The streetwise approach means getting to grips with the 'political' issues as well as the 'logical' ones. In the next two chapters, we'll complete our survey of the 'problem'. Then we can start to develop 'solutions'.

9 Firefighting and rework

We often ask IT managers we work with what they measure (we deal with measures in more detail in Chapter 17). A common area for measurement centres on the help desk. Many IT managers measure the number of calls, and the number of calls which are dealt with within a certain time frame. Indeed, many service level agreements (SLAs) have such measures embedded within them. Sophisticated help desk procedures and systems have been devised over the years which give confidence that, at least in this area, we are doing everything we can to present a positive response.

Numbers are data. These days we all know the difference between data and information. So simply having a chart which looks like Figure 9.1 does not mean we are doing a good job. Should the

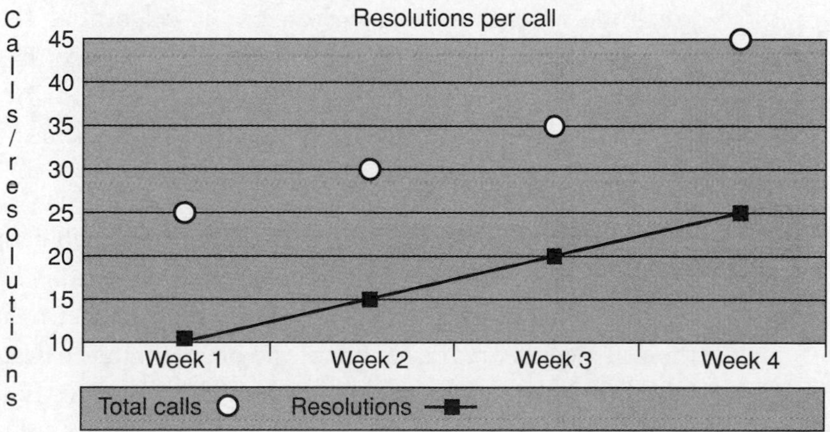

Figure 9.1 Calls to the help desk

number of calls be going up or down? If they are going down, then we seem to be sorting out people's problems. Perhaps, but this may mean that people are getting fed up with waiting, and simply putting up with their problems. On the other hand, if the problems are being sorted out, are these resolutions making any real difference to the business? Perhaps one of the unresolved calls is from the CEO?

The problem with so many of these kinds of measures is that they can mean so many different things. And one of the hidden messages which often lies behind such measures is a fundamental difference of opinion about what is going on.

Ask yourself the following question: 'In my time in the IT business, what have been among my most satisfying moments?'. For many, the answer will relate to times when they have been able to apply their technical skills to resolve problems which users have been wrestling with. One of the leading car breakdown services a while ago based an advertising campaign on the 'heroic' nature of their operatives. The catch-phrase which went with the campaign was 'a very, very nice man'. It summed up the sense of relief and gratitude of the rescued customers; it celebrated the technical problem-solving skills of their staff. We suspect that many IT people get much of their sense of self-esteem from similar problem-solving exploits. They may be the only times when users say 'thank you'.

Of course, the downside to this analogy is that, whereas in the car breakdown situation, those who are called out to help seldom have responsibility for the fault with the vehicle, in users' eyes, their IT people are the source of the problem in the first place. The year 2000 problem is a case in point. It's all very well for the IT function to say that, with great effort and devotion (at the expense of all those other things users have been told they have to wait for) they have killed the Millennium Bug. But who started it, if not the IT community?

Fixing problems may provide short-term relief, but it represents what the quality folk of the 1980s called PONC – the price of non conformance. PONC is the total cost to an organization of dealing with and fixing things which have not gone according to plan. It covers all of those activities which are about fixing, reworking, repairing, revisiting, tweaking, fire-fighting, and in any other way sorting out those things which, in an ideal world, would have been 'right, first time, on time, every time'. For the quality movement, PONC was the way in which they demonstrated that quality is actually cheaper than rework.

We have looked at a number of IT shops which keep timesheets to work out just how much time people actually spend in firefighting and rework (in other words, how much PONC there is). As you will expect, the levels are very high indeed. It has not been unheard of for IT people to break something in order for them to bask in the glory of fixing it!

Some excuses

So let's get the excuses out of the way first.

The rate of change in technology is so great that new versions keep overlapping and interfering with each other. What started off as a good solution soon gets knocked about by its interfaces with yet another version of the word processing package, or an upgrade to the e-mail system. This is part of the way of life these days.

Users keep changing their minds. This is exacerbated by these new toys, but ever since we started to use computers, users have had this annoying habit of asking for something, trying it, and then complaining that what they wanted was not what they asked for. Cartoons illustrating this adorn the walls of many IT department offices. It's the way IT people get their own back.

Some responses

In the eyes of the user community, IT is a seamless whole. Just as you are to blame for the Y2K problem, so you are to blame for any inability you show to keep pace with the rate of technological change. Users have lost faith in the 'it's not us, it's networking you want to complain to' response. Your job is to represent every aspect of IT, whether it's your department, another department, an outsourced function, a vendor, or any other potential player in the increasingly complex game.

A few years ago I visited an IT department which nicely illustrated internal strife. Some wit had amended the notice above the door of the networking team as shown below.

In this department, Help Desk personnel and developers 'knew' that all the problems of the users were to be laid at the door of the Networking Team. Problems which others could resolve themselves were a clear illustration of how 'stupid' the Networking Team were; those which they could not resolve were a clear illustration of how Networking caused problems.

No doubt such internecine strife has been drummed out of your IT department. If there are any final echoes of such strife, look carefully at them – they are breeding grounds of PONC.

From SCREAM to CREAM

Ten years ago one of the authors wrote a book for information centre managers in which he played with a couple of acronyms. He suggested that most information centre managers (often implicitly) would list their key functions as:

- Support.
- Corporate information access provision.
- Recommending hardware and software solutions.
- Education of users in end user tools.
- Advice and guidance on the potential of IT for the future.
- Marketing the information centre (not just promoting it).

The acronym made up of the initials of each of these was just right, since most information centre managers we knew were on the verge of screaming all the time. The idea that they would work their way to the bottom of the list, and actually devote time to developing a marketing approach to end user computing was bizarre – few of them had time to take a deep breath!

The advice we gave then is still valid. So long as support heads the list, the culture of firefighting and rework will remain. So long as support is seen as something to be eliminated, a culture of growth and development is possible. The aims of the quality movement were to remove PONC altogether; the aims of the IT function ought to be to do the same. This means working towards an ultimate goal where support becomes a thing of the past.

In the 'real world' this is unlikely to happen. But the probability that something will never fully go away should not prevent it being a target for elimination. Imagine a world in which research scientists stopped seeking cures for diseases on the grounds that diseases would never fully go away. For them, the vision is as unlikely to come about as any vision of a 'support-free' IT world. But they work as though the vision could become reality.

Firefighting and rework may never go away. But many IT managers may discover, if they are honest with themselves, that they are not putting as much effort into their elimination as they could.

10 Shattering the illusion

Part Two of this book has been devoted to asking one of the very big questions – do you really want to become streetwise?

We have not been kind. We have made suggestions and accusations which many readers will find offensive, or at least difficult to swallow. But our research suggests that it is in the nature of the IT psyche to remain the innocent victim of users' bullying, political intrigue and general lack of reasonableness. It is still the case that often very senior IT managers have a hankering for the good old days when they could just be left alone to enjoy their lonely pursuits.

If, deep in your heart, you know that reading core dumps is more what you want to do than to engage in the cut and thrust of senior business management, then the chances are that you have reached (or even surpassed) the level of seniority to which you are suited. You may, in that case, decide that there is no point in reading the rest of this book. You may be better advised to stay put and avoid making your own and others' lives a misery as you go in pursuit of a goal which is wrong for you. We are not all destined for senior management. Indeed, it is a good job that we are not. If you are one of those for which the path to senior management is not an attractive one, rejoice in what you are good at, and do not try to be what you are not.

But if you do want to break through, and are prepared to take the messages of the book on the chin, then here are a few thoughts to launch you into the next part of the book.

How you see yourself and measure yourself may need to change radically. Like Martin, you may be puzzled by an apparent inconsistency between your own perceptions of effectiveness and what others think about you. Don't worry, this is all part of emerging from the IT shell.

You will need to take time out, and to have the courage to face up to who you are and how you behave. Humility, honesty, self awareness and an addiction to feedback are part of the skill-set you will be exploring in the next part of the book. You may need to face up to some uncomfortable truths.

If you are thinking as you read this, 'But I haven't got time for all this ...' you may already be suffering from the kinds of defensiveness which prevent many IT managers becoming streetwise. If you always do what you've always done, you'll always get what you always got. Step back, and be prepared to see yourself through others' eyes. Build your strategy for success.

Part Three
Why won’t other people let me do my job?

11 Leading, managing and abdicating

You can't do it all alone. It is a rare IT department that is staffed by one individual. And no matter how hard you may try to keep your personal image polished, it is the activities of your staff as well as you that will create and maintain your reputation.

This is because, as a manager, you are responsible for the actions of your staff. That's why you need to manage them – or lead them. So what's the difference? And why does becoming a manager mean you can't carry on being one of the lads?

As a start in exploring these questions, try the questionnaire on pages 100–102. This is repeated in the Appendix for ease of photocopying. It's for your own use, however you may like to gather feedback from your staff too. No one other than yourself need see the results. So be honest with yourself. The purpose of the exercise is to help you surface some of your deeper assumptions about what being a good IT manager is, and to help identify how you use those assumptions in your managerial behaviour.

Of course, there's no reason why you shouldn't use the questionnaire as a means of getting feedback from your staff as well. This

is because management is more about what you do, and how staff interprets that, than it is about what you think you do.

It is not uncommon for managers to have widely different perceptions about their management style from those of their staff. We have even come across managers who are, in their eyes, very good at managing, but none of whose staff realize that!

So take your courage in your hands and use the questionnaire both to map out what you intend, and to find out how it comes out. The contrasts, if any, will be more valuable than your own self-perception.

Leadership questionnaire

Each of the following sets of statements concern different approaches to leadership and management. Please score each statement in each set by distributing 5 points among the three options.

For each statement in each set of three, please consider which reflects how you actually behave with your staff (not how you think you ought to behave). If only one statement represents how you behave at all times, score 5 for that statement and 0 for each of the other two in the set. If two statements represent how you behave, spread the 5 points between them (4 and 1 or 3 and 2) according to how closely they match your behaviours. In the event that you sometimes exhibit all three behaviours in a set, give each statement an appropriate weighting (3, 1, 1 or 2, 2, 1).

1a	It is important to have clear plans	☐
1b	I have provided my staff with a clear vision for the future	☐
1c	We work on tasks as they arise, rather than try to foresee the future	☐
2a	We take things on an ad hoc basis, preferring to deal with matters as they arise	☐
2b	In order to get the work done, I allocate clear areas of responsibility to each of my staff	☐

2c	I spend time with my staff ensuring that we all have a common vision for the future	☐
3a	By pulling together, we all ensure that the work gets done	☐
3b	One of my most important tasks is to motivate and energize my people	☐
3c	It is my job to 'steer the ship' and maintain control	☐
4a	In this changing world, I encourage creativity and create change within my function to anticipate the future	☐
4b	We learn by experience, and use that experience to remove the necessity for rules or routines	☐
4c	I take a systematic approach to the ongoing tasks of my function, creating routines which ensure efficient service and project delivery	☐
5a	The buck stops with me	☐
5b	Problems should be resolved or dealt with by those who create them	☐
5c	I give authority and responsibility to my staff, but always remain accountable	☐
6a	Before embarking upon activities, I spend time ensuring that my staff are committed to our chosen course of action	☐
6b	I insist on my people conforming to established standards	☐
6c	Everyone has their own best approach, with which I do not interfere	☐
7a	My people are all familiar with the terms of our SLAs, so that they can work within the appropriate contractual obligations	☐
7b	My people are so motivated that they naturally go that extra mile for the customer	☐
7c	Work patterns are relatively fluid around here; non-urgent problems rarely get to the top of the list	☐
8a	I take an interest in my people as individuals and understand what makes each of them tick	☐
8b	We tend to get on with our own work, and help each other out as and when necessary	☐
8c	My people look to me for impartiality and fair judgement in any differences of view	☐
9a	Even when we are busy, I encourage my people to consider the long-term implications of their actions	☐

Leadership questionnaire

9b	People work best on what interests them, so our work patterns tend to centre upon each individual's expertise	☐
9c	We are good at responding to the needs of our customers and resolving problems quickly	☐
10a	Plans and mission statements are not suitable for the way we do things around here	☐
10b	People in my function are all aware of our mission	☐
10c	Activities do not take place here without a clear plan of action	☐
11a	Everyone in my function knows their distinct area of responsibility	☐
11b	All my staff have the opportunity to contribute to our vision of the future	☐
11c	I believe in being one of the team; we all take our share of the workload	☐
12a	People often come to me with problems because they know I can solve them	☐
12b	I lead by example and am respected by my staff for my technical expertise	☐
12c	People describe me as an inspiring person	☐
13a	My staff and I get on with our jobs, and let the business get on with its work	☐
13b	Innovation is one of my most important areas of focus – and not just technological innovation!	☐
13c	It is a key part of my job to maintain equilibrium within the function	☐
14a	I help people to grow by empowering them	☐
14b	I may involve others in reviewing options, but decisions are ultimately mine to make	☐
14c	Decisions are best taken by people who are working on the relevant job; I try not to get involved	☐
15a	There's always a best way to do things, and I ensure that my people follow the rules which ensure such best practice	☐
15b	So long as my people are committed to the vision and aims of the function, I do not worry about exactly how they achieve them	☐
15c	My people are all experts in their own right; I trust them to take a professional approach at all times	☐

Score sheet

Transfer your scores from each question into the grid below, and total up each column to give you a final score for each leadership style.

Question	TM-score	LS-score	LF-score
1	1a	1b	1c
2	2c	2b	2a
3	3c	3b	3a
4	4c	4a	4b
5	5a	5c	5b
6	6b	6a	6c
7	7a	7b	7c
8	8c	8a	8b
9	9c	9a	9b
10	10c	10b	10a
11	11a	11b	11c
12	12a	12c	12b
13	13c	13b	13a
14	14b	14a	14c
15	15a	15b	15c
Total			
	TM-score	LS-score	LF-score

Now plot your own profile by marking your TM-score (traditional management) on the left arm of the triangle in Figure 11.1; your LS-score (leadership) on the top arm; and your LF-score (laissez-faire) on the right arm. Join the dots for your complete leadership style profile.

The profile you have created on the leadership triangle identifies the degree to which you see yourself operating in three different 'zones' or styles of management.

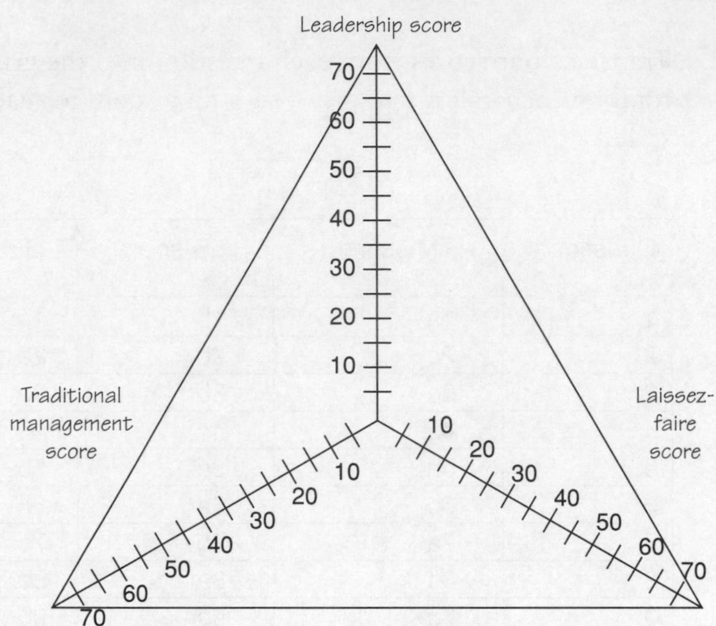

Figure 11.1 Leadership profile scoring chart

Traditional management

Your score out of 75 suggests how much of this kind of management you do. We have called this 'traditional management'. This is because it is the kind of management most often taught in traditional texts and on management courses.

Some key words and phrases which go with this style are:

- Systems and task orientation.
- Creating and sticking to rules.
- Monitoring and measuring.
- Process oriented and job allocation.
- Fitting people to jobs.
- Treating people as a resource.
- Creating certainty, regularity and consistency.

It takes as one of its principles that authority is associated with seniority or rank. The relationship between manager and managed is one of authority. The manager has power. Exercising this power means identifying (or guessing) what really motivates people to do as they are told, and then making sure that the 'carrots' or 'sticks' are clearly identified.

'Traditional management' attempts to eliminate the unpredictability of human behaviour in order to ensure that people within an organization do the things they are asked to do, and thereby help the organization to achieve its goals. The 'traditional' manager receives from some place a set of objectives, and marshals their resources (including the 'human' resources) in the pursuit of those objectives. It is based upon a set of assumptions about organizations and people.

One of the key assumptions it rests on is that the 'rational' goals of the organization and the 'rational' goals of each individual can be brought into line through rules and processes. The 'messiness' of emotions and personal dreams get in the way, and are therefore driven out. The 'ideal' is for each human being to be a completely rational part of a broader set of activities, each of which is part of an overall, systematic and tidy grand plan.

The IT profession has grown up within this set of assumptions. Our job has been to design and create the systems which will make our organizations efficient and effective. It has rarely been part of our brief to take into account the personal and individual needs of the people within the systems.

Now you may say that, over the years, we have often taken people into account. You may have your own particular stories about how you have helped avoid an implementation problem by pointing out aspects of proposed systems which will cause distress, or even precipitate strikes by groups of workers. That's great. But these are the exceptions which prove the rule – systems first, people to work within them second.

If you have scored high on this scale, don't take it personally. This is what you have been taught to do by your experience in IT and by the advocates of traditional management. If it makes you feel uncomfortable, it may be because it feels like you're losing your identity and sense of belonging which you felt before you took on the levels of managerial responsibility you now have. If this is the case, you may find that you have scored fairly high on the second scale – laissez-faire.

Laissez-faire

Your score out of 75 suggests how much of this kind of management you do. We have called this 'laissez-faire'. This is because it takes a very hands-off approach to the task of management, and allows a great deal of licence to staff.

Being one of the lads is a habit which is hard to break for some IT managers. The pressures of traditional management to distance oneself and become less personal are often resisted by those in IT management who have a deeper personal need to be liked or to join in. This resistance is often manifested in the style of management we have called 'laissez-faire'. Managers who adopt this style often explain it as leading by example.

Some key words and phrases which go with this style are:

- Being a member of the team.
- Sharing out the responsibility.
- Hanging on to technical expertise.
- 'Us' versus 'them'.

- Anti-bureaucratic.
- Letting people do their own thing.
- Focus on jobs rather than purpose.
- A need to be liked.

One of the symptoms of high scorers in this style is an inability to clearly articulate and live by the difference between empowerment and letting go altogether. Delegation, which is a major platform upon which true empowerment rests, is not something which comes easily to many IT managers. In this style, delegation manifests itself as abdication, when managers allocate tasks, often unfamiliar ones, and then offer no help or guidance. It is not uncommon for these tasks to be snatched back when these managers perceive that those delegated to are struggling, cannot do the job as well as they can themselves, or are simply not doing the job in the 'right way'.

In many cases, the argument is that it is quicker to do a job yourself than to teach someone else to do it. They also find it difficult to accept a lesser standard than they could deliver themselves, or an alternative style or approach. They often carry with them the mindset of 'only one right or best way to do this job'.

Put down that screwdriver if you want to become streetwise. If you find this too hard, ask yourself again, 'do I really want to be a senior manager?'. Or do you want the trappings of seniority without the responsibility which goes with it? There is nothing inherently wrong in a high score on this scale; it simply suggests that what you truly want from your working life is the sense of belonging, affiliation and friendship which may seem unattainable from outside this style of management.

Before trying to confirm that view, let's look at the third style, which we have called 'leadership'.

Leadership

Your score out of 75 suggests how much of this kind of management you do. We have called this 'leadership'. This is because it is the style which is most actively built upon the notion of leading rather than managing or abdicating. Leadership only works if people actively follow you and support you. You can't do leadership on your own.

Some key words and phrases which go with this style are:

- Mature and robust.
- Empowering and enabling.
- Inspiring and motivating.
- Creating a vision.
- Effective delegation.
- Bringing out the best in others.
- Treating people as people.
- Creating trust, honesty and integrity.
- Developing people to their full potential.

Leadership shares with abdication a strong sense of belonging, and takes a personal approach to management. It shares with traditional management a sense of responsibility for achievement in the often harsh world of organizational life.

Leadership is built upon the realization of the potential of those who follow. It exercises delegation effectively, and recognizes that organizations are made up of people who use systems to help them, rather than of systems into which people are expected to fit. Because leadership starts with people, it provides a firm training ground for the kinds of political acumen which this book is all about.

But to achieve the capabilities associated with this definition of leadership demands the development of high levels of interpersonal skills, and a maturity and robustness which is rarely developed through the kinds of training and education traditionally provided within the IT community.

The 'ideal' profile on our leadership triangle is a high score at the top of Figure 11.1 (leadership) with a little of the other two styles. This is because the streetwise senior IT manager builds their reputation on the active followership of their staff, and the trust, honesty and integrity which underpin a successful and valued IT function.

We write in much more detail about this style of management in Chapter 27. Truly to understand how leadership works depends upon foundations we will be laying down in the next few chapters.

12 Recruiting into the tribe

In earlier chapters we described the IT stereotype. Why does it persist? The IT tribe needs new people all the time. Like most tribes, IT brings into its ranks those who fit in well, and who will not taint the purity of the bloodstock. So is the IT stereotype's continued existence as much a result of our recruitment strategies as it is of outsiders' prejudices?

At the time of writing, recruitment is a key issue. There is a perceived shortage of good people to be had, and many IT managers are tearing their hair out trying to attract sufficient resources to meet the ever-increasing demands of the business.

Most IT managers are constrained by what they can pay their staff, and therefore expectations set by advertisements in the computing press may well be beyond your own budget. Indeed, you may be right to be sceptical, since these figures could well be over-inflated. Maybe no one ever really pays the top of those scales. But in such matters, you are up against expectations you cannot meet.

IT managers occasionally assume that the only way to keep up with the market is to match salaries with the best payers. There is more to life than a fat pay cheque at the end of each month, and many HR managers are very helpful in drawing up packages which meet other needs as well as money. However, Martin's negotiations with his HR Director have not hit the mark.

There are two angles to this chapter. The first looks at how we recruit into the ranks of our departments. How we do this is largely under our own control. The second looks at how the most senior IT person is recruited into an organization, especially where this IT person is brought in at IT Director or CIO level. This is where the recruitment strategy can have a big impact on the political clout at the top of IT.

Growing your own tribe

'Comfortable cloning' (for a more comprehensive look at this, see 'Putting Your Company's Whole Brain to Work,' by Dorothy Leonard and Susan Straus, *Harvard Business Review*, July–August 1997) is a process which most of us unconsciously go through when we recruit people. It means recruiting people like us. In its simplest form, it means 'left-brained' people tending to recruit other 'left-brained' people, because they like their sense of order and logic, and have suspicions about any 'right-brained' applicants who exhibit disorder and subjectivity in how they present themselves. Meanwhile, 'right-brained' people will welcome the creativity and openness of other 'right-brainers', and see 'left-brained' applicants as dull and potentially frustrating to work with.

At the conscious level, many of us try to kid ourselves into believing that we avoid such preconceptions, saying that we deliberately look out for people unlike us so that they can complement our strengths.

But part of the problem in this is that we are like each other and unlike each other in many different ways. The idea, borrowed from physics, that 'like poles repel, unlike poles attract' is, like so many ideas from the sciences, applicable only in a narrow sense. Human interactions are far more complex than the attraction between magnets.

We'll delve deeper into the implications of this in Part Four. For the moment, we'll concentrate on the kinds of skills, qualities and attributes you might want to look for when recruiting into your IT department.

Skills for what? The competencies of the IT function

Before looking for specific skills, it may help to be clear about what the IT department ought to be good at. After all, skills are only as good as the contribution they make to an overall set of organizational abilities.

We'll call what the IT function needs to be good at 'competencies'. When we talk of skills, qualities or attributes, we'll be referring to things individuals have or acquire. We'll look first of all at what kinds of competencies your IT function needs. Then we'll explore what this means for your recruitment strategies.

We have researched the key competencies of the IT function, and have identified nineteen which we have sorted into four categories:

- *Competencies which can transform business thinking, and enable IT to be a business partner*:
  1. Have impact and influence on business thinking;
  2. Establish credibility as having an equal voice within the business to that of all other functions;
  3. Innovate to enable competitive advantage;
  4. Effect and manage business change including technical, organizational and people issues;
  5. Build and manage internal/external relationships at all levels.

- *Competencies which add value to the business, and enable IT to be a change agent*:
  6. Select, motivate and develop IT people (technical, managerial, business, people skills);
  7. Allocate IT resource effectively (right people, right jobs);
  8. Monitor and evaluate future trends;
  9. Monitor and evaluate business benefit;
  10. Understand customer expectations and perceptions.

- *Competencies which deliver the core job of IT as a service function*:
  11. Align and deliver IS product supply with business need;
  12. Develop and maintain an effective and flexible systems architecture;
  13. Evaluate and select supply options;
  14. Establish suitable control mechanisms and measures;
  15. Manage risk and plan for continuity;
  16. Build and maintain a robust, reliable and responsive infrastructure.

- *Additional competencies which work at all levels*:
  17. Establish and maintain a positive and healthy culture within the IT function;
  18. Communicating effectively at and between all levels;
  19. Individual personal visions and the will to pursue them.

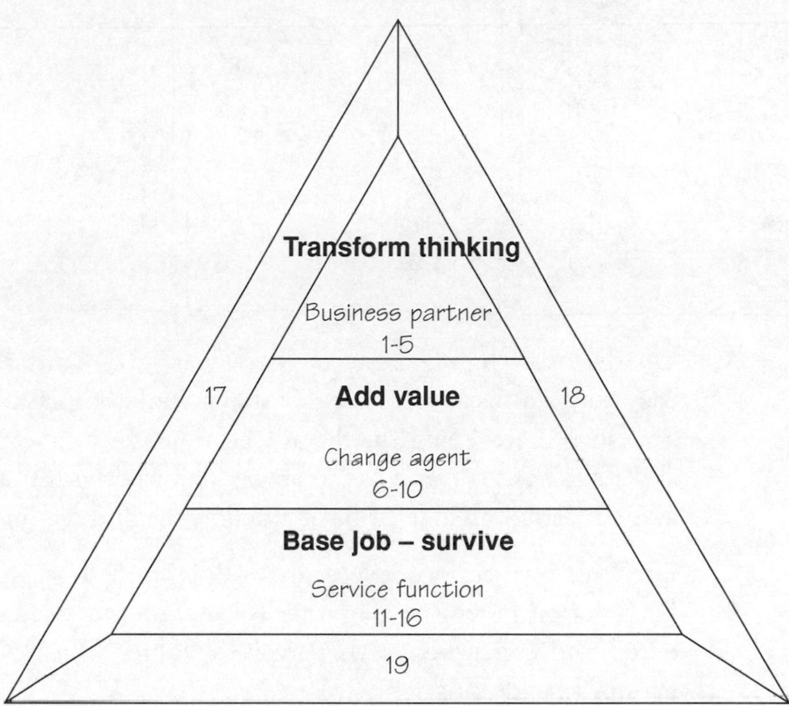

Figure 12.1 Generic competencies of the IT function

The specific skills, qualities and attributes which you need in your IT function to deliver to these competencies will be manifested in individual members of staff. Clearly, the skills, qualities and attributes needed to deliver competencies 1 to 5 are very different from those needed for competencies 11 to 16. Competencies 1 to 5 demand leadership and senior management capabilities.

But not all skills, qualities or attributes are easy to teach. Take, for example, having an impact and influence on business thinking. This demands leadership, empathy, resilience, creativity and so on. These are not qualities you can pick up from a course or two. For some, they are either part of your natural characteristics as an individual or they're not.

Skills for what? The competencies of the IT function

On the other hand, many of the lower level skills are relatively easy to train. Report writing, systems analysis, planning methods and so on, are being taught all the time. Even specific technical skills such as C++ and Java can be acquired within a few weeks, given a certain degree of basic intelligence and technical aptitude.

For your own staff, consider the following. If I want to create an IT function in which everyone is customer-focused, market-oriented and concerned with perceived value, what kinds of skills should I be looking for?

On the one hand, you'll want technical skills which will enable you to set up and run systems, and to provide efficient support when things go wrong. On the other, you'll want your people to be able to see things through the customers' eyes, to appreciate the concept of value as customers define it, to be able clearly and without patronizing to communicate with customers. Now consider this:

> Which is harder: to train someone in a specific technical skill who already has good interpersonal skills coupled with aptitude for technical matters, or to train a technically competent employee in interpersonal skills?

Whatever you want the answer to be, it is simply this. People who do not already have good interpersonal skills and qualities are very, very hard to train in those areas. People with good interpersonal skills can be quite quick at gaining technical skills.

So how do you balance the technical with the interpersonal in your recruitment? How confident are you that you know what good interpersonal qualities or aptitude look like? It's very easy to test someone's capabilities in a technical area – give them a screwdriver and away they go. But is it so easy to test for the more 'human' qualities?

Of course it isn't. But it is neither impossible nor undesirable. The fact is that time and again, senior IT managers recruit people in their own image – comfortable clones. They excuse themselves by arguing that they depend upon high levels of technical expertise to deliver to their customers. But in many cases this is just an excuse for failing to develop in themselves the courage and capability to bring on board recruits who can challenge and change the IT stereotype.

Look at your own recruitment strategies. Are you, in the balance of technical and interpersonal skills you demand of your recruits, simply ensuring that the IT stereotype will be reinforced in the next generation? Or are you genuinely taking in people who have the aptitude and attributes to deal with the political issues which have held IT back for so long?

Recruiting at the top

Once we reach the very highest positions in IT, the skills, qualities and attributes which we have referred to largely as 'interpersonal' become not only desirable but crucial. There was a recent survey of CIOs and IT directors who have left their jobs under pressure from their employers. These people were asked why they did not succeed. The number one reason they gave was the politics. No other single reason came even close.

This survey is appropriate, because further research suggests that most senior IT people who leave their jobs are pushed rather than leave voluntarily. Many of them are pushed far earlier than their colleagues at the same level who are in finance, or marketing or human resources. There is yet more research which suggests that many of the most senior IT people who leave before they are pushed do so 'before they are found out'. Indeed we have come across a number of these people who almost make a living out of being light on their feet. Their CVs have been rewritten many times to suit the changes in circumstance. And like genetic code which has been copied millions of times, each copy has subtle but significant variations from the previous version.

Senior IT people are, therefore, a wandering tribe. But this kind of wandering is not a feature of the IT psyche at all. So why has it come about?

It is now common practice for this most senior post to be filled with the help of recruitment agencies, or headhunters. When a new CIO or IT director is needed, the CEO, the HR director or someone else works closely with the headhunters to specify the job description which will find the ideal person to fill the post. This job description reappears (suitably edited to sound attractive) as the job advertisement.

We and many others have done some research into the nature of advertisements for the most senior IT posts in this country. The conclusions we have all come to is that, unlike advertisements for the most senior posts in any other function, the IT director or CIO seems to need high levels of technical expertise or experience to get past first base.

It seems that, even if you want to put down that screwdriver, those who would offer you senior posts do not want you to put it down.

Take, for example, Figures 12.2–12.5. They are a random selection of extracts from recent newspaper advertisements for senior IT jobs. Each is exactly as published.

Information Technology Director

£six figures, plus executive benefits

'Significant desktop technology strategy, design, development and implementation experience, preferably NT-based.'

Figure 12.2 Job advertisement 1

IT Director Designate

c.£85,000, car, executive package

'...you will have established a classic IT career record to date with experience in an IBM environment.'

Figure 12.3 Job advertisement 2

Director of IT

£60,000, plus bonus and benefits

'...the successful candidate will possess a knowledge of relational database tools and will be experienced in EDI implementation, voice and data communications and the internet/intranet.'

Figure 12.4 Job advertisement 3

IT Manager

£45,000 + comprehensive benefits

'To succeed in this position, hands-on knowledge of NT and/or Novell implementation and administration is essential.'

Figure 12.5 Job advertisement 4

It seems that, no matter how high up the corporate ladder you seek to climb, you have to take your screwdriver with you.

So what is driving this serious barrier to the development of a business orientation for senior IT managers? There are a number of factors at work. We believe that the three major factors are the naivety and fear of technology of many non-technical chief executives and directors; the lack of a professional qualification for senior IT people; and the motivations of the headhunters.

Technology has become a critical part of the life of most businesses. If the IT fails, the business often fails. Yet most senior business people have very little understanding of the underlying technology. This worries them in ways that not understanding how people tick (which is a concern presumably delegated to the HR professionals) does not. With this kind of technophobia comes a psychological need for reassurance. And this reassurance has to come from the man or woman at the top of IT.

There is no recognized professional qualification which the most senior IT person can acquire. The finance director will normally be a chartered accountant, and through possession of this qualification will have proven their technical capabilities. When they go for the top job, the aspiring Finance Director is not expected to prove their technical expertise; the qualification says it all.

Those within the organization seeking to appoint their new IT Director will often be at a loss. Whether they turn to the IT people (who will advise on technical requirements), their HR people (who will panic) or their CEO (whose teenage children will blind him or her with science), they will rarely have the confidence to put aside the technical and concentrate on the leadership and business acumen of the candidate.

The headhunters, to whom they turn for help, know that focusing on technical considerations is folly. They have seen more than enough evidence to prove that time and again IT people in the most senior positions fail because their technical expertise is no compensation for a serious lack of political and leadership skills. Any manager at this level of seniority needs political skills, business skills, interpersonal skills… . Without them, they join the massed ranks of the disillusioned, forced out through being too good at the wrong stuff. So why don't the headhunters tell their clients this?

We asked some of them. The answer is simple. Headhunters make their money out of new appointments, not stability. By keeping this advice from their clients, they can appear technically well-versed, and honest, knowing all the while that they are helping to put in place people who will almost inevitably fail. But that very failure brings another commission.

This may sound cynical – libellous even. But our sources are the headhunters themselves through personal interview.

So how do you help break out of this loop? To start with, focus on bringing in more balanced skill sets into your own IT function. Don't allow the business to see only anoraks and geeks flooding into the IT department. Use the people skills of your new recruits to help break down the IT stereotype which the recruitment strategies are perpetuating.

Secondly, continue your own personal development. Role model non-technical behaviours. And in so doing, help your colleagues recognize the value of technical awareness balanced by people skills and commercial and political acumen. Be streetwise. This does not mean being defensive. It means bringing right-brain balance to the left-brain dominance of the old-fashioned IT tribe.

13 Talk to me

Among the wonders of modern technology for which many IT people feel proud is the advent of e-mail and voice mail. These inventions have transformed the lives of many people in business. They are the kinds of tools which are in full use by both IT and non-IT people. They may be seen by many to be the common ground on which business and IT people can meet. After all, there can be little difference in the ways in which these tools are used by both communities.

This may be true. But there are aspects of the ways in which these mail systems are being used which are thoroughly negative. It is likely that among the worst perpetrators of this kind of misuse are many non-streetwise IT managers. Consider the ways in which the IT stereotype will use e-mail, for example. (And while you do so, consider your own and your staff's use as well.)

Hello, are you receiving me?

For a start, e-mails are now being sent across offices in which sender and receiver can see each other, and could, therefore and without much effort, talk to each other. Like children playing with their first toy intercom systems, such users are more excited by the technology than the relative benefits of the 'new' system.

But more sinister is the way in which the IT stereotype, as well as some real users, are hiding behind their screens, using the availability of e-mail to reduce human contact.

The most common excuse we hear for this is that by committing what you say to writing, you cover your back. In cases of dispute, the fact that you have sent an e-mail is taken as evidence of having done what you should do. But as George Bernard Shaw once reminded us, 'the greatest problem with communication is the illusion that it has been accomplished'. The practice of sending an e-mail assumes that it is the reader's responsibility now, not the sender's.

In the simple, black and white world of the IT stereotype, the sending of an e-mail is an unassailable defence. But in the real world of organizations – of people – such blinkered behaviour is better seen as a means of avoiding responsibility; of passing the buck. 'I've sent you an e-mail, so now the monkey's on your back, not mine' ('Management time: Who's got the monkey?', William Oncken, Jr and Donald L. Wass, *Harvard Business Review*, November–December 1974). This is the sub-text of such defensiveness.

The plague of e-mails

There's a plague of e-mail out there. Like so many contagious diseases, it has spread so fast that many people have caught it before they even knew of its existence. So devious is this disease that one of its early symptoms is a sense of pride in having caught it. This is shown in the way many managers 'complain' (a better way of describing it is boasting) of having so many e-mails to deal with. With a deep sigh of feigned regret, such managers turn to their screens to 'deal with' their e-mails. Peace at last. They can get back to solitude and the interaction between self and screen, and avoid the complex challenges of real human interaction.

But this willingness to catch and spread the e-mail disease merely exacerbates the problem everywhere. The more that managers give in to the symptoms, the worse it gets. The less time managers have for other things. The more likely they are, therefore, to pass that buck along the ether. If you have an exponentially increasing number of e-mail communications to deal with, you are going to devote exponentially less time to dealing with the human aspects of communication. The softness and subtlety of tone of spoken language is missing. And so is face-to-face, collaborative relationship building. It leaves no time for networking.

Instead, the culture of brevity and a business-like approach has developed, along with more and more ways of passing that buck, of stemming the tide of responsibility which is flowing towards each of us, as our colleagues do the same to us. Bucks are passing with amazing density along the networks of our organizations.

One of the problems this is causing is the essentially crude nature of keyboard and screen-based communications, especially those constructed in the name of business. Human beings evolved as gregarious creatures, sensitive to the thousands of modifying effects of non-verbal communication (often simplified to 'body language') between people when they talk, and the emotion created by the richness of our language. Talking to each other is poetry. (For more on this idea, you might like to read 'The human moment at work', Edward M. Hallowell, *Harvard Business Review*, January–February 1999.)

Body language

Non-verbal communication includes such rich signals as tone of voice, pitch, pace, eye contact, body postures, hand waving, leaning forward or back. The list is almost endless. When we talk to each other face to face, it is estimated that over 80 per cent of what we communicate is achieved by these non-verbal signals. They enable us to communicate subtleties, to soften the blow of bad news, to let people know we are sympathetic to them as we share difficult information, and to establish and maintain rapport way beyond the demands of the task in hand. Such signals are psychologically of enormous value to all of us in the rough and tumble of social life.

E-mail messages cannot convey such subtlety. The little smiley faces attached by some people are desperate attempts to fill this gap, but are of so little worth that they can only conjure up derision in many who receive them. How does one check sincerity in an e-mail message?

In Part Four of the book, we'll look more closely at how effective communication can be achieved. It depends upon a thorough alignment of intent and action. It demands good interpersonal and communication skills. It builds upon face to face contact. Its strongest foundation is a desire in all communication to achieve a positive outcome for both (or all) parties. This is called win-win.

Communicating for win-win

Achieving win-win does not rely upon a formula. It depends upon subtle interactions between people. It is 'negotiation' in a positive sense. It is a series of subtle interplays between people as each finds out more about the other's needs, concerns, wishes and fears. It works at many psychological levels at the same time. For this reason, the superior architecture of the female brain makes this kind of activity easier for them.

There are fundamental differences in the structure of the brains of men and women. The 'logical' left hemisphere of the brain is connected to the emotional, imaginative, and sensitive right hemisphere by a bundle of fibres known as the corpus collosum.

Women's brains have a much thicker corpus collosum, enabling a greater level of communication between the two hemispheres. Whereas men can use the relative lack of 'interference' from the right hemisphere to concentrate on technical, logical and unemotional aspects of life, women can read situations better than men, especially how people they are talking to are responding emotionally. Many men (and especially our IT stereotype) miss out on these clues even when they are face to face with people.

So when they revert to e-mail, they simply don't have a clue what they are missing out on, and go headlong into covering their back and passing the buck.

As each of us does it increasingly to others, more and more two-way communications become games of winners and losers. The aim of many such extended e-mail campaigns is to win by proving a point, by leaving the monkey on the other's back. The 'send' button becomes a kind of weapon; it is used to 'fire off' responses. And like most weapons, once the trigger is pulled, there's no going back. At any one time there are likely to be a fair number of these extended feuds going on in most organizations. How many of them are you involved in right now?

So why, given the enormous risks of getting into fruitless and destructive battles which come with e-mail, do so many people seem to catch the disease?

For one, it is thought by many to be part of the western culture of business to minimize the personal and maximize the impersonal. Comparison with the Japanese way of doing business provides some evidence for this.

The Japanese way

Japanese business people do considerably more communication face to face than through the written word. Their approach is to try to arrive at consensus before proceeding with a project. This is acknowledged to be a slow process at first, but the payback comes from a committed team once a decision has been reached. The Japanese know that commitment is something we make with our whole selves, not just our intellect. This is one reason why they put in a great deal of effort to establish and nurture relationships between business people. Relationships are built upon real talk, not written one-liners.

Interestingly, Japanese organizations do not suffer from the culture gap between business and IT which we have been describing and addressing in this book. This is due in part to the Japanese habit of ensuring that all managers, as they rise up the hierarchy, spend time in each of the different parts of the business. All user managers have experience of working in IT; all IT managers have worked in most of the user departments. They know each other's languages. They have not lived in stovepipes.

It is also partly due to the relative lack of dependence on written material in business. It is suggested that, due to the much larger and more complex character set in the Japanese language that they have not adopted technology-based written communication in the office as much as we have in the West. The Japanese place greater reliance upon verbal agreements, which both necessitate and encourage trust in people's word. They have learnt how to build and nurture relationships across many different parts of the business. They know how to talk.

14 Where are you when we want you?

The importance of the human element

One of the biggest mistakes many IT managers make is to assume that users simply want an IT service. This is an easy mistake to make. After all, some users have been known to say that what they want is for IT to be 'invisible'. It is relatively easy to infer from this that the best way to run IT is to stay in the background and remain unseen.

But this would be to miss the point. Remember the IT stereotype. If users expect, when dealing with IT people, to be confronted by people like this, it's no wonder that they would rather keep them at arm's length. But when they have a problem, users are *people* with problems, not the problems themselves. In other words, try to get yourself and your staff into the mindset which recognizes that there are no IT problems until they have an impact on people, whether these be users or customers. Therefore, the golden rule is:

> Fix the person first, then the problem

As one senior manager said of his IS department, 'IT need to use more charismatic people to get more user sponsorship, and to make friends in the business'. IT is not just about technology – it is about the quality of service overall which people in the business feel they are getting. Good relationships have a significantly beneficial impact on business effectiveness.

The central role of the help desk

This often comes naturally to the kind of individuals who are attracted to work on the help desk. Although help desk staff are not always able to solve users' problems, they often take an interest in them, and give the message that they care. In so doing, they foster good relationships.

However, where levels of service are not perfect (and where are they ever perfect?) it is the help desk staff who bear the brunt of user frustration. Especially where change in systems is taking place, the number of calls to the help desk can increase enormously. It is often the case that help desk staff cannot deal with many of these calls, and have to rely on second- or even third-line support for help.

But to users, IT is IT, and they can become extremely frustrated when their problems cannot be resolved immediately. In many cases, despite the willingness of the help desk staff to help, if they could, their own back-up comprises teams of technically competent experts whose attitudes to users are often less than ideal.

It's all very well keeping these sub-human techies away from direct contact with users, but unless they, too, are highly motivated to focus on the person before the problem, they can undermine the slow but important development of trust and positive relationships with users. The point is that, when second-line support fails to deliver, it's often the help desk staff who get it in the neck. All their good work is destroyed by their own colleagues' lack of interest or concern.

The constant abuse from frustrated users, and feelings of helplessness felt by many help desk staff takes a serious toll on their morale. For some, the work can become a constant nightmare, with evenings being used up simply trying to recharge depleted emotional batteries. Home life can be adversely affected, and, consequently, their ability to deal with already difficult problems at work deteriorate.

Some users are aware of the stresses under which their help desk staff are working, and no longer put calls through because they feel sorry for them. They know that, on balance, their calls will create more stress and problems. They are therefore prepared to live with the frustrations of their systems. This can have unintended consequences.

We have come across situations just like this. Users, caught between the desire to help the help desk people, and the lack of back up they actually receive, are turning to alternative sources of help. This seems to signal success to the IT departments, as they see a reduction in demand for help desk services. So their help desk staff are reduced in number. At the same time in these organizations, IT management continues its drive to improve its efficiency. Staff are told that the plan is to work on reducing the time spent on each help desk call – to eliminate the 'niceties'. In other words, help desk staff are required to cut out the 'irrelevant chatter' with users, and to get straight down to the problem and its resolution. In at least one instance we have researched a new help desk manager is planning to listen into calls to ensure that these new rules will be followed. That way it is believed they will be able to increase throughput and thereby improve the help desk service. Help desk staff are distraught, as the conversational aspect of their job is what makes it worthwhile for them.

Research constantly shows the criticality of a human touch in users' perceptions of the value of a help desk service. It also shows that, to motivate staff to provide this kind of human touch means treating help desk people with respect and dignity. After all, they are the human face of IT for many users.

The impact on senior IT management

All this may seem to be of low level importance to the aspiring streetwise IT director. After all, everyone knows that the 'real' role of the most senior IT person has to do with strategic matters, not the tactical, day-to-day grind of help desk responses.

The problem is that your credibility as a provider of strategic thinking will be influenced by the quality of service right at the lowest levels of your 'hierarchy of needs'.

In Chapter 5, we borrowed from Abraham Maslow this concept of hierarchy of needs. Used originally as a means of helping managers recognize that workers' needs have to be satisfied at a number of levels, this concept applies just as well to the relationship between IT service providers and their customers.

Our research in many organizations shows that it is almost impossible for the most senior IT manager to achieve the kinds of credibility they need to attain high levels of influence without attending to the perceptions of service quality which are represented by these 'low level' activities. Consequently, you may find it worthwhile taking a personal interest in these perceptions.

The case of the help desk turn around

Our favourite true story concerning the human face of IT management comes from a senior IT manager with whom we worked recently. After attending one of our management development programmes for senior IT people he went back to his organization to find that, at one site, the help desk had a poor reputation and was viewed as delivering a very bad service to the users. Rather than try to deal with the 'problem' (the perceived lack of responsiveness of the help desk), he decided to fix the people first.

He deliberately left the help desk alone, wanting to test the ideas we had presented on our course. He made no effort to improve the actual responsiveness of the help desk. Instead, he went out and among the users. He talked to them, listened to them, asked about their concerns and the impact of the help desk service on what was really important to them. As he listened and learnt, he built rapport with the users. Their perceptions changed.

Within a few weeks, people at the site were talking very positively about the improved help desk service. The CEO of the organization heard of the turn around and asked the IT manager to work closely with him on a number of initiatives, including presenting change projects to the company at large. From villain, the IT manager became a hero. Yet he had done nothing to the help desk itself.

He had changed perceptions. In the end, it is all down to perceptions. Is a 98 per cent uptime better than a 94 per cent uptime? It would appear so. But the value of uptime does not reside in the numbers. It resides in people's perceptions.

Our sample IT manager had recognized what so many IT managers miss – that IT services are provided by people for people. Most of the time this is irrelevant. But when things go wrong, it becomes vital.

Service beyond the help desk

You are in the services business. It is helpful to look into how those who have trodden this path before you have been able to learn about providing excellence in service delivery. One lesson they have learnt is that the perceived quality of a service is measured by the overall *experience* a customer has, and not just by the component parts. In other words, if the experience is good, the service is good.

To make sense of this, consider for a while what you would expect from travelling business class on an airline. Don't think of the physical attributes of the service, such as the aeroplane, the food or the seats. Think of how you are served by the people. And don't focus on the things you would expect or take for granted. Think of what would make that service memorable, and make you want to use that airline again.

We have run this exercise many times with IT people. The outcomes are very similar. The kinds of thing people look for in an exceptional service are:

- They are made to feel that they matter.
- They feel that the service providers care about them as people.
- They receive personal/individual attention, often tailored to recognized needs.
- The service is end-to-end and seamless.
- People smile at them.
- People anticipate and respond to their needs proactively.
- When things do go wrong, they are open and honest, and offer alternative solutions.

There are a number of interesting factors about this kind of list. The first is that additional budget is not a key issue. It is not necessarily expensive to provide what feels like an excellent service. The second is that what works in the airline industry works just as well in any other service provision. Reflect for a moment, how do your own users judge the service you offer them? Yet time and again IT people overlook these crucial influencers of perceptions of value.

Inferring quality and value

There are at least two levels on which we can judge quality and value. The first is by taking objective measures, such as hours, minutes and seconds; numbers of events; speed of delivery; and so on. These are what are often measured scrupulously by IT people. They are also often the stuff of service level agreements (SLAs).

The second is by putting ourselves in the shoes of customers and sharing the overall experience with them. Since the quality of a service will be judged by the overall quality of their experience, it is worth using the analogy of how you would judge an experience of flying with an airline to seek out ways in which this level of assessment is likely to be made of your services to your customers.

This second level of assessment is often overlooked. This is partly because it is hard to measure, compared to the quantifiable measures of uptime and service delivery. But it is also overlooked because it seems 'biased', 'unscientific', or 'simply a matter of opinion'. We're back to that familiar territory of 'organizational politics'.

Opinions as political statements

In the earlier chapters of the book we talked of politics simply being the differences of opinions and values of individuals. In a 'free' society, it is perfectly acceptable for people to see things differently. Of course, politicians spend extraordinary amounts of airtime on radio and television trying to influence others' opinions. And in so doing, they often refer to the 'first level' data in support of their arguments. But most politicians know that politics is about opinion, not data.

What forms a political opinion is not data but values and attitudes. Values and attitudes determine whether 30 per cent of a nation's budget should be spent on defence, or 40 per cent on education. Values and attitudes determine whether German cars are better than Japanese or Italian cars. Values and attitudes determine whether 95 per cent uptime is an acceptable level of service, or whether 80 per cent of IT effort should go on maintaining the status quo. Therefore values and attitudes determine whether an IT service is a good or a bad one.

In which case, IT directors who expend a great deal of their energy in tracking first-level measures, and ignore how they can influence the second-level 'values and attitudes' are doing a disservice to themselves, their departments, and to the overall image of IT in general.

Balancing service orientations

Try to make sure you achieve a balance between a more traditional 'technical' orientation and one focused upon managing people's perceptions of your reputation overall. Clearly, no product or service will survive for long if it fails to deliver a level of value which people can feel good enough about to judge as 'good'. The decline of the British motor car manufacturing industry illustrates that the loyalty of traditional buyers is not enough on its own.

Therefore, you would do well to maintain at least some of your focus on resolving technical problems.

You will also do well if you attend at least as much to the interpersonal elements of problem solving. Fix the people first, then the problem and your reputation will be enhanced.

Perceptions can be managed – or they will manage you

The human mind is capable of dealing with enormously complex problems. However, it has also learnt the art of short cuts. The very existence of stereotypes is evidence of the human mind's capacity for eliminating the need to reassess every situation from scratch. If I've learnt that lions are dangerous, I do myself no benefit if I 'give this lion the benefit of the doubt'. The probability that this lion is not dangerous is low; the risk to me of testing such a hypothesis is very high.

Therefore, we have evolved the highly valuable ability to reduce the amount of data we need in order to make up our minds to a very low level indeed. It was very useful, during the long period of human evolution when we lived on the open plains of the savannah, to have this ability quickly to assess a situation. In those days, no one bothered much about the political incorrectness of stereotyping lions. Today we are blessed with very much the same brain architecture; in evolutionary terms, the arrival of civilization has hardly happened yet. Evolution has not (and will not for hundreds of thousands of years) made any fundamental changes to the instinctive ways in which we operate. Our evolutionary tendency for instant classification produces today's 'self-fulfilling prophecy'. (For more on this, see 'How Hard-wired is Human Behaviour?' by Nigel Nicholson, *Harvard Business Review*, July–August 1998.)

Depending upon our current attitudes to something, almost all new data is quickly assimilated into reinforcing these attitudes. It is not helpful to spend energy and time starting from scratch each time. Therefore, if we are interacting with a situation about which we have negative attitudes already, it is likely that we shall see the negative aspects of that situation. We look for the data which reinforces our already firmly held beliefs and perceptions. Consider how easy it is to see members of a political party which we do not agree with as being more arrogant, stupid, shallow, devious and even uglier than those of our own persuasion.

The same is true of IT services.

The vicious cycle (Figure 14.1) of poor expectations sets up a process in which it is hard to win. When users or customers expect poor service, they look for the negatives to support their expectations. Not surprisingly, they find instances of what they expect to see, and consequently give negative feedback, or set rumours of poor service in motion. Hearing these, your people get discouraged, and often assume that they can do nothing right. They try less, lose interest, and give up. Service deteriorates, and users or customers

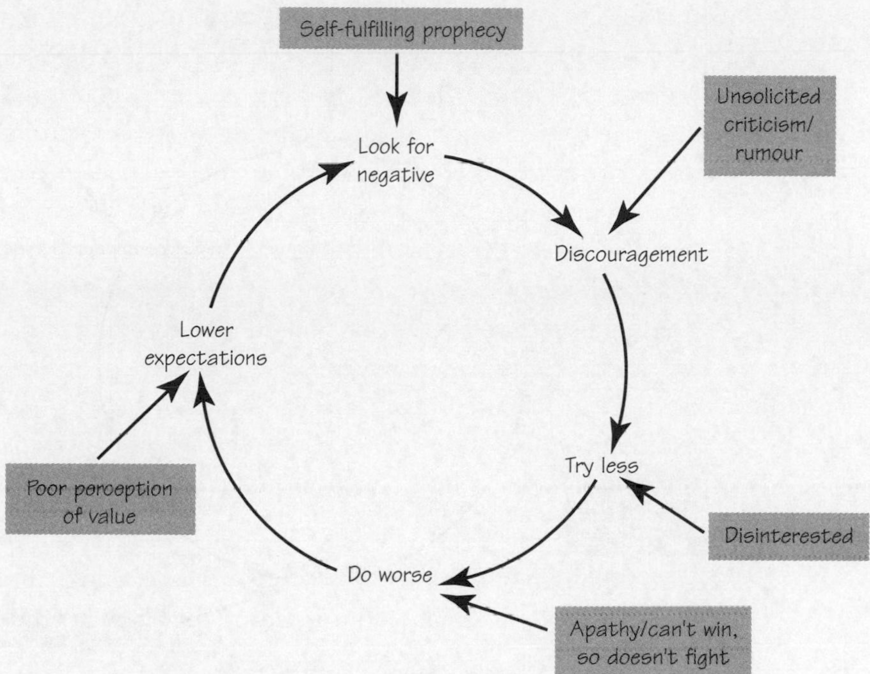

Figure 14.1 Vicious cycle

get even more fuel for their perceptions. The cycle continues.

But the same kind of mental phenomenon can be of benefit to IT. Figure 14.2 shows the same process in reverse.

The virtuous circle is achievable. Positive feedback creates motivation to do well, and, in consequence, performance improves. When you have this kind of self-reinforcing set of perceptions in the minds of your customers, most of what you do is interpreted positively. The 'same' level of service is now seen as good not bad. Perceptions are the reality.

How much is such a virtuous circle worth to you? Compare that worth to the effort you are currently putting into making such a circle a reality.

IT directors who spend time in their offices planning how to

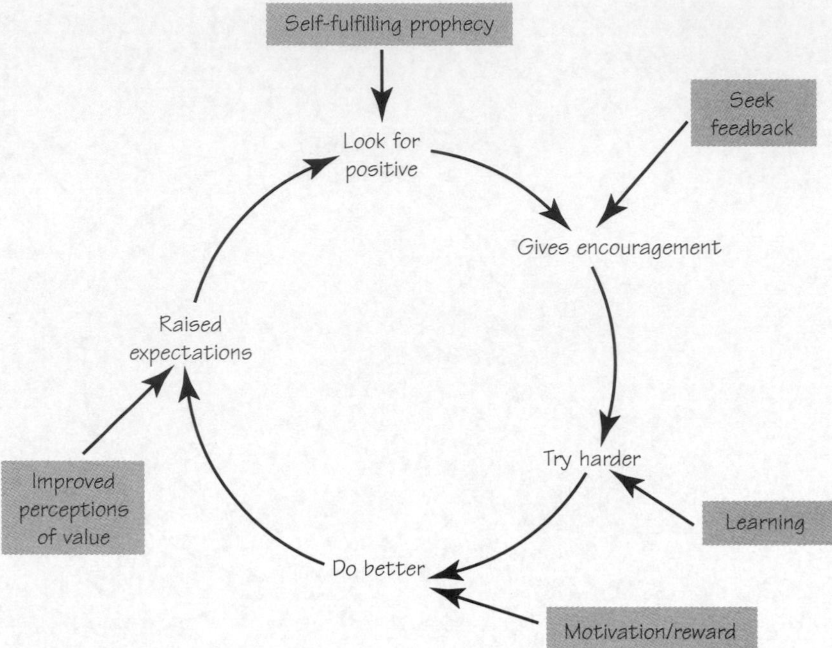

Figure 14.2 Virtuous circle

improve their services expend lots of energy for little effect. This is because they are pushing against the tide of the vicious cycle. Those who get out and about, and help manage perceptions expend lots of energy for great effect. These are the ones going with the flow of the virtuous circle. If the answer to 'where are you when we want you?' is 'in my office trying to do my job', then you are likely to be swimming uphill.

15 Lock horns and push

In the animal kingdom, the struggle for supremacy is represented nicely by the male deer. Two such creatures who come into conflict tend to lock horns with each other and push. He who pushes hardest wins. Might is right in this kind of battle.

Managers don't have horns to lock. But many of the interactions between them are of a similar kind. Two opposing ways of developing the business, or systems, will often result in their chief proponents engaged in head-to-head struggles. But now, instead of more and more muscle, more and more data are applied to the push. Voices often get raised in meetings, to add to the torque of the position. And like the Englishman trying to communicate with the foreigner, the same words are replayed, but just a bit louder.

It is part of the upbringing of many IT managers that it is primarily their job to come up with the 'right' answers. And once those right answers have been arrived at, to use their intellect to convince others about these answers. Faced with resistance, it is not part of the script that the IT manager should reconsider. After all, they will have done all the calculations already. Therefore, faced with obstinacy or stupidity on the part of others, the task is simply to push harder and harder until the 'truth' is acknowledged.

Many managers are unaware that, in their minds, there is no difference between the correctness of an idea and the fact that it's their idea. In other words, the difference between me and anyone else is that I am always right. The problem is that, if two people feel the same way, but each has a different opinion than the other, then there is no way out other than to lock horns once again.

Our evolutionary past has provided us with the determination (pig-headedness as some would describe it) to push through to victory. The 'warrior' in all of us needs considerable taming.

Solutions to such differences do not come from pushing harder, but from a two-stage reappraisal of the situation.

The role of different levels of inference

There are some things about which it is worth arguing, since by so doing, we may be able to establish 'the truth'. These are generally about 'facts', measurable phenomena against which we can apply widely accepted yardsticks.

There are others – inferences – which cannot be proven by such means. This is because they are matters of interpretation, opinion and inference.

When we make inferential assertions, such as that John is mean rather than thrifty, we are saying more about ourselves than we are about John. We are exploring what we mean by 'mean' and 'thrifty'. If someone has a different opinion about John, there is precious little point is locking horns and pushing, since there is no 'right' answer to push towards.

Most managers know this intellectually. However, it is not often that they will acknowledge how many of their assertions are 'simply' their opinion. The forcefulness of the push is in direct proportion to the degree of belief that, in this case, this is a matter of fact and not opinion.

The ways in which political issues are debated on radio and television illustrate this point well. Politicians lock horns and push. But how often have we witnessed, during such a debate, one politician conceding the argument to the other? The rarity of such events is not surprising. There is little value in working towards win-win in party political debate. Its purpose is not to arrive at a solution for all, but a win for one.

Organizational politics and debate

Organizational life is political, but not in that sense. There are very good reasons why you should be striving to achieve win-win rather than win-lose. After all, even if you believe you are right, you need to be clear in your mind whether winning this argument in the short term is worth the potential damage to good relationships which that might entail.

It is here that we begin to touch on some of the deeper concerns which we recognize IT managers have with organizational life. The idea that one might back away from a 'right' position for the sake of good relations is very difficult for some of them. It smacks of double-dealing, of chicanery, of duplicity and of doing dodgy deals. The anchor which has held them fast for all these years – that of complete commitment to 'the truth' is hard to cast off. Out there in 'doing deals land' lie all the risks and dangers which follow the rejection of the one true code.

This feeling of being cast adrift by letting go of the 'truth' can also, however, be described as immaturity. The fact is that organizational life is ambiguous and uncertain. Hanging on grimly to 'facts' alone is like hanging onto the side of a swimming pool – you're unlikely to drown, but you'll never learn to swim. In this analogy, the water is the world of inference. Good swimmers are able to recognize and deal with the inferences which comprise the water in the organizational pool. The dolphins in this world are those who know what lies in these waters, and are adept at swimming among them. Sharks are good swimmers, too, but their aim is to kill, not to collaborate. Dolphins are not afraid of sharks.

Going for win-win

Learning to swim with the dolphins means:

- Recognizing there are many different opinions about most organizational issues.
- Recognizing that other people are likely to see things differently.
- Having a genuine desire to work with others to achieve better outcomes than any single individual could come up with.
- Recognizing that, where you do want to influence other people, what influences you may not be what influences them.

One of the most important skills you need to develop to break out of the IT stereotype is that of understanding what is going on within organizational life. This means having the sensitivity to see the cultural influences on how people look at things.

16 Business priorities and culture – the unspoken agenda

One of the things IT people often say to us is that their lives would be so much better if users would only make up their minds about what they wanted, and were open and honest about their hidden agendas. In other words, many IT people see the problems they face largely revolving around what is (perhaps deliberately) kept below the surface – hidden from their view.

In this chapter and the next we'll explore this set of feelings. Here, we'll look at the nature of 'hidden agendas', since they play such a key role in people's political attitudes. In the next chapter, we'll look at ways of dealing with the frustrations of unclear and unprioritized sets of demands on IT resources.

The 'hidden' agenda

Those in IT who have felt for years that they have been left out of the political game seem to experience a sense of being excluded. They suffer from a similar feeling of paranoia: 'what are they saying about me behind those closed doors?'. In some cases, IT people can get it into their heads that the reason they are being excluded is that they (unlike their unscrupulous colleagues) do not approve of hidden agendas.

Just because something is not visible to you does not mean it has been deliberately hidden. In many cases, it is better to speak of 'unspoken' or 'unarticulated' agendas rather than hidden, since the latter implies some act of secrecy and subterfuge. Many agendas appear hidden simply because they have not been thoroughly communicated. It is not necessary for a lack of thorough communication to be a deliberate act of keeping things from you.

Communication is a two-way process. If you don't know something, don't always blame someone else. Many acts of communication are 'incomplete' simply because there are, in almost all communications, several embedded assumptions.

At the simplest level, assumptions are made about words meaning the same for you as they do for me. This is one of the major sources of 'jargon'. When an IT person says something like, 'open the file', they assume that the hearer interprets the word 'file' in the same way they do. They often forget that, for many who have not grown up with computers, a file is not a piece of software, but a physical object which lives in a cabinet.

Imagine a world in which you had to explain every word in every sentence. Communication would be impossible. We take it on trust that most of what we say is interpreted as meaning what we meant it to mean. People who share a common language can only do so if such assumptions are made, and are largely well founded. But, as with America and Britain, having the same words do not imply having the same culture.

It is when different languages appear to be the 'same' language that most confusions occur. When we are told something in French, we are alert to the fact that the words are different; when an American says he's put something in his 'vest pocket', we can forget that he is not referring to an undergarment. And when a senior colleague talks about our company's 'strategy' we may assume falsely that we are referring to the same thing. We may be thinking about a general direction which informs most of what we do in the organization, whereas our colleague may be referring to a document with the word 'strategy' in the title.

Some people are content to see 'strategy' as simply the cohesive framework which makes sense of the actions undertaken inside the organization – the 'implicit' strategy. This kind of strategy is visible to those who are looking for it. But if you are looking for a document rather than a set of actions, you won't see this kind of 'strategy'. And if you are looking for agendas which are always formally articulated and written down, you'll find few of these.

Most people's agendas are not written down. For many people, their own agendas are obscure and hard to piece together (a point we'll explore in some depth in Chapter 29). But this does not mean they're hidden. You just need the skills of identifying and understanding them.

The idea of a 'culture'

The complex pattern of such 'hidden' meanings is often what people refer to as a 'culture'. Organizations are said to have 'cultures'. These comprise the ways of thinking, the language and the accompanying assumptions about meaning. And since we can 'walk the talk', cultures include the unspoken as well as the spoken meanings.

Someone once said that 'what you do speaks so loud I can't hear what you're saying'. This suggests that our cultures are as much about the 'language' of 'implicit meanings' as they are about the words we speak. If you cannot see the culture of the organization in which you operate, you're less likely to be heard or understood. This is why it is important, if you want to become 'streetwise' to develop the skills of understanding the implicit meanings which make up the culture, and which explain those unspoken assumptions we may be tempted to call hidden agendas.

There are many different models of organizational culture. The purpose of these models is to map out the various components which are important to understand if you want to understand the 'whole' of the culture. From the point of view of the streetwise IT manager, the purpose of exploring a model like this is to identify what you need to be aware of if you want to be a 'member' of the culture.

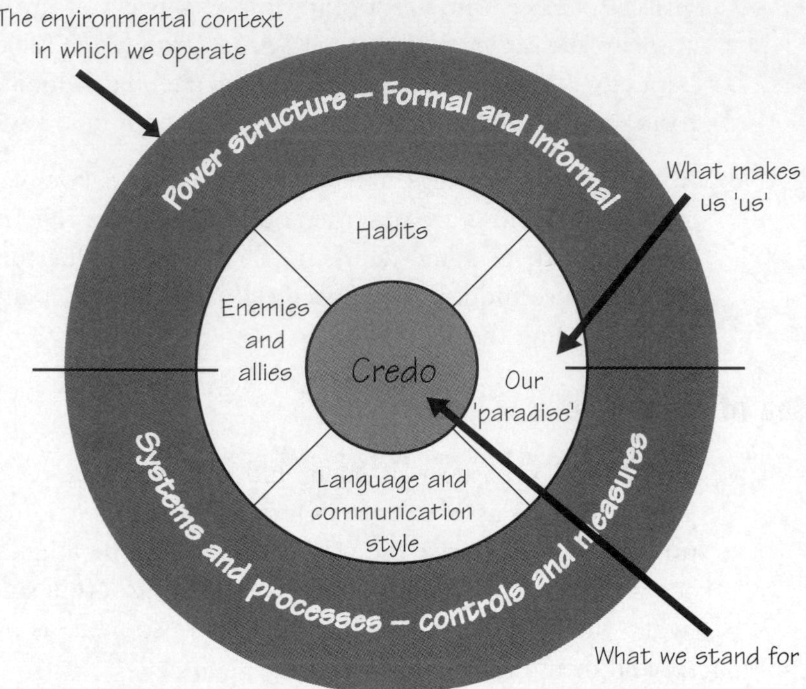

Figure 16.1 Cultural strata

In the model shown in Figure 16.1, the key elements of an organizational culture can be mapped. Different people may have different perceptions about what each element should contain, but we often find that people who share a common language within an organization can quickly identify the key elements within the model.

The outer ring of the model is where you write down the power structures, both formal and informal (who has the power, and what gives one power), and the systems and processes, along with how people and performance are measured and rewarded. If in doubt, ask some of your 'streetwise' colleagues about their perceptions of what is important 'round here'.

The middle ring contains four deeper cultural elements. The habits of an organization may be things such as Friday lunchtimes at the pub, rewarding people for specific actions, treating the 'customer as king', and so on. They describe 'the way we do things around here'.

You learn a lot about your organization by asking people who they see as friends or enemies. All too often among IT people, enemies are typified by people in other departments rather than 'the competition'. While friends are those who may simply share the same enemies!

Language and communication style reveal a great deal. This is why we keep suggesting adopting the language and communication styles of your senior business colleagues. As anyone with teenage children will know, language is a powerful tool for defining the boundaries between 'in-groups' and 'out-groups'. Many business people see the jargon of IT people as a more or less conscious means of reminding them that they are a different tribe.

'Our paradise' represents the ultimate vision and goals of your organization. By asking this question you can often unearth the deeper motivations which people are driven by.

The core of the model, the 'credo' is that set of beliefs and values which are shared by members of an organization, that operate unconsciously, and actually underpin what people do and how they behave. You may like to contrast this with the often sterile 'mission statement' or 'corporate values statement' that adorns many organizations' walls but have no impact.

The streetwise manager is in touch with all these elements of the culture of their organization.

An example of an organization mapped out on the same model is shown in Figure 16.2.

This is a real example of an organization which is in the financial services business – an investment bank. The main benefit of using such a model is not so much the output – the words in the figure

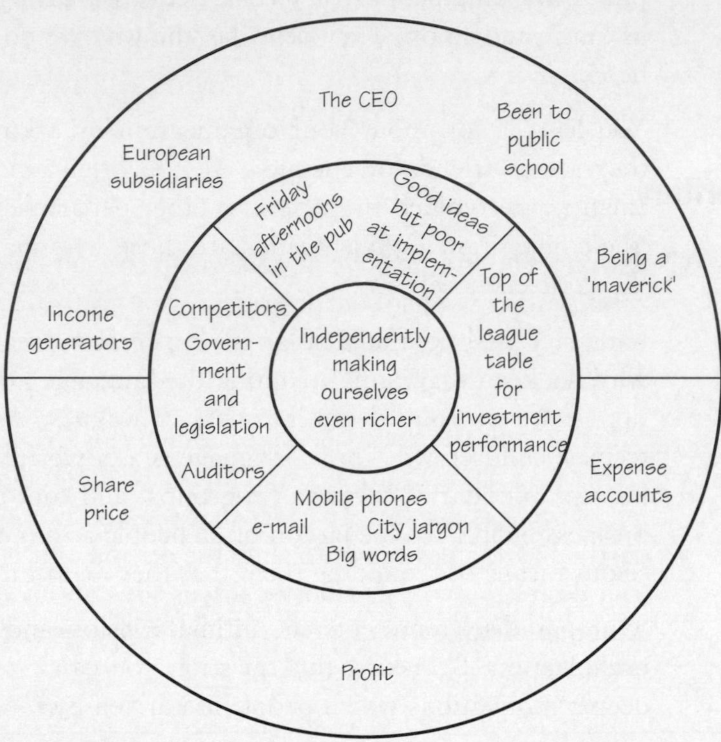

Figure 16.2 Cultural strata in action

– as the work which you do with others in describing the organization. This involves some revealing discussions, and means entering into some often uncomfortable debates.

As you talk about the underlying 'drivers' of the business or organization, you often uncover significant differences of perception and opinion. Moreover, when you do agree, you may not like what you are finding out about yourselves. This is all to the good. Time and again, the problems which beset organizations are those which ought to have been noticed years ago. The roots of problems are so obvious to all but those who live with them, day by day. Was it any surprise, for example, to find that, eventually, trying to run a major clothes and department store without changing room facilities or without accepting credit cards would not work? Everyone knows this apart from (until recently) the people running the business itself!

The priorities

Anyone who is intimately in touch with the culture of their organization is also aware of the priorities for the future. The need for and barriers getting in the way of change in many organizations are embedded in the culture. Anyone with political acumen can see this.

Most organizations can be mapped like this. Many management teams read these cultural situations with a common understanding of what is needed. The fact that they do not articulate this is partly due to a desire not to state the obvious. (It is often also due to a desire to avoid conflict or discussions about sensitive issues, although it takes a degree of cultural awareness to recognize where these conflicts or tensions will emerge.)

When you are living in a log cabin which is being invaded by snakes, it is not always helpful to pester others for a policy on reptiles. What people are more likely to want is action to get rid of the snakes. Yet many IT people are so concerned to have policies, statements and strategies handed to them that they are unaware just how irritating and irrelevant their demands appear to their colleagues.

This brings us back to the 'phantom IT strategy' of Chapter 3. The IT strategy is implicitly written in the culture of the organization. The priorities are there to be seen by all.

Not everyone can see it

In some cases, the culture needs to be described more overtly. There is no reason why a senior IT person cannot engage in constructive dialogue with their colleagues about the priorities and needs. Several very successful IT people we have worked with have done just this. But they have not sat back and sulked at the absence of a strategy. They have gone out and talked to each and every one of their colleagues about the priorities. In so doing they have helped their colleagues surface the assumptions they have made, and they have created for themselves a 'value-adding' role in articulating the implicit strategies of their organizations.

One such IT director was so successful in this that he was invited to become the CEO of his organization, an offer he accepted willingly.

Multiple cultures

Clearly, in so far as cultures are manifested in language, the different 'jargons' of different functions within organizations suggest they may have different cultures. So what is an organizational culture, and does an organization have one or many such cultures?

Differences between cultures are differences of degree. Although some writers have taken the approach which classifies cultures into distinctive sets, these are heuristic devices more than reflections of some objective 'reality'. The approach we take is to suggest that, for you, the aspiring streetwise IT manager, there could be a number of cultural differences within your organization of which you need to be aware.

Sometimes we work with both the IT people and the marketing people from the same organizations. In some cases, we work with this mix of functions from a variety of organizations at the same time. When we do so, we usually ask them to characterize each other's 'sub-cultures'. In other words, we ask the marketing people to describe the IT culture, and vice versa. The results are informative.

In a nutshell, the marketing people reproduce close variants of the IT stereotype. At the same time, the IT people produce another stereotype – that of marketing people. In each case, the stereotype is pretty consistent. Given the wide range of people in each of these functions, we are clearly being treated here to people's perceptions of the 'sub-cultures' of IT and marketing. They do not speak the same language.

And yet IT people often seem to assume that marketing (and other non-IT) people do (or ought to) speak 'IT'. They don't. They see the world through different lenses. If you want to sell refrigerators to Eskimos, know their cultures. Only that way will you truly understand their needs.

17 Breaking the taboo – marketing IT services

In the previous chapter we introduced the idea that it was a mistake to sit and wait for the business to set the IT agenda. We explained that it was up to IT people to understand the priorities by appreciating the cultural imperatives, and to work with senior people in the business towards articulating and checking those priorities.

In some senses, this has already started the process of introducing marketing into the IT function. If you want to market IT services, the first thing you need to do is to understand the cultures into which you want to 'sell'. But there is more to marketing IT services than this.

The stereotypical IT manager is analytical, and driven more by curiosity than a desire to serve. Martin's response to increased demand may be a little over the top, but, like almost every one of these cartoon stories, contains elements of what IT people have actually said to us over the years. One of the things they have consistently said is that they wish the business would make up its mind what it wants from IT.

The business agenda and marketing IT services

Culture watching is not enough on its own to establish the business agenda. You need in addition a clearer idea of what key users actually want for the future.

Wouldn't it be nice if all the business people got together and wrote a 'strategy', from which we could develop our own response? In Chapter 3 we suggested that you do not try to write an IT strategy. Let's reinforce that.

Bleating about a lack of priority setting, or a clear agenda we can respond to is a bit like a major retailer shutting up shop in a huff because all its customers have not had the decency to get together and draw up a list of all the things they will want to buy from the shops over the next five years.

Millions of businesses get by without such a stark mandate from their customers. It's called marketing. It's what good IT managers do. You don't have to call it marketing, just so long as you take appropriate steps to work with your customers to arrive at some sense of what they want from you, and how you are going to go about delivering it.

Marketing by walking about

This sub-heading is shamelessly derivative. It will irritate some readers who dislike:

- Anything which they have not thought of themselves.
- Cheap imitations.
- So-called 'witty' aphorisms which over simplify.
- The original phrase (management by walking about).

Many of the reasons why some senior IT people are so bad at marketing are embedded in these kinds of emotional responses.

It is in the nature of the IT stereotype that marketing is cheap, dishonest, subservient and alien to the precision, accuracy, honesty and objectivity of IT. This is the 'taboo' of the chapter's title.

One of the strongest messages of this chapter is that marketing is not about techniques, it is about a mindset. If you are a dyed-in-the-wool IT traditionalist, then you'll have difficulty with some of this chapter. But if you skip it, you'll miss one of the most crucial steps in becoming a streetwise senior manager.

Features, advantages and benefits

When marketing people say, 'people don't buy drills, they buy holes', they are illustrating this mindset. To the literal-minded IT manager, it is just not true. You can't go into a shop and ask for a hole in your kitchen wall. The statement is not meant to be taken literally, however. A great deal of marketing is about using language and thought in other than purely literal ways. If you want a translation, 'people, when they are buying drills, are probably thinking about the reasons why they are making the purchase – the benefit to them of making the investment'.

One of the complicating factors in this kind of approach is that it generalizes. Clearly, there are some people who are technically-oriented who may buy drills because of the technology itself. The 'holes not drills' statement is about the majority – what motivates most buyers, and not the 2.5 per cent 'early adopters'.

And here's one of the big problems. Many IT people are excited by the technology itself. Many would buy drills rather than holes, just like the father of one of the authors, who had a collection of over 500, many of which had never been out of their boxes. (Incidentally he also had over 100 chisels.) And many would buy hardware and software without a clearly defined outcome, value or benefit. Liking technology for its own sake, they can tend to overlook the fact that the other 97.5 per cent of the population are 'hole buyers' not 'drill buyers'.

One of the *features* of a highly networked IT environment is that it can operate without paper at any stage of the process. An *advantage* of this is that people can do away with paper copies and files. A *benefit* of this would be… .

And here's the rub. A *benefit* is a response to a clearly stated need, and not something which may, perhaps, be good for you.

Imagine you are being sold a car (and imagine you are not a technical wizard, but just an ordinary punter who knows nothing about what goes on under the bonnet). The salesman tells you that the car delivers 256 bhp due to its 24 valves and turbo. So what? Now he says, these *features* allow you to do over 140 mph, and to go from 0 to 60 in less than 5 seconds. If (but only if) you are a speed freak, this may resonate for you. But if you are not interested in such recklessness, your first impressions will be along the lines of, 'so how much does this testosterone substitute cost?', 'so how will a jail sentence for consistent speeding feel?' and 'so how many miles per gallon will this thing really do?'.

In other words, the *advantages*, not being a response to what you need or want, raise in your mind issues of cost (financial and other). That's how your customers feel about IT.

Unless you are selling them *benefits*, they will be either uninterested or put off by the disadvantages. And *benefits* are worryingly woolly things. They are things like 'peace of mind', 'feeling important', and 'being able to hand everything over to someone else'.

Benefits are often quite personal things. But they cannot be ignored, since it is against these (often unspoken) criteria that we are actually judged. Some people are taking the concept even further. Nearly fifty years ago, American psychologist James Gibson came up with the concept of 'affordances', the talents and capabilities a product affords to a human user. The concept covers both the 'innate' properties of a product, and the uses that it can be put to. Kettles which change colour as the water heats up, and users who choose toasters on the basis of how they fit into the kitchen decor, rather than for their toasting abilities are examples of affordance (*Professional Engineering*, 10 March 1999, 23–24).

The value of thinking in this way is that it helps designers, and providers of IT services, to ask users what affordances they want from a product or service first, and then design the product or service to provide those as simply and clearly as possible.

Marketing as manipulation(?)

Some IT people we have spoken to seem to have the idea that marketing is about manipulating people's minds. Based loosely on the notion, introduced in the 1960s, that marketing people use 'hidden persuaders', IT people have formed the impression that the primary role of marketing is to persuade people that they need something which they don't.

Ironically, IT people are far more guilty of trying to do this than most marketers, who have discovered that their job is far more about identifying and meeting needs and wants than it is about trying to create artificial needs and wants.

Educating users

This is why, when IT people say that part of their job is to 'educate' users, they are so far off the mark.

Your customers may wish to know about possibilities; they may even convince themselves they'd like more information about technology itself. But they do not need educating about what they want – the benefits they are seeking.

Where people make a mistake is in thinking that customers who cannot or will not clearly articulate what they want are in need of education. They may need some sensible, human dialogue, it is true. But this is talking not educating.

Because so much of the dialogue between IT people and users is stilted, uncomfortable and artificial, you often end up with a set of 'benefits' which are questionable, such as 'response times' and 'resilience'. These are learnt phrases. What they say is: 'Go away and stop pestering me; it's pretty obvious that whatever I ask you for you'll either not understand, or be unable to deliver. So I'll say a few words in your language and maybe you'll leave me alone.'

Now this is one thing that marketing people have got right. They know that some of the benefits which buyers want cannot be fully articulated – they would not be 'politically correct'. When car makers, for example, describe their luxury cars in terms of performance, reliability, comfort and so on, they know that most of their (male) buyers are really looking for 'ability to impress women', 'ability to impress the neighbours', 'lots of toys to play with', and 'leg room in the back'.

The advertisers, who work more in imagery, are able to have a greater impact and far more directly address these kinds of buyer benefits. That's why companies spend so much on advertisements that create images and impressions, but which say very little about the features of their products. The buyers just aren't interested in these.

No one 'educates' buyers about these deeper desires. Successful people simply get to understand them and respond to them.

This is not to say that 'leg room in the back' will be a key buying criterion of IT services. But you can be sure that the real criteria for judging levels of service will be more like 'leg room in the back' than they will be like the bland and meaningless 'performance'.

Chunking up

If you don't know, for your key influencers, what is the equivalent of 'leg room in the back' for IT services, then you have to try to find out. And now you have to throw away yet another of the old faithful maxims.

In the past, IT people were taught to differentiate between 'wants' and 'needs'. The theory went that you should not simply respond to what people want, but should educate them about what they need, and then deliver that. Wants were seen as frivolous, unnecessary and expensive, while needs were business-oriented, task-related and still expensive.

The relationships we form in business are not fundamentally different from those we form in our social life. Although it has been popular in business schools to pretend that humans don't populate organizations (organizations are populated by robotic 'roles' according to most books on business and management), people are still people even when they are at work.

Therefore, consider the following interaction between a husband and wife:

Wife: 'I need a new dress for that party'.

Husband: 'You don't need a new dress, you only want one'.

You may have witnessed or even experienced this kind of interaction. You may have learned from it that it produces negative outcomes. Yet this is what IT people have been taught to say to users. Is it any wonder that many users see IT as arrogant, insensitive, patronizing and lacking in streetwise skills?

They are used to being dealt with by account managers, salespeople and consultants who have learnt a thing of two about getting under the surface. They use the skills of 'chunking up'.

This is a questioning technique which is wondrously simple to describe, but very hard to do well. Like playing the piano, you need to practise.

It consists of asking customers a little more each time about what they will get from some feature or 'benefit'. Take a user who has asked for a system which will get a set of forms out by Friday lunchtime. You now ask what that will provide them with – what that will do for them. When you get the answer to that, you ask the same kind of question again – what will *that* get them, and so on, until you have arrived at some irreducible value. It's what they really want.

In some respects, this is not unlike the process we all went through in our systems analysis days. The difference is that 'chunking up' is aimed at getting further, and it is unashamedly personal. In the end, all those 'business' or 'organizational' benefits are seen as such only so far as they contribute to each individual's personal goals. The fact that these goals are often unspoken does not mean they are not there, or are not underpinning our opinions about almost every aspect of our lives as managers.

Chunking up, when it is done professionally, brings mutual benefits. The user is helped to think though what is important to them. The questioner gets a much clearer picture of the kind of world the customer wants to inhabit, and therefore, how IT services can be delivered to create this world. Badly done, however, and it appears intrusive, overly personal and patronizing.

Which brings us back to the IT stereotype. And why, in some organizations, we have heard that users have set up macros in their e-mail systems to automatically delete any new mail which comes from their IT departments.

What does the face of IT look like in your organization?

In a recent research programme, two IT departments which had raised their credibility with their users were investigated (see 'A credibility equation for IT specialists' by Barbara Bashein and M. Lynne Markus, *Sloan Management Review*, Summer 1997). The researchers wanted to know how this improvement had come about. The outcomes were startling.

The IT people in these organizations told the researchers that their improved credibility had come from impressing business managers with dazzling technologies or with behind-the-scenes preemptive solutions. But those same business managers attributed IT services' improvement to some of the 'soft skills', like being good team players, using common language, demonstrating patience and being willing to hold hands.

You may not be fully aware of how your customers see you, even if your reputation is good. But you can be pretty sure that your IT function is measured by very few of your customers on the whizbang technology you provide them with.

If your organization is anything like most of the others we have worked with, most of what will make you successful comes from how you and your staff behave towards your customers, and not from the physical manifestations of your business, like hardware, software, logos or mouse mats with witty reminders.

The things which a marketing approach demands include a sense of individual responsibility on the part of all your staff. This means no-one saying to a user, 'sorry, that's not my area of expertise; you'll have to phone so-and-so'. It means everyone in your department being able to spot opportunities to go that bit further to meet the needs of customers.

People remember the exceptions. If most of the exceptions are IT disasters, the inference is that the IT function is no good. If the

exceptions comprise better than expected service, the inference will be formed that IT is OK in our organization.

Focus your friendliness

Being nice to everyone is not marketing. We are not suggesting that you send your staff to charm school. All we are asking for is a little human communication. If this is hard to do for everyone, then focus your resources.

Draw up a list of your twenty strongest critics; now draw up a list of your best people (measured in terms of their interpersonal skills). Match them up, and tell your people to make their number one priority to change those critics' image of IT. Get them to refurbish IT's reputation.

People buy from people they like. This may not be fair. It may not be politically correct (especially where issues of gender insinuate themselves into the equation). But it is not your job to change human nature. It is your job to understand how human nature (whether we like it or not) deeply influences everything we do. And this is as true in the workplace as it is at home. People do not stop being human when they go to work, despite the best efforts of bureaucrats.

Let us reiterate. This is not manipulation. It is being human.

Marketing, done well, is simply rediscovering how people feel, think, communicate, perceive and respond to how others meet those needs. It isn't difficult to describe.

But if you've spent years suppressing all this, it may take a bit of work rediscovering it. That's where Part Four of this book comes in.

18 Suppliers and consultants – the wolves at the door

Introduction

As if dealing with internal relationships were not enough, you also have to deal differently these days with outsiders, such as suppliers and consultants. In the old days, it was a clear situation. It was heads down and charge – and may the best man or woman win.

The problem is that there is now a great deal of research evidence to suggest that adversarial relationships like these are ineffective. The name of the game, according to the latest research is 'co-opetition'. In other words, rather than fight, we have to learn to get on, even with those who may be direct competitors.

The partnering approach

You may be a little concerned that we are suggesting something along the lines of Little Red Riding Hood giving the big bad wolf the benefit of the doubt. It is written in the folklore that suppliers and consultants are the big bad wolf. Don't trust them, is the message of the past. So what has changed to make these wolves so trustworthy now?

Part of the change lies in the increasing competition between the suppliers and consultants. With technology changes such as de facto standards, lower price per mip and increased levels of technology awareness, especially among the younger people, the mystique which some of the more unscrupulous suppliers and consultants relied upon is fast disappearing.

It is also true that these former wolves are learning the lessons of the adversarial past. Imagine you are negotiating with someone who you can easily beat down. It may be a supplier in a very competitive market place, or a salesman new to the job, and unaware of the tricks of the trade. You have a choice. You can either take advantage of the situation and defeat the weaker 'partner', or you can try to make a deal which is good for both parties.

In the old days, the answer was simple. If you can do them down, then do so. You may never have such a chance again. Many smaller suppliers, often with brilliant and promising products and services, have been forced out of business by these tactics. Short-term gain has led to long-term loss.

Even when they have been able to survive damaging contractual terms, 'losers' can often find ways of 'getting their own back', such as creating dependency and walking away, or delivering a level of service which meets the strict terms of the contract, but leaves a lot to be desired.

The quality of service (is not strained)

Remember how we discussed the quality of your services to your customers? We suggested that you can make an enormous amount of difference to the perceptions of quality simply through how the service is delivered. Attitude influences quality.

Poorly treated suppliers, especially those whose profits may be under threat by hard negotiations on your part, will deliver a poorer service. They'll do everything you ask of them, and you won't be able to put your finger on it. But there'll be something not quite right about it.

If they are supplying something which will have a knock-on effect to the service you deliver to your customers, guess who's going to suffer most in the long run?

Treat suppliers and consultants as partners. In the long run, this will make your service to your customers the better. Most of them know this already. But it takes two to tango. And if you won't partner with them, they will find it hard to partner with you.

What are they providing?

Many adversarial relationships become so because neither party has the ability clearly to articulate what each is delivering to the relationship.

Of course, at the 'literal' level, this is not true. They are providing a service, and you are paying for it. But the problem lies with what we described in the previous chapter. You are not buying a service from them, you are buying what that service could deliver. We're back to drills and holes.

Be very sure about the outcomes – both practical and emotional – which you are looking for. Take, for example, one 'classic' use of consultants.

You know how it is. The CEO won't listen to you. So you delve into your consultancy budget, hire a big name, tell them exactly what you want them to say to the CEO (which is what you have been trying to say for years), and step back. In go the consultants, and, frustrating though it is, achieve in one presentation what you have been trying to achieve for months, years maybe.

In this case, what are you buying? It's clearly not expertise or knowledge, as you've provided those to the consultant. It's not 'the right answer', for the same reasons. In this case, it seems that the thing you are buying from them is 'credibility'.

Here's another 'marketing' term. We could have introduced it in the last chapter, but felt you may have had enough marketing speak for one chapter. But it is such an important phrase that we can't leave it out altogether.

The term or phrase is 'value proposition', and it may have exactly the same impact on you as other marketing phrases. Why can't people use the Queen's English? Probably because the Queen's English means so many different things to different people that the risk of misunderstanding outweighs the benefit of avoiding these new, clumsy terms.

So we'll stick to 'value proposition' to describe the (often unspoken) things someone wants from spending their money. Things like 'holes in my kitchen wall', 'peace of mind when driving my family' (for Volvo drivers), and 'being recognized as having style' (for some designer label wearers) are value propositions.

Delivering a credible message is the value proposition in the case of the consultants we described earlier. Ultimately, it is the value proposition you buy, so getting it clear is a very good idea.

Different kinds of value proposition

It is often when buyer and supplier have different perceptions of the value proposition that lack of trust arises. Take the classic gripe about consultants – that they are taking your money in order to sell you their next job. This is dependency.

You are unlikely to see this as the value proposition. However, many such value propositions are best explored at a deeper psychological level. Many manufacturers of big, fast cars know more about their value proposition than some of their customers would like to admit. Many consultants know more about theirs than some of their customers would like to admit.

We know clients for whom the value proposition between themselves and big-name consultants is best described as 'being too busy dealing with these big boys to have time to deal with the trivia in the office'. They thrive on this kind of association, and are prepared to spend lots of their company's money meeting this psychological need. This may be an extreme case. But it is closer to the 'truth' lying behind many relationships with consultants than the 'official line'.

Consultants deliver a wide range of value propositions. These can be classified in a number of ways. For example, three broad kinds of consulting are:

- Providing a pair of hands.
- Being the expert (it's like going to the doctor).
- Coaching (you keep the problem, you provide the solution, but with coaching help from the consultant).

In each case, the underlying value proposition will clearly be different. Unless, that is, your underlying value proposition is so hidden from you that you sign up for one kind of consulting when you really needed to sign up for another.

It is this kind of misunderstanding of the underlying value proposition which makes partnering so difficult. Time after time consultants know that a client's need is for long-lasting care and protection. The client is (effectively) asking for a dependency relationship to compensate for problems or inadequacies. The client will not admit to themselves that this is the value proposition, as it would be damaging to their self-esteem and credibility.

When the dependency becomes obvious, it is often the consultant who is blamed. But that's OK. They have thick skins, developed over many years of dealing with such clear demonstrations of denial and projection.

Be honest with yourself, and you'll be more honest with them

Being streetwise with suppliers and consultants is not about outwitting them; it's about not outwitting yourself. You have to be very clear and honest with yourself about your motives, and about the value proposition. What, in the end, are these people supposed to be delivering to you. Just like you and your service to your customers, they will be measured, ultimately, not on the overt terms and conditions of the contract, but on how they deliver to the underlying value proposition.

It is partly for this reason that we do not advocate drawing up detailed and complicated contracts with suppliers and consultants. These documents suffer from the same shortcomings as SLAs. They miss the point, and they encourage an adversarial relationship.

Establish good personal relationships with suppliers and consultants. Treat them with respect and honesty. Make it clear what it is you want from them – in terms of outcomes and not inputs. And keep the dialogue and the relationship going. The chances are that at least a part of the value proposition will only be possible if you meet regularly and talk freely.

It's all about relationships again

Those who would pretend that business gets done without human intervention are mistaken. Those who pretend that human intervention is not about relationships are also mistaken. And those who pretend (often to themselves) that they can be purely rational and business-like in their relationships are the most mistaken.

Suppliers and consultants are not a strange species with whom you have to establish new and different ground rules. They are just another group of human beings, trying to go about their businesses. Their business and your business can be of mutual benefit – each can get value from the other.

We believe that you weaken that potential value the more you try to strengthen it through artificial means such as binding contracts. Think of the impact on trust you would have if you said to someone you were planning to marry, 'let's draw up a binding contract covering every possible act of treachery we could imagine committing on each other'. We know some people have entered into such 'prenuptial' contracts. We don't think they're a very good idea – for a marriage or for any other kind of human relationship.

19 Let someone else do it for a change

In the previous chapter, we discussed the 'value proposition' of suppliers and consultants, suggesting you make sure you and they are fully aware of what it is you are buying from them. What if you could deliver that value proposition yourself? Should you?

The idea of a profit centre

Part of the problem many IT functions face is an overall lack of focus on the value they deliver to their customers. It is said that, where IT is a cost centre, the business places IT in the same category as building maintenance and other service functions. It sees high cost and little value added. IT will be perceived as expensive, and business users will wonder if they are getting value for money. This is the ideal situation for hostile outsourcing.

Sometimes user departments are not even keen to justify IT expenditure. It is dealt with in this case by one central budget. In this environment IT will be taken for granted, and users will expect to receive everything they ask for, when they ask for it. Anything less than this will be perceived as a poor service. Expectations will soar, and IT will be in a no-win situation, receiving mixed mes-

sages from users (spend, spend, spend) and from their masters (money is a scarce resource – be frugal).

The solution which some have gone for is to set IT up as a profit centre. Here IT can contribute to the bottom line of the business, and thereby justify their existence by selling services outside, and proving their worth in the market place. Trying to deliver a good service internally as well as making a profit externally is rarely possible. But at the very least, it does make the users justify their needs, just as they would for any bought in service, and this should give them a better idea of the value of IT services.

There is irrefutable logic at work here. Far from trying to do everything for everybody, all at the same time, and with no consideration for the cost to the organization as a whole, the profit centre allows you to develop some clear strategies for focusing on delivering value.

Although the idea of the IT profit centre is plausible, and has been around for well over ten years, it has not been taken up widely by the IT community. It seems that businesses don't like the idea of their IT people having the potential to set up virtually monopolistic means of pulling even more (wire) wool over their eyes, and to make a fortune while they're at it.

If anyone is going to do that, it ought to be strangers, the outsourcing companies.

The rationale for outsourcing

The outsourcing phenomenon is part of a wider trend in businesses to focus effort on core areas of competence. As we said in Chapter 8, in years gone by, Cadbury's would make the boxes into which they packed their chocolates; and NCR made the screws which held together their early generations of cash registers. Now, Cadburys and NCR know that there are people out there who are better at making boxes and screws than they are.

There is no fundamental business difference between outsourcing and buying in boxes and screws. It may feel different if you were once responsible for fulfilling a function, and now someone outside is doing it instead. But the rationale is simply to identify what you can do better than anyone else, separate that out from what others can do better than you, and to outsource the latter. This frees you up to focus your scarce resources on the things you can do best.

Bear in mind that, in this comparison of what each can do better than the other, it is the ultimate 'value proposition' which we are exploring. If, as in one case we worked on, the value proposition of the internal IT function was their subservience to the whims of key business managers, then an outsourcing company was unlikely to fulfill that function well. They would be far more concerned with contracts, service delivery, and a whole host of 'rational' factors than learning to jump when told.

Outsourcing – planned or hostile?

If you have not already drawn up a list of elements of your service which are suitable for outsourcing, and another list of those unsuited, you should start now.

Most IT functions which suffer from hostile outsourcing do so because they have taken an all-or-nothing approach. Their logic was that any 'partial' outsourcing deal would be the thin end of the wedge. Once an outsourcing company gets its foot in the door, there's a slow but inexorable take over.

But pulling up the drawbridge to keep the enemy out is another example of IT people burying their heads in the sand. It may be true that some outsourcing deals have taken the following form.

The CEO is worried about IT but cannot put his finger on it – it's all jargon, unfulfilled promises and escalating costs. He plays a round of golf with a director from an outsourcing company, who suggests to him how much he can save if he outsources, and how his dual problems of not understanding how IT works, and the language of his IT people will dissolve into history. Clearly, what this director is being good at is finding the value proposition – 'take away my need to try to deal with technical people and help me understand what I'm paying for'.

So the outsourcers come in. The terms of the contract cover the base services, but do not allow for unexpected extras. The base contract is cheap. Extras, when it becomes apparent that the base service in inadequate, prove to be very expensive. Over time, the extras add up to a very expensive deal overall. The base contract (the part which the CEO bought on the golf course) was a loss leader. The profit comes from the extras. By the time everyone has seen through the trick, it is virtually impossible to revoke the deal. No one has breached any contractual terms. But you have turned over all your hardware, software, communications and people to the outsourcer. It would be a mammoth task to build your capabilities up again, and step in to save the day.

These kinds of nightmare scenarios have happened. But avoiding them is not achieved by head-burying. You need to take control, and accept that there are some aspects of your job which will soon (if they are not already) be better done by someone else.

Take your telecoms network for example. Unless your business deals with data traffic which would put a strain on the networks of a moderately sized developing country, you cannot afford to maintain the expertise to keep it in-house. You need the services of a managed network organization. That's their core business. That's their job, and they will do it better and cheaper than you, whilst removing a large headache for you.

There will be many others like this. Your job is to construct a clear strategy for selective outsourcing, before the decisions are made on golf courses without you.

What should be outsourced?

If you need any tools to start the task of sorting out what you should let go of or hang on to, you could turn to the applications portfolio we introduced in Chapter 8. You should be seriously considering outsourcing those activities which you plot in the bottom half of the model. You should be planning to retain until your dying breath those in the top half.

It is the activities you perform in the top of the portfolio which form the basis of your organization's sustainable competitive advantage. Outsourcing these would be business suicide. But by the same token, not outsourcing those activities which others can perform better and cheaper (and which are in no way unique or a source of real advantage for you) is bad for business. It ties up expensive resources (you and your people) in doing things which add less value than their costs.

Of course, this exercise in determining which elements of your activities plot in which parts of the portfolio is easy to 'fiddle' We have known IT people who have tried to squeeze almost everything into the Strategic box in a desperate (and pathetic) attempt to keep outsourcing at bay. Remember, the meaning of 'Strategic' here is that this system, application or activity changes the nature of how you do you business, and provides your organization with genuine competitive advantage; it does not mean anything which is important enough to ruffle a few feathers. When IT people do misclassify everything like this, they only demonstrate their ineffectiveness as senior members of the business.

Choose your outsourcers wisely

Outsourcing is more than a business deal. It is a kind of partnership. As we said in the previous chapter, partnering is about people.

Research by outsourcing consultancies have shown that, like all forms of partnership, those which work well do so because of the success of the relationships between the key individuals. And since individuals tend to reflect their organizations' cultures, you need to be sure that your chosen outsourcing company is compatible with yours in terms of your respective cultures.

You may find it helpful as you weigh up the pros and cons of different outsourcing partners to use a tool like the culture map we introduced in Chapter 16. Draw up one for your organization, and another for the potential partner's. It will not take years of precise analysis to tell you how close the two align, and where, if anywhere, the stresses and strains will appear.

Where you do find achievable levels of compatibility, take the same open, honest and collaborative approach to surfacing and dealing with those contentious issues that we have advocated between yourselves and suppliers and consultants. The same principles apply.

You and your outsourcer should both be in pursuit of the same goals. So long as you have been open and honest about the value proposition, there is less room for misunderstanding. You need to make the profit and risk sharing aspects of the relationship less threatening by questioning and challenging what may become damaging differences in assumptions about what is acceptable and what not. Be open about your values, and your vision for the future – if you can be clear about these.

If you cannot, don't worry. This key issue will be dealt with towards the end of the book.

Part Four
Becoming streetwise

20 Shades of grey

Talking to computers and talking to people

The roots of the challenges you face in getting to the top lie in the nature of your history as an IT person. It is in the nature of IT to work with precision and certainty. Those of you who, like the authors, remember having to submit (what a wonderfully rich word in this context) punch cards to the compiler, and wait for its judgement, will also remember how unforgiving compilers are. There is a right answer, and wrong answers will be rejected.

It is not surprising that those attracted to IT in the first place will be people for whom this kind of relationship with your work is seen as a challenge rather than a prison. IT people love to take on the compiler and win; those unsuited to IT see the compiler as a stupid moron which cannot see anything but what is thrust under its nose.

You see, most people (those who don't choose to work with computers) rely heavily on the ability which humans have, but most computers don't, to infer from incomplete data what people are saying.

Research into the human mind (or brain, if you prefer) shows how we humans have a remarkable capacity for 'filling in the gaps'. For example, when presented with the image in Figure 20.1 we see a triangle. It isn't there.

When we listen to people talking, we can understand what they say, even if there are gaps in what the ears actually pick up. A great deal of what is said comes from unconscious monitoring of these gaps, and of the body language – the non-verbal communication which our brains are tuned into.

Figure 20.1 The phantom triangle

Computers can't do this. To communicate with them, you have to say everything you cannot imply it. You have to say everything through the right medium (for most computers, it's the keyboard), rather than being able to 'send' signals through a mix of media such as words, tone of voice, posture, gestures, facial expression and so on. When we communicate with other humans, we automatically use all these media at the same time. This enriches the communication, and enables us to work with the enormous subtlety which reaches its apotheosis in the arts.

Many IT people we know find it hard to understand what others have against computers. If you like the purity, precision and rigor of communications with computers, you may not realize that you are in the minority. Human beings have not evolved to work like this. You are different. And the years you have spent working with computers will have served to reinforce this difference. Not wrong, necessarily, just different.

Where it starts to feel 'wrong' is when you want to gain recogni-

tion at the most senior levels of management, and they won't let you. Until then, IT people often rejoice in their differences. They see their mastery of computers (upon which we all increasingly depend) as a sign of superiority. But that specific superiority does not let them into the inner sanctum. That's when IT people start to think there must be some line of code which they haven't written into what they do. Once this line of behavioural code is written, they will slide easily into their entitled senior management roles. After all, they are intelligent enough.

Tell me what I need to do

We recently received an enquiry from a senior IT manager which we felt summarized nicely the kinds of question we are often asked. In essence, the enquirer said that he wanted a seat on the board, because IT is critical to the future success of his company. He said: 'I've tried pointing out the business benefits of new technology, I consider myself to be in tune with the business, I network as effectively as I can – but I still report to the Finance Director. What should I do next?'.

Like many of his peers, this IT manager has done all the right things, and cannot understand why he's not on the board like the most senior people in finance, marketing and so on.

Many of the people we work with are motivated by the same thing – they want a seat on the board. Many also sign up to our management development programmes because they believe that our course will provide them with tools and weapons for their campaign. In other words, they come looking for a prescription.

This is a bit like a compiler asking for the 'right' code. It is an attitude which is underpinned by the assumption that there is a 'right' way to achieve this goal, and that this has somehow been withheld from them. We are asked to provide that prescription.

The truth is not out there

The first key lesson is that solving this problem does not depend on acquiring something from the outside. The truth is not out there, it's in here (in other words, in each individual IT manager, distinctively, and uniquely). You cannot simply go out there, get hold of the lines of code, or the tool, or the method, and simply apply it, graft it on.

While you are looking out there, you're overlooking the source of the challenge, which is in the history you have lived, the assumptions that history has generated within you, and the consequential reputation you have built yourself.

Clearly, as we said in the very early chapters of the book, the IT stereotype is not of your making; you may the 'innocent victim' of that general perception. But the solution for you lies in challenging the version of the IT stereotype which applies to you in your organization. It starts with you being prepared to acknowledge that you have to do something differently, not just everyone else.

Seeking prescriptions or applying discretion

The very act of seeking a prescription betrays one key element of the challenge. If the goal is to be invited into the inner sanctum, you need to be aware of the significant transformation in thinking this entails. It means crossing a threshold between prescription and discretion.

For most of our managerial lives, discretion is limited. Clearly there are decisions to be made. But the scope of our choices will be limited: by procedures and rules; by precedent and what we expect our boss would want; by the cultural realities (the way we do things around here); and so on. Choice there may be, but within relatively tight (and comforting) boundaries. There are brakes on the machine we are driving, which mean that we can go wrong, but (usually) not horribly so.

Once we cross the threshold into senior management, our decisions are no longer prescribed in anything like the same way. We have a much greater degree of choice – indeed, that is what we are there for, to exercise choice. If similar rules applied to decisions at the most senior level, any half decent manager could do the job. (The fact that almost everyone in an organization says they could run the company better than the bosses who do does not mean they could do so.)

Once you get across the threshold, you are no longer comforted by rules; you are exposed to real and unguided choice; you are watched closely by everyone (staff, customers and shareholders); and your decisions can have major impact on organizational success or failure. It is nothing like writing lines of code for an unforgiving compiler, because, once you know the rules, you can satisfy the compiler every time. You can never do this for unforgiving press, public, staff, stock market analysts… .

So what makes this so different?

In chapter 15 we introduced the notion of different 'levels' of inference. At one level, there are facts, objectivities we can measure and generally agree on by appeal to an independent set of rules. At another, there are opinions. When we asked is John mean or thrifty, we were not asking about John and his behaviour so much as about the person to whom we asked the question. There is no 'right' answer to such a question *if you assume the question is about John.*

Much of what we do before we cross that threshold deals with facts and measures. To be sure, there are areas in which our opinions are important. But once you are dealing with long-term futures, the are very few facts to work with. If you have to take decisions based on what is likely to be the case in five years (or ten or twenty years), then you are unlikely to be able to appeal to many objectivities to help you.

This is more than simply having the knack of being a good guesser about the future. It is about working with ambiguity and complexity.

Ambiguity and complexity

What makes a perfect marriage? Now show me one. For every 'perfect marriage', it is not hard to reinterpret the data to present it as fundamentally flawed. Divorce lawyers know this. They will tell you that they can present any marriage in ways which clearly demonstrate an irretrievable breakdown.

What makes a perfect business? Now show me one. For every 'perfect business', it is not hard to reinterpret the data to present it as fundamentally flawed. Journalists and industry analysts know this. And millions of pound of shareholder value can be gained or lost on these kinds of interpretations. It is not the accuracy of the interpretations that counts (what would constitute accuracy, when there is no absolute truth against which to measure it?) It is their persuasiveness.

IT people have not grown up in an environment which values persuasiveness over accuracy. Try persuading a compiler. Consequently, IT people tend to feel that there's something morally suspect about winning through persuasion.

Accuracy and factual truth depend upon a limited set of rules and an agreed goal. For computer programming, the right way is defined by the goal – a robust and working program – and the rules – the language in which the program is written. You don't need to debate about it.

When governing a business, both the rules and the goal are questionable and imprecise. It is a matter of opinion whether the goal is profitability for shareholders, job satisfaction for employees, providing products and services which do good for the world, defeating the competition, or anything else, or even any combination of these in whatever proportion you like. This is complex and ambiguous.

Even if the goal is clear, the 'rules' of how best to get there are uncertain. Organizational life involves messiness and confusion. It involves unpredictability. It looks tempting as though, were we clever enough, we could predict the future with the accuracy with which we can predict eclipses of the sun. But we can't.

If you go into senior management with the deeply rooted desire to work towards such predictability ('because there *must be* a right way') you will miss the point. If you go in with the recognition that this is an art and not a science, you will be preparing the ground for dealing with uncertainty, complexity and ambiguity.

The case of King Lear

The lasting appeal of Shakespeare's plays is partly due to the universality of the problems he addresses. King Lear is useful, for example, because its questions do not have 'right' answers. Unlike the detective novel, which loses a great deal of its appeal the second time we read it (we know who dunnit) King Lear's relationships with Goneril and Regan, with Cordelia, with Gloucester and Edgar are the stuff of human existence. There is no right answer to the question 'Was King Lear to blame for his own fate?', since each answer tells us more about our own beliefs and values than about King Lear.

Like many kings of the day, Lear had a court jester, the Fool. This character kept telling the kind of things he didn't want to hear. For many readers of the play, the Fool is a hero, because he sees through the hypocrisy and intrigue to which the king is blind (the more worldly-wise Gloucester has his eyes plucked out for similar perceptions). Hero he may be for this reason, but Fool he remains.

The Fool was neither king nor prince. He stuck to what he saw as the truth, because he had no political role to play. Unlike the Fool in King Lear, anyone who aspires to senior management must be prepared to turn away from the simple (but naive) commitment to 'the truth' and embrace the shifting, ambiguous world of 'multiple truths'.

The role of belief

Because Shakespeare had the knack of painting characters we can relate to so well, some people may be afraid that moving across the threshold into senior positions means turning your back on what you believe in.

Nothing could be further from the truth. The apparent contradiction here lies in the difference between what we believe and what we believe *in*.

What I believe tends to be about the world out there. I can easily be shown that the perceptions I have, which have led to those beliefs, are flawed. I change what I believe. However, what I believe in are my underpinning values. These drive me, and strongly influence my opinions. When asked the question whether John is mean or thrifty, it will be my underlying values which will make me answer one way or the other.

Where there are no rules to break, and where there are no truths to rely upon, we turn to our values to guide us. One person's set of values is no better or worse than another's (although we like to think our own values are good – we perceive other people's values as 'good' to the degree to which they are the same as our own).

Because of the impossibility of demonstrating the relative merits of value sets, and because executive decisions are highly influenced by the values of those executives, most conflicts at this level are conflicts of values – just like the conflicts in King Lear. In assuming the mantle of responsibility which goes with senior management we do not turn away from values, we embrace them as our primary guide.

In later chapters, we'll explore how you can increase your effectiveness when relying on values rather than facts. First, let's look at what a more values-oriented approach entails.

21 Say hello to the rest of your brain

As Martin is discovering, this 'right-brain stuff' is not easy, especially if you approach it through the 'left-brain' habits of a lifetime.

Recently, brain research has shown that the naive split into 'left-brain' and 'right-brain is far too simplistic to represent how the brain actually works. It's much more complicated than that. Yet as a 'model' that contrasts between the different kinds of activity we use our brains for, it can be helpful. In other words, this chapter is not a lesson in neurophysiology, it is an exploration of the enormous variety of ways of seeing, thinking, feeling and behaving which are available to us, and which are influenced more or less by the architectures of our individual brains.

Therefore, when we refer to right and left in this chapter we are not referring to actual locations in the brain, but to differences about styles and approaches characterized as 'right-brained' and 'left-brained'.

Martin's problem, in the cartoon at the start of this chapter, is that his intelligent terminal (all 'left brain') is reminding him that right-brained approaches are not better than left-brain, but different. And because they are different, they have to be judged in different ways. If you are seeking the right answer to a problem for which 'the right answer' makes sense, then taking a left-brain approach is fine. But if you want to explore possibilities in ways which may lead you to the unexpected, your 'left-brain' will try to get in the way.

So what's all this 'right-brain/left-brain' stuff about anyway?

For the purpose of this chapter, we'll call the logical, factual part of our personalities the 'left-brain' stuff, and the imaginative, values-driven part, the 'right-brain' stuff. And we'll separate out four key elements of each 'side' of the model (brain) to illustrate how the 'stereotypical' IT manager tends to favour the left-brain over the right. Then we'll explore the effect of this 'lopsidedness' on approaches to senior management, and advise you on ways in which you may want to even up the balance between the left and right parts of your (model) brain.

To make sense of this 'lopsidedness' simply remember that most people in the world are right-handed or left-handed. This means that, almost without thinking, and so long as their culture does not prescribe which hand to use for what tasks, people will favour their 'stronger' hand for important tasks. For right-handers, they will normally write and do precise tasks with their right hands, which is likely also to be stronger. They rarely consciously choose which hand to use; it just comes naturally. For right-handers (of which there are many more in the world than left-handers) the left hand's role is to provide support and back up.

As we look at the 'left'- and 'right'- brained options, think of them in this way. Most people in the world will favour (almost unconsciously) the left or right option. They will use the other option in support, and as back up. The same brain architecture which makes us right- or left-handed is responsible for making us left- or right-brained for each of these options.

We'll start with the different ways in which 'left-brained' and 'right-brained' people see the world and how they make up our minds. Then we'll touch on how these differences affect lifestyles, and how we deal with the outside world.

Pictures of the world

Our perceptions of the world are built from two distinct sources. The 'left-brained' source comprises our perceptions of things in the real world, facts, data, the here and now, and the impressions we get directly through our five senses. People who naturally favour the left-brained approach are down to earth, practical people. They learn through experience, and have little time for flights of fancy. They go about things in a sequential manner, following directions rather than hunches. And they develop strategies from the bottom up, gathering relevant data and using those data to provide a firm and solid foundation for the way forward. When they solve problems, they take the attitude that, if you can gather enough information about the problem – its nature, causes, effects and so on, the solution will fall out naturally.

The 'right-brained' source comprises our perceptions of potentialities. It is the part of the brain we use to make intuitive leaps, and have those 'aha' moments when things fall into place. We use it innovatively, creatively, and to imagine the future. People who naturally favour the right-brained approach are creative, visionary people. They learn through seeing patterns and connections, and have little time for what they see as 'tedious' practical tasks requiring concentration and application. They go about things randomly, following their intuition. And they develop strategies from the top down, identifying the vision or goal first, and then looking back from that goal to how they are going to get there. When they solve problems, they take the attitude that the less data they clutter their minds up with, the more likely they are to arrive at a creative solution through lateral thinking.

IT people, like most of us, use both 'sides' in their work. But it is in the nature of the profession and most of its inherent tasks, that the left-brain approach is taken. Even multi-tasking is built from a series of linear, sequential components. Underlying our whole approach to information technology (especially in the West) is a left-brained way of perceiving. If this is how computers have been designed to work, it is not surprising that people who favour working in this way will tend to work with computers. (By contrast, people who do not favour working this way are often technophobes rather than technophiles.)

Making up our minds

A second pair of options relate to how we make up our minds about things. On the 'left' side lies the approach which works with logic, principles, rules and objectivities. Here, people deal with problems based upon precedence and 'laws', such as the laws of physics, of maths and of logic. Working towards the 'right' decision means looking at the process of getting there. The outcome is determined by that process, and not by what the outcomes will mean or imply for those affected.

The right-brain works differently. It looks beyond decisions and judgements to the outcomes these may have. It works subjectively and asks what impact various decisions or outcomes will have, and how those impacts relate to the decider's values. 'Right-brainers' will avoid conflict and confrontation, and will aim to create harmony in relationships. When a problem arises, the left-brain's instant response is to seek a solution; the right-brain's approach is to empathize with the owner of the problem. Its rationale says that, for anything to be a problem there must be at least one person for whom this situation is undesirable. So the right-brain seeks ways of appreciating, sharing and empathizing with the owner of the problem, giving the 'tender loving care' so they will feel better, and capable of finding their own solution to the problem.

So the left-brain can work comfortably on 'problems' in the abstract, isolating the problem from its owner. In the search for scientific truths, and for information systems solutions, this tendency to abstract from the particular to the general is a strength. It's how IT works. Again, not surprisingly IT attracts people who favour the left-brained approach, and who can be excited by and motivated by the search for solutions to problems.

As we have suggested at various points so far in the book, there is a downside to this. Unless the right-brain is developed as a strong supporter to the dominant left-brained problem-solving mode, IT people will have more difficulty relating to people who have problems than to the problems themselves. Hence, for example, the frequent complaint from business people that their IT people provide a technically competent service, but one which feels unsatisfactory. This highly dominating left-brained style is a key cause of the vicious cycle we introduced in Chapter 14.

Pairing up the options

The activities of getting our pictures of the world and making up our minds pair up together to form a central style or approach to many of the tasks we perform in our lives and our work. This produces four quite distinct styles.

Those who favour both the left-brained approaches to building pictures and making up their minds are highly practical and logical people. These are the *down-to-earth* types. They deal with problems logically and sequentially, and they rely upon their ability to accumulate information and experience, to prove the cases they want to promote. Their potential weaknesses lie in a lack of imagination and sensitivity to people.

Those who favour both right-brained approaches are creative, imaginative people who are often unsympathetic to technology. These are the *idealistic* types. They are people who follow their values in everything they do, and the apparent lack of logic or sequence in their intuitive leaps can frustrate the practical types. They rely heavily on their intuition, and are happy to build their strategies for life and business on very little supporting data. Their potential weaknesses lie in a lack of patience with what they see as boring routine, and a naivety in their hope that, in time, the imperfections in people will be resolved and the world will become the ideal place they would like to create.

Some people favour the right-brained approach to building their pictures of the world, but the left-brained approach to making up their minds. These are the *theoretical* types. They make big intuitive leaps, and prefer to work with patterns rather than detail, but are also excited by problems and logical solutions. They work on strategies rather than tactics, and love to create and work with theoretical models rather than facts and data. Their potential weaknesses are a lack of connection to the 'real world', and an insensitivity to the impact of their 'great ideas' on other people.

Finally, there are those who favour the left-brained approach to building their pictures of the world, but the right-brain in making up their minds. These are the *caring* types. They are practical, but the focus of their practicality is the care of other people rather than technical problems. They have little time for theory or day dreaming, and are forever seeking ways of making individuals feel better. Many of these people go into caring professions such as nursing, teaching small children and customer service jobs. Their potential weaknesses are a lack of imagination and an unwillingness to engage in strategic thinking or theoretical exercises.

So what? The role of fuzzy thinking in technology

The influences these aspects of brain architecture can have on organizational thinking, on career choices, and many other aspects of our lives are far from trivial. Take, for example, the long-term lack of success in developing artificial intelligence in the West. This reflects the fact that information technology has been developed largely on the left-brain model. IT has been the kingdom of the *down-to-earth* types, who have built IT, bottom up, logically and sequentially from simple principles. The most simple principle underpinning Western technology has been 'A or not-A'.

Partly because Eastern philosophy has always been comfortable with the underlying principle 'A and not-A', it is the Japanese and Koreans who have successfully broken through with 'fuzzy technologies'.

We are not saying that IT people in the West could not have come up with the technologies which have become almost commonplace in washing machines, camera lenses, air-conditioning systems and hundreds of other world-class products we are now importing from the East. Just that it is less likely they would do so; they are temperamentally inclined to attack problems by working harder at their strengths (data and logic) rather than relying upon their less favoured approaches (imagination and a sensitivity to outcomes, impact and real benefits of 'affordance').

So what? The role of influencing

What influences people differs according to their styles. *Down to earth* people are more likely to be convinced by proof, while *idealistic* people are more influenced by an appeal to their values. *Theoretical* people want the big picture – for the whole argument to make sense; while *sociable* people want to see how something will benefit real people, right now.

Even if you as a senior IT manager do not share the same personality characteristics as the IT stereotype (which lies in the *down-to-earth* types' domain), you may have been led unsuspecting

The down to earth ones	The theoretical ones
• Be organized and structured • Be practical and realistic • Work logically and systematically through your analysis • Offer proof and evidence	• Show how it fits into the bigger picture • Ensure the theoretical base is sound • Appeal to my intellect and imagination • Be a credible source of information
The sociable ones	**The idealistic ones**
• Be clear and explicit, don't just imply • Show me how people will benefit • Demonstrate immediate and practical results • Show me respect	• Engage with my personal values • Paint pictures and draw analogies that have meaning • Be passionate and engage my imagination • Show me how it will contribute to the 'greater good' of human kind

Figure 21.1 The four influencing styles

down the route of trying to influence people in just the same way as the *down-to-earth* types would.

This is not to say that the *down-to-earth* types' approach to influencing is wrong. It is just ineffective if you are trying to influence someone of a different type. Most of us grow up believing that other people will be convinced by the kinds of arguments which convince us. Therefore, until someone is kind enough to point out that this is not the case, they continue to put forward their cases in the same way. What is worse, when that doesn't work, they tend to exaggerate.

Let's imagine a *down-to-earth* type trying to influence an *idealistic* type. In preparing his case, he will gather a great deal of supporting evidence, develop a logical, sequential argument which brings into play all this relevant data, and take the process carefully and incrementally from start to finish. It will be logical, detailed, and faultless.

But it may not work. If he has a second chance, he may make things worse by bringing even more data next time, and by developing an even more detailed case. What he has failed to understand is that idealistic types are not convinced by more data and better arguments. They are convinced by creative approaches to the future which will appeal to their imagination and produce an outcome in line with their core values and beliefs. They would favour a presentation which starts at the end – one big picture of the world. Their imagination can tinker with it. With the data-driven approach, they may have dropped off to sleep before you get to the 'punch line'.

You may have been there yourself. Many people, when they come away from this kind of presentation or conversation having failed to get their point across put the failure down to 'a political decision'.

What's a 'political decision'?

In a sense, all decisions are political. No matter how logical a case may be, decisions about the relative importance of cost, quality, ease of use, impact on the environment, staff morale and a whole host of other factors still underpin business choices.

These are the 'political' decisions which are the stuff of being a main board director. Logic and data are not enough.

Some of the *down-to-earth* types we have met in IT have had difficulty in understanding the subtlety of this point. They have said that they do use their right-brains a lot in trying to influence others. We ask them to show us – to try it for real. Time and again, it has proved too difficult for them without a fair amount of guidance and development. The psychological strength of our favoured approaches is so great that, for many people, they cannot even see how far they have to go to develop balance between these and the less favoured parts of their brains or personalities.

Without this genuine development, decisions and activities which call upon the right-brain are dimly appreciated. But until they have been more fully developed, people don't always know what they're missing. For example, many male managers we work with say, when presented with the 'model', that their favoured style of making up their minds is right-brained – values-driven, subjective, and focused upon the impact on people. The evidence they produce to 'prove' it is that they love their children.

This is like saying I must be left handed because I scratch the back of my right-hand with my left hand. You cannot love your children with your 'left-brain'. If you love them at all, it calls into play your right-brain. But you can still be overwhelmingly left-brained in all the other aspects of your life, including, and especially, at work.

It is often this dominance of left-brained approaches, coupled with such a dim appreciation of the alternatives we have represented as right-brained which lies at the heart of many IT managers' frustrations. Not all main board directors are right-brained, but few are as exclusively and overwhelmingly left-brained as the stereotypical IT manager.

A few final words on the brain (for the moment anyway)

The IT stereotype is plagued by two more left-brained approaches. The other two pairs concern how we deal with the outside world, and our lifestyles.

Dealing with the outside world

Everyone has heard of extraversion and introversion. Few realize that these are another pair of approaches like right- and left-handedness. The extraverted part of our personality is the part which deals with the world out there – people, things and activities. The introverted part is that which we use to introspect, to reflect and so on.

One manifestation of the differences between favouring extraversion and favouring introversion shows itself in how we think about important issues.

For people who favour extraversion, 'two heads are better than one'. They tend to prefer to tackle important issues with other people, feeling better when thoughts and ideas can be expressed out loud, and explored with others (if there's no one around, they'll even talk to the cat). They are comfortable with saying the first thing which comes into their heads, because, in their view, this is not the answer, but just another idea to kick around. For extraverts, other people add value, and extraverts therefore build networks of friends and acquaintances. This provides them with a steady stream of people with whom to bounce ideas around whenever they need. In return, extraverts make themselves available to others, keeping their doors open and happily dropping what they are doing to help another or to join in with a debate. They find it hard to concentrate for long on one task anyway, so interruptions are often welcome.

On the other hand, introverts believe that if an issue is important enough, it should be thought through before being presented to the world. They are uncomfortable with what they see as 'slick' answers, and will prefer to say nothing than be seen to be blurting out nonsense. They are only prepared to articulate thoughts once they have had time and space to think things through properly. For introverts, then, other people get in the way when there's something important to work on, so they send out (often unconscious) signals which say 'leave me alone, I'm busy'. Extraverts often misinterpret this as unfriendliness (perhaps directed at them personally), and see introverts as shy or aloof. Introverts are independent, preferring to deal with problems by themselves.

Most IT people are introverts. Most main board directors are extraverts. It is in the nature of corporate governance that ideas are shared and discussed, with the resulting decisions being characterized by cabinet responsibility. Introverts can join this club, but it is harder for them.

There is even less scientific validity in 'placing' one of these options in the 'left-brain', but we'll do it to make a point. For the sake of argument, let's call introversion a left-brained option, since it relies more on introspected intellect than it does on human interaction. As we have said about other aspects of our personalities, we're not suggesting that introversion actually does operate in the left hemisphere of the brain, but it seems to make sense to put it in that part of our model.

Lifestyles

Some people favour decisiveness, others spontaneity. The decisive ones tend to be relatively organized and in control. They make investments in systems and processes to make life easier for them in the future. For example, they may create a videotape index which enables them quickly and without hassle to get at the tapes they want to see. They make plans and stick to them, preferring to know what the future will bring, and helping to control the future through their plans and schemes. Completing things gives then satisfaction. They like decisions, because decisions take them forward, and remove uncertainty.

The spontaneous ones don't like decisions because they close down options which they'd prefer to keep open for as long as possible. Completing things does not give spontaneous types satisfaction, once it's finished, it's no longer available for yet further amendment. Spontaneous types therefore finish fewer tasks, including the development of systems and processes like videotape indexes. For spontaneous types, the surprise at finding that they have something on tape they had completely forgotten far outweighs any frustration at being unable to find the film or programme they started to look for.

Spontaneous types welcome distractions. Faced with an invitation to play, when there's work still to be done, decisive types will do the work first, preferring to have everything 'done and dusted' to allow them to play without the burden of unfinished work hanging over them. Spontaneous types, on the other hand, are quite happy to play now and deal with the work later; they can therefore appear to be more sociable, as they respond positively to more invitations to 'come and play'.

Completing the 'model' decisive types follow the 'left-brain', while spontaneous types are more 'right-brained'.

More IT people are decisive than spontaneous. Creating systems lies at the heart of the job, and projects are about getting things done. However, it takes spontaneity to feel comfortable with ambiguity and complexity.

The full monty

The IT stereotype is characterized in this chapter's model as a combination of introverted, practical, logical and decisive. There's nothing inherently wrong with this combination of approaches. Indeed, this combination can be very strong in getting things done. When strategies are already in place, rules have been set, and tasks have to be planned and carried out, this combination can be very productive. The problems start when each element starts to amplify the others, and works to exclude the potential balance from extraverted, creative, value-centred and spontaneous approaches.

Some people have this combination of extraverted, creative, value-centred and spontaneous approaches as their natural style. Few enter the IT profession; even fewer, if they do enter, stay.

One reason for this is that the very nature of working more with technology than with people serves to reinforce the behavioural tendencies which go with the introverted, practical, logical and decisive set of approaches. The tasks, the pressures, the daily experience of working with computers, all make IT people more like IT people day by day. When they have to call upon the other side of their personalities, as they do when they want to enter the inner sanctum, they not only find it hard, but they also find it hard to understand why they find it hard.

You may remember our enquirer in Chapter 20 who asked: 'I've tried pointing out the business benefits of new technology, I consider myself to be in tune with the business, I network as effec-

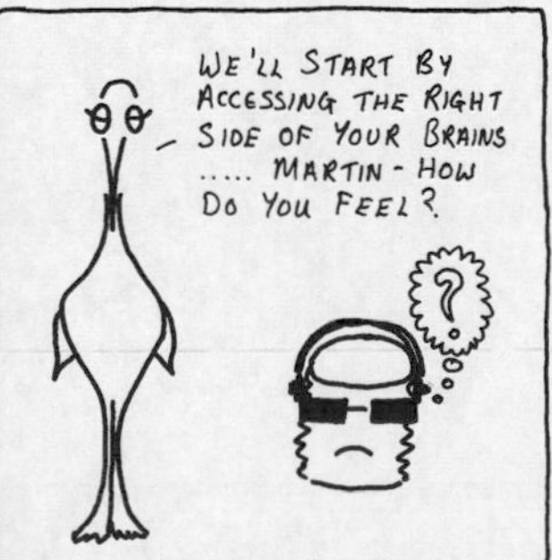

tively as I can – but I still report to the Finance Director. What should I do next?'. He is attacking his problem through the left side of his brain. Even if he knows this, and wants to do something different, he may have difficulties in doing it.

22 Blowing the whistle

Let's take a look at one important issue in IT management which illustrates how IT attracts people who fit the introverted, practical, logical and decisive pattern, but also how the set of behaviours characteristic of this personality type feeds back into how IT is run.

The IT project and the boiled frog

In Chapter 4 we reviewed IT project management. IT projects are notorious for being over budget, late and vary far short of their original promises. We suggest that one reason for this is that IT projects set out with unrealistic promises in the first place, and go from bad to worse.

IT people are taught (often by other introverted, practical, logical and decisive people) good principles of project management. This suits the stereotypical personality, as it encourages them to (for example):

- Draw up detailed plans.
- Put in place hard measures of progress (project milestones).
- Break down the project into small, manageable chunks.
- Allocate clear roles and responsibilities to individuals.
- Specify deliverables at the conclusion of each project phase, and request sign-off for each.
- Produce many and detailed progress reports.
- Develop a costing schedule, built up from the component parts of the project plan.

- Add in contingency for things which they cannot imagine at the moment, but which may take time and resources to deal with.

Projects come under scrutiny by the business, and one of the first things to go is the contingency. After all, according to the business, IT projects have been going on for so long now that, surely, IT professionals can anticipate all the pitfalls and challenges well in advance. They do learn from experience, don't they?

This is the thin end of the wedge. It's pointless and painful to run through yet again what happens thereafter. In extreme situations such as the London Ambulance system disaster, the Stock Exchange Torus project, and many others almost as infamous, things just go from bad to worse. Like the proverbial boiled frog, no one seems to be able to blow the whistle on these projects.

What it takes to blow the whistle

For a start, many such projects receive very senior management attention. To blow the whistle means drawing attention to oneself from some very high quarters. What is more, many IT people remember previous encounters with very senior people. Somehow or other their well worked, detailed, and watertight proposals were taken apart in ways they could not understand. Dare they try that again with what would be a very unpopular proposal, fraught with political overtones? No.

So it takes seniority and credibility, things many IT people lack. But it also takes a different set of approaches. When you want to blow the whistle, you may need to call upon the extraverted, creative, value-centred and spontaneous approaches.

Imagine your organization has decided to implement a new marketing system. You have been out to the market with a limited budget and bought what looked at first sight to be an 80 per cent solution. As time progresses, however, things start crawling out of the woodwork. The company has gone into continental Europe and your system has to work on other European languages and legislation. The way the package was written and structured was more complex than you thought, so there's a greater degree of dependency on the suppliers to help with modifications; their services are proving highly expensive. Finally, the business users have gone back on what you were convinced they had agreed to, and are refusing to modify the way they work to fit in with the

package solution. You are asked to modify the package to fit in with them.

There are significant sunk costs in the project already. The new marketing system will (according to the official line) provide a competitive edge which will take the company into the next millennium. But you have to deal with all this with a reduced budget, and with deadlines which have been shortened. This is because the Marketing Director has found out (on the golf course) that the competition is already 90 per cent of the way to implementing a system which will steal a march on your competitive edge. You mutter that, if it's so important, maybe they'll give you more money and more resources. However, by now the message is coming back that you've already overspent, you're producing a 'me-too' system, and there's little point in trying to get senior management attention for this project because there's more pressing items on their agenda right now.

The classic response to this kind of situation is to turn to one's strengths. For the stereotypical IT manager, this means getting their head down to work hard on revising plans to deal with a challenging set of requirements. There must be, they think, a right way to solve this problem, so let's stick as far as we can to the broad plan, but make adjustments and amendments. The last thing we'll do is 'can' the project – finishing is too attractive a goal.

So attractive is finishing that it overshadows the original objective of the project, which was to increase competitiveness of the organization. Now, even though this is not overtly acknowledged, the prime objective becomes to finish. You and your colleagues may not even realize it, but this shift has happened so many times. Systems are driven to completion even at the expense of bankrupting the company.

What about an alternative scenario? You network with as many people as you can to share your concerns. You throw away the plans and brainstorm new ways of achieving 'similar' outcomes (in terms of the value proposition, not the system). You debate with influential people about the impact on them of these alternative scenarios (and not the elegance or logic of the answers), and you remain open to radical new ideas no matter how 'committed' you feel to a course of action.

Doing it well, not going through the motions

Some IT managers we have worked with say that they do all this. In many cases, this is the same self-delusion as the 'logical' type who claims to be a 'values' type because he loves his children.

Blowing the whistle in these ways means drawing upon aspects of your personality which may not be easily accessible to you. This is not to say you shouldn't try it. It is to say that it will take years of practice.

Sometimes we have offered this kind of advice to 'stereotypical' IT managers. They have told us that they have tried it, but it doesn't work. This is like someone saying: 'Someone advised me that playing the piano can produce beautiful music. Well I tried it once, and it doesn't work'. As the construction worker said to the man who asked how to get to Carnegie Hall, 'you gotta practice'.

23 All stressed out and nowhere to go

Some people are claiming that IT management is now one of the most stressful occupations. Figure 23.1 is a selection of headlines from the computing press over the past few years.

Given the problems we have been describing in this book, especially those associated with projects (see Chapters 4 and 22), it is not surprising that people in senior IT positions are suffering from the pressures of work.

But it is not just the pressures of IT work which are the cause of stress among so many IT managers. It is more the interaction between the pressures and the style of the 'typical' IT manager. Something happens where the pressures of the work of IT managers meets their personal style. In other words, it is the mix of the following which creates negative reinforcement and creeping stress:

- The high expectations placed upon the IT community by the relentless hype of the IT suppliers, and the ease with which with children can manipulate their own PCs.
- The pressures placed upon IT management for delivery.

'Directors pushed to breaking point.' *Computer Weekly*, May 1997

'Stress at work: At breaking point.' *Computer Weekly*, October 1996

'Growing work pressures hit directors' home lives – 65 per cent of IT directors in the UK felt under such stress that their home lives suffered as a result.' *Computer Weekly*, December 1997

'Stress levels among IT staff increase.' *Guardian Financial Services*, July 1996

'IT brains stress to impress.' *Computing*, February 1998

'All stressed up and nowhere to go – IT management has become more stressful than divorce.' *Computing*, January 1998

Figure 23.1 Press coverage of IT stress

- The psychological make-up of many IT managers.

In other words, IT managers unwittingly bring much of the stress upon themselves.

Psychological indicators of stress

There are many research projects in which questions are asked about stress and psychology. It is clear now that there are some styles of personality which are more prone to stress than others. People who are more likely to suffer from stress, and the consequential illnesses, including heart disease often display the following characteristics.

Intolerance of ambiguity

People who find it hard to deal with situations in which it is hard to be certain what is 'the right answer' use a fair amount of psychic energy trying to reconcile different views. In chapters 15 and 20 we looked at the notion of inference. There are many situations in managerial life (especially at the more senior levels) in which opinions and inferences play a major part. There is ambiguity in the statement 'John is not mean, he's thrifty', and people who find this kind of irresolvable dilemma uncomfortable are more prone to symptoms of stress.

Focus on rigid, single approaches

Some people are relatively closed to the notion of 'divergence'. This means that they tend to seek 'perfection' in answers to questions, or ways of doing things. Those who live their lives dependent (even if they do not realize it) upon sets of rules and principles often feel that allowing for a variety of ways of seeing and doing is 'sloppy thinking'. Their efforts constantly to eliminate this apparent redundancy of thought add stress to their lives.

View short-term perspectives only

It is often the case that circumstances force us to deal with the here and now almost constantly. IT managers chasing their tails over projects which are falling short of their goals often find it very hard to raise their eyes above the short-term horizons they have been set. However, among these managers are those who, if they are honest with themselves, are temperamentally inclined to 'firefight' and to remain focused upon the immediate issues of the day.

Miss nuances and complexities in situations

Those who are likely to focus on the 'one right way, and now' will be less prepared to see the subtleties of organizational politics. Taking things literally will mean missing the complex interactions of visions and ideas, values and opinions. One of the main reasons many IT managers are branded with the IT stereotype is their apparent literalness where, often, a more 'right-brained' approach is expected.

Lose fine distinctions in judgement

One consequence of an over-literal approach is the lack of awareness of the ways in which subtle alternative viewpoints can alter the judgements we make. Overlooking the unintended consequences is a classic reason for many IT project failures.

Less consultation

The research also shows that those who are more likely to follow their own judgements, and ignore the possibility of exploring ideas with other people, are more prone to stress. IT managers often do like to consult with others, but, when the going gets tough, and they fear that consultation with senior user managers will be linked to negative feedback, they can tend to withdraw behind their barricades and 'go it alone'.

Tendency to rely on old, inappropriate habits

IT people are taught to be systematic in their approaches to their work. 'Methodologies' are often the frameworks through which they find comfort and certainty. But following such methods can become habit-forming, and new situations (especially those at senior levels) call for very different styles. What may have been helpful in a more mechanical set of tasks (such as systems design or project management) may be very out of place when you are trying to reconcile apparently incompatible sets of values.

Less creative

IT people are often hurt when they are accused by others of being less creative. Yet much of the apparent 'creativity' of IT lies in finding more and more ingenious ways of following rules. The creativity they exhibit is the narrow focus of the left-brained approach, rather than the genuine, lateral thinking creativity of the right-brain.

These indicators seem to point to the stereotypical IT manager being more likely to suffer from stress than other types. The IT stereotype is characterized in the model developed in Chapter 20 as a combination of introverted, practical, logical and decisive. Research into people who suffer from heart disease shows that people who demonstrate these characteristics are statistically more likely to suffer from this major consequence of stress than those who are inclined towards the extraverted, creative, value-centred and spontaneous approaches.

It is certainly true that, when the pressure is on, many IT managers we have met do seem to want to lock themselves away from the outside world. Ironically, it is often IT which lets the world into the IT manager's hideaway.

Focus on outcomes, not process

One example of how the stereotypical IT profile exacerbates stress is in the habit of trying to solve problems, often by yourself, by looking at the process to the exclusion of the outcomes. Let's explain what we mean by this.

When users complain that they are not happy with some aspect of the service they are receiving, typically you, the IT manager, will look at the service, and seek to find ways of improving it. You will probably try to sort it out by yourself, have faith that your thorough examination of the facts, and your sense of logic will throw up a solution, and you will then put in place the appropriate systems or processes to ensure that errors will be eliminated and/or the improvements will be implemented.

Take the following example in which users do not believe they are getting value for money. In response, you review your metrics and your monthly reporting (which is already fairly comprehensive), and you decide you need to add a function point comparison, and benchmark yourselves against other similar organizations' IT functions. That will prove it to the users, you think, that you are doing a good job.

Actually this makes the situation even worse. They are fed up with facts and figures. They just want to be made to 'feel' important, that they matter, and that you care about their problems. When they feel better about you they will start to feel that they are getting value for money. Address how they feel, not the stark, abstract and ultimately meaningless figures.

Compare this numbers approach with the case of the manager who 'improved' his help desk service by doing quite the opposite.

He took himself out of the office, talked to people, ignored the details and the logic, but empathized and reviewed what outcomes people were looking for. He kept an open mind, not closing down when he thought he had the answer. By doing so, he took an enormous amount of pressure off himself, whilst at the same time making the users feel significantly better about the service.

Throughout this exercise, this manager did not try to explain, excuse, 'educate' or impress upon people how difficult it is providing a good service. He let the users talk. He was adopting an outgoing, creative, empathetic and spontaneous approach to the problem. Contrast this with the 'typical' introverted, practical, logical and decisive stance. Neither is right, but there are some situations in which, for the sake of your health, you may want to consider breaking the habits of a lifetime.

What gives us stress

Although there are situations which seem to cause stress in everyone, some people are stressed by situations which others find quite tolerable:

- Introverts are more stressed by interruptions, for example, than extraverts.
- Practical types may be stressed by being asked to deal with a problem by starting with a clean sheet of paper. Their preferred style is to deal with a problem by exploring its nature, its causes, its component parts; starting with nothing but ideas can be very disconcerting. Contrast this with the creative types, for whom data about a problem can get in the way; a clean sheet of paper is, for them, the ideal.
- Logical types can be highly stressed by personal and emotional problems, since these are not susceptible to logical solutions. People with such problems are seldom looking for answers at all – they need to talk, to be listened to and empathized with,

sensitively and with compassion. Trying to provide answers is missing the point. The value-centred types, by contrast, find such situations easy and natural to deal with.

- Decisive types can be highly stressed by uncertainty, delay in decision-making and apparent vacillation. On the other hand, spontaneous types can be stressed by rapid closure, and being tied down by rules and regulations.

Try to be clear about what it is that makes you stressed – not only the obvious situations like pressure at work, but the situations which may be peculiar to yourself. Try also to find out what makes those around you stressed. You may discover that many of the things you are doing to them causes them stress, even though they may be the very things which you feel comfortable with.

Imagine, for example, you have an introverted, practical, logical and decisive approach. You are trying to work alongside someone who is inclined towards the extraverted, creative, value-centred and spontaneous approaches. Your independent, sequential, logical and decisive style may seem perfectly appropriate to you. When you parcel out tasks and get on with your own; when you go at a problem by seeking out and analysing all the relevant data; when you design a solution which makes perfect sense but ignores the feelings of those who would implement it; and when you close down on what seem to you to be silly alternatives, you may be giving your colleague an extraordinarily hard time.

Put the boot on the other foot, and imagine your colleague insisting at all times on sharing the whole task rather than parcelling out sub-tasks. Imagine your colleague wanting to throw away all your precious research data. Imagine your colleague insisting that the solution be based on what individuals want rather than what is appropriate and efficient. And imagine your colleague constantly throwing away ideas and starting down a new road, even when you thought you'd reached an agreed course of action. Add to this the likelihood that your colleague will turn up late to meetings, come apparently ill-prepared, keep going off at tangents, will keep suggesting bringing irrelevant ideas (and people) into the project, and will act as though the workplace is a social club rather than a serious place of focused achievement, and you may be feeling the kinds of frustration you may be causing to them.

Many of the stresses suffered by IT managers can be put down to this simple question: 'Why can't everyone be like me?'. Before trying to reduce the stress levels you are suffering, please take time to understand what makes you stressed, and therefore, what specific strategies for stress management will work for you.

The human moment

If some of the causes of stress among IT people are specific to their personal styles, others seem genuinely to emerge from the nature of IT itself. For all the enormous progress IT seems to be providing for society, it does bring with it its own dangers.

Over fifty years of research into the neurochemistry of the brain, and its influence on mental health, have assembled a significant amount of evidence to show that we do harm to ourselves if we don't regularly communicate face to face with other human beings. From an evolutionary point of view, human beings have come to depend upon talking, touching, and close, regular proximity. When we are in direct positive communication and contact with people, beneficial chemicals are released into the bloodstream, which reduce stress and promote feelings of well-being.

Extended periods of isolation from other people allow the release of harmful, stress-related chemicals. The more we are alone, the more we do things for ourselves, the busier we are doing our personal tasks, the more we are creating self-induced stress. Although this affects extraverts more than introverts, in the long term, even introverts need human contact to stay sane and healthy.

Ironically, the rapid growth of the use of electronic mail, telephone conferencing and ISDN communication links is having a detrimental affect on our mental well-being. As prime users of information technology, IT people are at the leading edge of the kinds of chemically-induced stress syndromes which result from busy work done without regular doses of sociable, human contact.

Throughout the book, we have been suggesting that one of your major tasks for becoming streetwise is to go out there and network. It may look as though this will simply add to your burdens. But the more you do it, the better you'll feel, and the stronger you'll become in coping with those jobs which really do demand your personal and undivided attention.

Plan out your time. Make sure that if you do have some jobs to do that will keep you locked up and away from other people, you generate for yourself plenty of opportunities to recharge your hormonal batteries by spending time talking to others. And while you are doing so, remember that the more you play with ideas without closing down, the more you take on board alternative views and approaches, and the more you seek new and creative ways to do things, the healthier you'll be getting. In the next few chapters, we'll develop these ideas further.

24 Lighten up a little

Many of the psychological indicators of stress we referred to in the last chapter are the other side of the coin from a sense of humour. People who are characterized by intolerance of ambiguity, incapacity for seeing nuances, and who believe in single, rigid approaches to problems are often lacking in a sense of humour.

But hold on, you may say. Surely the IT community can't be accused of lacking a sense of humour. After all, IT people are among the most avid disciples of Dilbert and Dogbert.

Let's try to sort this one out. Cartoons of the Dilbert variety are often ways of safely venting hidden anger. Reading them and nodding in rueful agreement can become a way of reinforcing the 'victim' mentality which some IT people are prone to. The problem, many such cartoons suggest, lies with 'management'. In some cases, cynical cartoons which replay the follies of other people, entrench ideas rather than lighten the mood.

This chapter is about fighting the stress, not helplessly or nervously demonizing the 'enemy'.

What's the point of having a good laugh?

Laughing is not a way of avoiding the issue. Laughter delivers positive physiological benefits. It reduces the amount of the stress hormone, cortisol, and increases the infection-fighting lymphocytes in the blood stream. It reduces the heart rate and blood pressure, and makes the muscles in the chest and shoulders contract, which relieves the tension that builds up there.

In other words, laughter strengthens your ability to deal with stressful situations. Not surprisingly then, when you laugh, you are less likely to fall prey to feelings of depression and helplessness. It is difficult to be stressed when you are laughing.

Like many emotions, those associated with laughter are contagious. Good humour can spread throughout a group – so long as people are prepared to be receptive. When people say, 'this is too serious a matter to laugh about it', maybe the proper response is, 'this is too serious a matter *not* to call upon laughter to help us out'.

The 'joker' is one of the most widely recognized characters in myths and legends of all cultures. Unlike some of our modern communities, pre-literate cultures recognized and celebrated the power of humour in dealing with problems.

Who's laughing at whom?

Genuine humour depends upon a willingness to let go. Laughing at the misfortunes of others is a grim surrogate for genuine humour, which starts with oneself:

- Question: How can you spot an extraverted programmer? Answer: 'He looks at *your* shoes when he's talking to you.
- Question: What do you call an IT manager in the boardroom? Answer: The man who's come to fix the overhead projector.
- Question: What does a systems analyst use as a contraceptive? Answer: His personality.

The point is we are all human, we are all fallible. Some people deal with their fallibility by being defensive, pretending they have no significant faults. Others – those who have learnt to 'lighten up a little' – use their fallibility to their advantage.

This is one reason why we have created our own cartoon strip to illustrate this book. The humour is directly related towards the fallibilities we have come across time and time again in working

with senior IT managers. Fortunately, when we use the cartoons with them, most of them recognize the relevance, and take the humour in good part. After all, development starts with recognizing developmental needs.

Humour, pictures and creativity

Why cartoons? One reason is that one of the authors can draw. Another is that cartoons tap into the visual senses as well as the verbal. Martin is, by his abstracted form, capable of representing each and any of us. Terminal One is the archetypal alter ego for IT people. And the other characters each convey a deeper message than could be conveyed through more conventional means.

One of the key points of pictures is that they speak directly to the 'right-brain'. They are like analogies and metaphors – symbolic representations of universal problems, concerns, hopes and aspirations. Like metaphors and similes, as Professor Helen Haste of Bath University says, they 'not only allow the framing and organization of ideas, but also give us a fast and effective way of communicating those ideas to others' (*Sunday Times* 'Brainpower supplement', 1998).

In Chapter 21, we talked briefly of 'intuitive leaps', those non-linear progressions through the brain which we use to be creative and imaginative. Intuitive leaps are the very stuff of the human mind. The brain is 'organized' into massive neural networks, with our billions of neurons all communicating across the networks in what often seem like random ways. Take the following example:

> Time flies like an arrow, but fruit flies like a banana.

As you read this sentence, your mind follows the sequence down what turns out to be a mistaken path. As you realize that what you took to be another verb is meant to be a noun, the neurons in your brain called on their electro-chemical fuel to help them make the intuitive leap from flying fruit to little flying creatures. For some readers, this will have caused a smile, or even a laugh. That's an intuitive leap in action.

Dealing with ambiguity in this way is a great deal of what humour is about. Humour, along with the intuitive leaps associated with it, 'exercises' the mind, and helps us to be more creative. The more connections we can make between our personal neural networks, especially where those connections take us into sudden and complex shifts of direction, the more we are learning to become comfortable with ambiguity and uncertainty.

Being comfortable with ambiguity and uncertainty is one of the prerequisites for success at the top of organizations, success in the uncertain arena of organizational politics.

Some role models

Not many IT managers graduate to the position of CEO, except in IT companies themselves. We have met and extensively interviewed most of those who have reached the position of CEO in non-IT companies in the UK. One of the most noticeable characteristics most of these rare creatures have in common is a willingness to be self-critical. This is not the same as the self-deprecation we see among some less happy IT people, but the comfortable acceptance of personal limitations.

This is associated with a relaxed sense of humour. Our interview tapes are liberally punctuated with laughter, as our erstwhile IT managers who now lead their colleagues have shared with us the funny side of the climb to the top. They don't take themselves too seriously, using their intuition both to bring about the physiological benefits of positive chemical secretions in their brains, and to find creative solutions to apparently intractable problems.

They are comfortable with their shortcomings. They know the IT stereotype and can laugh at it. We also know the 'management development' stereotype, and often make light of this as well.

None of us is perfect. Those who would strive for the impossible – personal perfection – are missing the point. Our aim should be to become the best possible version of ourselves, and to share with others the humour of our imperfections rather than try (vainly) to cover them up.

Being liked is better than being perfect

Success in organizational politics is about building trust and alliances. It is about being liked more than being perfect. What makes us likeable is being human, fallible yet strong enough to see ourselves as others see us. This personal honesty, which we will explore in more depth in the next chapter, is most obvious in those who can laugh at life, and laugh at themselves. Having a sense of humour is attractive to others.

So lighten up a little. It will give you strength to carry on, and massively enhanced interpersonal skills. In organizational politics being liked is better than being right.

25 IQ is not everything

Most people in IT are very clever. Many have high IQs, and Mensa is probably over-represented by people from IT. If you've got it, flaunt it.

But it seems that being clever is not a guarantee of political success. Winston Churchill is reputed to have been a bit of a duffer at school. Yet many very intelligent people seem to have difficulty getting on among 'lesser mortals'. Martin is very clever. But his route to the inner sanctum seems blocked.

So could it be true that Martin's wife has some of the answers?

Too clever by half

In his now famous book, *Emotional Intelligence* (Bloomsbury, 1995), Daniel Goleman describes story after story of people who had great intellectual powers, but who were unsuccessful in life. Later, in his follow up work, *Working with Emotional Intelligence* (Bloomsbury, 1998, p. 31), he adds that in a comprehensive survey of hundreds of competency models in active use in large numbers of corporations, 'emotional competencies were found to be *twice* as important in contributing to excellence as pure intellect and expertise'.

It may well be the case that people who rely heavily on their intellect in their work may leave their emotional intelligence underdeveloped. The more they develop intellectual skills, the more they neglect those very characteristics of human behaviour, which would otherwise guide them to success. If you tend to relax by playing games like minesweeper, you may be doing the development of your emotional intelligence a great deal of harm.

What is emotional intelligence?

Goleman and others have written at length about the various manifestations of this 'catch-all' we are calling emotional intelligence. Like so many aspects of human behaviour, there is no 'right' or comprehensive definition of the term. In later writings, Goleman seems to have been tempted to call anything that contributes to business success 'emotional intelligence'. This may not be very helpful.

To make things simple, we will stick to a set of characteristics that we have borrowed from Goleman's work, and have found useful. These are:

- Self awareness.
- Self management.
- Focus.
- Empathy towards others.
- Social skills.

Self awareness

It may sound unlikely, but some of the IT people we have met seem to know more about their jobs than they do about themselves. They keep themselves so busy, and identify so closely with their busy tasks, that they seem to lose touch with themselves as people. One of the most noticeable aspects of this is how many of them find it hard to get in touch with their feelings.

Human beings have acquired the capacity to block out their feelings and emotions, especially male human beings in our industrialized culture. It may seem that such people have no feelings, as Martin seems to think. However, our emotions are associated with the never-ceasing activity in the lower reaches of our brains, to which our consciousness cannot directly gain access. In other words, we are having emotions every moment of every day and night.

At night, they may show themselves through dreams, although some people claim not to dream. Research onto brain activity and 'rapid eye movement' (REM) sleep shows that everyone dreams, even if, when people wake up, they can't remember their dreams. Some researchers suggest that people who do not remember their dreams are unwittingly repressing the messages their unconscious minds are trying to send about their emotions, because, during the day, we can effectively shut most of them out.

This does not mean, however, that our emotions are not affecting us. It simply means that we may be unaware of the effects our emotions are having on us, subconsciously. Suppressed emotions can surreptitiously affect our judgement. Not being aware of the feelings which may be having these effects on us could be dangerous, especially where we are tackling a politically complex problem.

Here's where it really matters. When we are trying to solve a logical problem (using our thinking function, as we described in Chapter 21), the ability to shut out the 'noise' from our emotions is very helpful. The 'traffic' of communication between the part of our brain where our emotions are dealt with, and the part of the brain where we consider the impact of those emotions, 'drives' directly past the part of the brain where we do logical problem-solving. In school we learn how to shut out the noise of this traffic to enable us to do mathematics and other 'hard' stuff.

However, the problems we need to solve in organizational politics are not logic problems. We need to be clear how we feel about them, as logic alone cannot help us. Political problems are problems about values and beliefs. And our values and beliefs are about how we feel, not how we think. Shutting out our emotions while we are dealing with political problems is highly dangerous.

One reason why some IT people find organizational politics so hard is that they claim that everything they do is 'for the good of the company'. They see more senior managers appearing to feather their own nests, and taking 'the good of the organization' less seriously. This, for the politically naïve IT manager, gives organizational politics its bad name.

The reason this is naïve is that it begs the question what is good for the company. There is no absolute set of guidelines or rules that tell anyone what 'the good of the company' actually is. There are measures aplenty which you can appeal to – profitability, full employment, market share, shareholder value, employee satisfaction, customer delight, growth, competitive edge, return on capital employed – the list is potentially endless. Deciding among such measures is the political problem. There are no right answers. So how do you choose?

By going after what you want, what you believe in.

In the absence of any 'objective' choices, the best choice is to follow your beliefs, values and emotions. This looks illogical, and, in some sense, it is. It is logic tempered by values and emotions. And if you don't know what it is you want or believe in, you'll make a pretty poor custodian of organizational success.

Keeping in touch with your emotions makes you more likely to know what you want, and therefore what you 'ought' to do. It will 'feel' right because it will be in harmony with your vision and values. We'll revisit this question of values in the next chapter.

Self management

'Know thine enemy'. For many people, one enemy is their tendency to get in the grip of negative emotions – anger, depression, desperation. Ironically it is often the people who seem to have few emotions in the normal course of events who get gripped by these episodes.

As we said earlier, everyone is having emotions all the time. People who block them out become a stranger to them, and are therefore less capable of dealing with them when they break through the barriers they erect against them. Emotionally intelligent people often spend a few moments every now and again simply monitoring how they feel, and considering how, positively and constructively, they can either capitalize on or deal with their emotions.

Take a situation in which someone makes a mistake. The emotionally illiterate approach is to rationalize your actions and suppress your feelings, pretend it didn't happen or that someone else is to blame, and try to erase the event. People around you will pick up your negative reactions and adjust accordingly. They will feel embarrassed, and will (more or less consciously) mark you down as a prickly character, someone who may not be good to be around in a crisis, and someone who may not have the courage to face up to or admit to problems.

Contrast this with the emotionally intelligent response, which is to redirect the energy that comes with frustration and potential anger into humour. You admit the failing, make light of it, and generate positive emotions out of the crisis. It is possible to find something good in nearly every situation, even if it is merely saying, 'well at least I know not to try that again'.

No one is perfect. If your treat your imperfections light-heartedly, you will generate the energy to improve; if you try to hide or deny them, you'll carry them around with you as a burden which everyone else will see better than you.

The difference between confidence and arrogance is that confidence is knowing what you can do well; arrogance is not knowing what you can't do well. Emotionally intelligent people are confident; emotionally illiterate people are often arrogant.

Managing emotions means knowing your limitations and setting realistic goals and targets. It allows you to avoid making hasty judgements, as you consider carefully how you feel before you speak. It allows others access to how you feel, so that they can understand where you are coming from (instead of having to draw inferences about your feelings and values from your behaviour). And it allows you to act with integrity.

Because different people have different values, and because there is no 'absolute' arbiter of one set of values over another, it is impossible in our pluralist society to say that one set of values is 'better' than another. Acting with integrity in our culture does not mean following one set of values over another. It means making it clear to others what your driving values are and being true to those values at all times.

In times of change, uncertainty and ambiguity, your values may be the only constant guide. Be open and honest about your values, and you will help create an environment of trust and openness around you.

Focus

Think negative thoughts and you will weaken yourself. Think positive thoughts and you will gain strength. And this will include the strength we call determination against all odds.

We are not suggesting that the power of positive thought will achieve the impossible. Self-help guides are often a turn-off because they suggest that we can think ourselves into becoming super-humans, people we can never aspire to be. However, we do recognize that, due to the electro-chemical secretions in the brain which accompany emotionally-charged perceptions, thoughts and musings, we can influence our competence through how we manage our minds.

There is a great deal of evidence, from firewalking to rigorously conducted scientific experiments (see, for example, *Flow: The Psychology of Optimal Experience*, by Mihali Csikszentmihalyi, Harper & Row, 1991), to show that we humans can control our minds and bodies far more than most people in our society actually do. The power of positive thought has gone beyond the 'mumbo-jumbo' stage to a key tool for success, used by very large numbers of notable leaders in business and elsewhere.

One of the most fascinating things about this ability to 'get into the flow' is that it is available to everyone, it takes just a few seconds of concentration, and it is free. Here's how it can work: Close you eyes, and concentrate on creating in your mind a 'perfect place'. This 'creative visualization' can take you to a real place from your past experience, or to some imaginary perfection. One of the authors, for example, transports himself at these moments to the South Downs in summer. The skylarks are in full flight, the wind is rustling the long grass, and the smell of gorse in blossom lightly pervades the air.

The positive hormones secreted in the brain during one of these brief experiences are a sufficient 'dosage' to prepare you for most challenges at work. Indeed, it prepares you to go beyond the commonplace and seek out new creative challenges; it prepares you to learn and grow.

Positive attitude and a sense of focus on where you are going are different from task-orientation.

Focus is strategic; many IT managers we have met waste their energies on tactics. Focus requires a vision; many IT managers we have met have no vision. They may have a mission, and pursue this with vigour. But having a vision, as we shall see in the next chapter, is fundamentally different. Emotionally intelligent people have visions; many can live happily without a mission.

Empathy towards others

As Martin sits alone, contemplating how to become streetwise, he's sliding backwards. Emotional intelligence, a prerequisite for political success, cannot work in isolation. It is exercised in the company of others. And its fuel is empathy.

This simply means considering the feelings of others, and being able to sense and understand their viewpoints. It sounds easy, but,

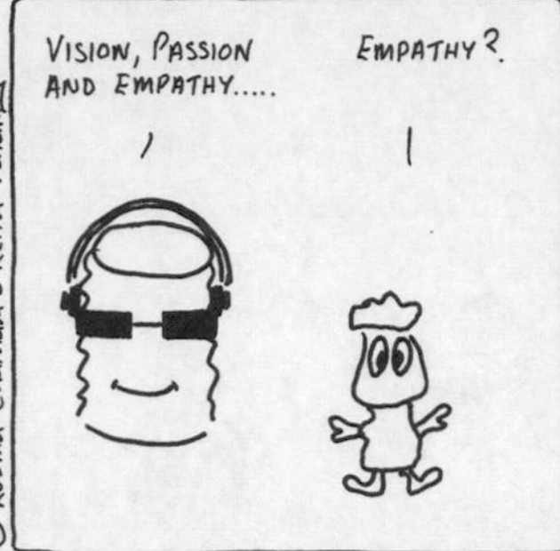

for many male, middle-aged, IT managers, this is the hardest part of all. The reason for this is that it calls directly upon their feeling function (see Chapter 21). And you cannot develop your feeling function through your intellect. The harder you try, the more elusive it gets.

There are ways in which you can develop empathy. None alone is guaranteed to be successful, but as a set of developmental activities it may be worth considering.

The first step is to develop your coaching and mentoring skills. This means true and effective delegation. One reason why many IT managers have difficulty in delegating is that they cannot shake off the belief that they could do the job better than the person they delegate the task to. This kind of approach betrays that their primary focus is upon the job rather than on the person to whom they have delegated. True delegation focuses upon the person not the job.

Try, next time you delegate, forgetting the job altogether. Focus instead on how the person to whom you have delegated is feeling, how they are progressing, and share with them their joys and frustrations. Track how they are learning and growing. Let them focus on the job; your focus should be exclusively on them. It will not be easy, but it will help develop your skills in empathizing.

Next, learn how to give and receive effective feedback. There's more on this skill in Chapter 30.

Third, try and become fluent in body language. Some writers suggest that up to 80 per cent of our communication is non-verbal. Those who would question this often overlook just how rich our (often unconscious) non-verbal signals are.

We have come across IT managers who are almost completely illiterate in body language. They just can't see the most overt and obvious signals. Few of us are fully conversant with the language, but all of us can become better at reading the signals we all send out.

The skill is inherent as much as learnt. Most of human evolution took place without language. Over millions of years we learnt how to read non-verbal signals because that's all there were! And without language to transmit this skill, it seems fairly obvious that, like many other pre-linguistic skills, most of our ancestors' body language skills were innate rather than taught. There are some skills that we just don't have time to learn the hard way.

So down there in your unconscious lies a whole range of abilities to recognize and respond to non-verbal signals, to read emotions in facial expressions, and to interpret feelings through body posture. Empathy is largely non-verbal, so communicating in body language is highly appropriate. All you have to do is re-learn. And there are many books to get you started. Just don't rely on the books alone, however, since most of them are written in words. One CEO we know took up amateur dramatics in order to develop his ability to read others, especially the audience.

Finally, developing empathy is significantly enhanced through the arts. When you read a work of fiction, watch a film or perform in a play, you are inviting your empathetic skills to play along with you. As you associate with the hero (or villain), as you share the plight of the protagonists, or as you get into role, you are putting yourself in someone else's shoes. This is empathizing in safety. It is excellent practice.

Practice in empathy is important. You have to mean it – to be sincere. It is so easy to try too hard, and to come across as insincere. Empathy is a skill that is more akin to being able to play a musical instrument than to being able to do mathematics. Once you have mastered the latter, you're there. The former can be excruciatingly painful for the listener until you master at least the basics. But even once you can play a passable tune, there's never a point at which you have got it absolutely right. The best musicians practise day in and day out. Empathy is like this. It's hard work.

Social skills

The previous four sections were the foundations for the fifth area, which is where the pay-off occurs. Becoming streetwise means being able to build mutually beneficial and harmonious relationships with a wide range of people. Some of these people will be very congenial; others will be hard to get on with. If you have mastered the arts of self-awareness, managing emotions, focus and empathy, then you have a fighting chance of building the necessary networks of supporters and allies to make it 'on the street'.

One of the keys to success at this level is the ability always to find a win-win in every situation, no matter how apparently intractable it may appear. Achieving win-win means knowing what you want, empathizing enough to work at finding out what will work for the other, and having the creativity and patience to work towards positive outcomes for all parties.

This is a complex process, which we will elaborate in more depth in Chapter 30. But the most important contribution to achieving win-win is not your intellectual capacity for problem-solving. It is your willingness to go the extra mile to seek benefits for people who may have irritated you time and again over the years. This calls on all the four previous elements of emotional intelligence.

You need to be aware of how you feel about the other person; you need to manage your own emotions for positive benefit; you need to focus on the mutually beneficial goal and have the emotional strength to put up with what are likely to be a series of set-backs; and you will need to get under the skin of the other person to see things through their eyes as clearly as you see the situation through your own.

Martin and his wife

So how can Martin's wife help, as she suggests in the cartoon at the start of this chapter? The chances are that, if Martin conforms to the stereotype of the IT manager, his wife conforms to the stereotype of the IT manager's wife. She will have a significantly higher emotional intelligence than Martin, who has got by on his intellect so far. Statistically it is likely that Martin's wife will be more of the *caring* type (see Chapter 21), which will mean that she will have many of the attributes of emotional intelligence already in place from an early age. She is also likely to have the inherent 'brain architecture' which enables her to read and respond to emotions in others which research has shown to be common to the majority of women.

She will be much more in touch with her emotions and can role model for Martin how to be open and honest about her feelings. She will have learnt over the years how to manage her emotions and channel them to avoid unnecessary conflict. She's become adept at defusing hostile situations, and at changing the mood of the family from potential conflict towards serenity and happiness. She is less task-oriented and is much more in tune with who she is and what she is all about. She'll have been empathizing deeply with others since she was a little girl, and she will have a network of people with whom she gets on comfortably.

She can help Martin, but only if he learns to stop telling and start listening and watching. He'll have to swallow his pride, but, without that willingness, he'll never develop his emotional intelligence anyway.

26 The road to Damascus

Where is Damascus? Unless you're on the 'right' road, you may miss the shining light.

Each of us has a right road, and each has many opportunities to 'see the light'. But, in our experience, many IT managers find themselves so buried within their projects, tasks and service provision that they lose sight of why they are there in the first place. None of us is born to a career, and, in the fullness of time, our little successes and failures count for very little. I have not come across many headstones in graveyards with inscriptions such as, 'Here lies Martin; he brought in his projects within budget'.

Politically successful people often appear to be very busy too. But most of this busyness is aligned with what they are trying to achieve beyond each individual task or project. In other words, they have a 'master plan' (however vague and lacking in detail it may be) and they stick to it. Each activity into which they throw themselves contributes to the pursuit of the goal – and does so immediately and directly.

Many of us throw ourselves into tasks which contribute only marginally to our longer term aspirations and goals. But this is not to be wondered at if our goals and aspirations are so vague that we cannot articulate them, even to ourselves. Many busy IT managers have dreams and aspirations which have become so dimmed by project goals and departmental targets that they can no longer illuminate the road to their own personal Damascus.

Vision or mission?

In the previous chapter we differentiated between a vision and a mission, but did not explain this difference. In short, a mission is a means to an end; a vision is an end in itself. For an individual, therefore, a vision is a picture of what they are all about, who they are, and what makes them the kind of person they are. Their mission may be, for example, to become the CEO of a large corporation. But unless that mission is in service of a broader vision, which includes responsibility, authority and power, then the mission is likely either to fail, or, if achieved, not produce the sense of satisfaction you envisaged. Without the underpinning vision, the 'successful' mission leaves a sense of being, as yet, unfulfilled.

Many people suffer from this mismatch between their (often implicit) mission and their (often unarticulated) vision.

This is often because they have not taken the time to ask themselves the fundamental questions, 'Who am I?' and 'What do I really want?'. You may like to spend a few minutes asking yourself this question, and using it to start to draw up your own vision.

The reason for doing this is simple. This book is about becoming streetwise. It is aimed at helping you to become skilful in the boardroom, and to break through a number of barriers which may have got in the way of your achieving seniority and success in your business life. But unless you are very clear that this is what you want, you may think about taking on board the messages of the book, but the chances are, you'll go no further. Because something in your unconscious will tell you not to bother.

Let us suppose you fight back, and do not listen to the messages of your unconscious. You may achieve the goals you have set yourself. But, again, if these goals are not part of your true vision, you'll end up better paid, but more frustrated than before. So take time to go through this little exercise and ask yourself, at the end, 'Do I really want this?'.

Creating your vision

Imagine achieving a result in your life that you really want. For example, you see yourself having the kinds of relationships which you always wanted to have, or living in a place where you always wanted to be. Don't worry at this stage if this vision seems unlikely or even impossible. Just imagine yourself achieving this outcome. Use your imagination to describe to yourself in words or pictures the vision you have imagined, using the present tense as if it is happening now.

To help create this vision, you may want to consider a number of themes:

- *Life purpose* Suppose that your life has a unique purpose – fulfilled through what you do. What would that purpose be?
- *Personal qualities* If you could be exactly the kind of person you wanted what would your qualities be?
- *Material things* What would you like to own?
- *Home* What is your ideal home?
- *Health* How important is physical fitness to you – enough to stay healthy, or do you want athletic prowess?
- *Relationships* What types of relationships would you like to have with friends, family and others?
- *Hobbies and personal development* What would you like to do in terms of personal learning, travel, reading or other activities?
- *Community* What is your vision for the community or society you live in?
- *Work* Finally, what is the ideal work environment for you? Does it match the vision of the streetwise IT manager?

How easy is it for you to visualize your vision? Do you think it's really close to what you want from life? If it is a difficult thing to do, there may be a number of things getting in the way:

- You may find it hard to imagine having what you want.

Imagining you could have anything you want may not be easy. Many people find that it contradicts what they learnt in childhood, which was that wanting leads to frustration. Unconsciously gearing themselves up to avoid disappointment, they shy away from any object of their deeper wishes, saying to themselves, 'It'll never live up to expectations anyway'. Others may feel they have to trade it off against something else – they can have a successful career *or* a satisfying family life, but not both.

For now, you are trying to articulate what your vision is. The question of whether it is possible is irrelevant at this stage. If there is something which underlies our drive for fulfilment, it is better to know about it than to pretend it doesn't exist. What makes something possible is, at least in part, being able to imagine it.

- Some people generate their visions based on what they believe other people would want for them: a parent, a teacher, a supervisor, or a spouse. Concentrate on what you want. If what comes into your head is that you want a good relationship with your partner, you should include it only if you want it for yourself – not because you think your partner would want it.

- Some people assume that what they want is not important. They draw out whatever comes to mind quickest, to get the job done. Treating this visioning activity as just another task is missing the point. It is as much the process of thinking and imagining as the outcome that is important.

- Sometimes people who try this activity start half-heartedly because they think they already know what they want. But by going through the exercise again, you may create a new sense of what you want especially if you have not asked yourself this question for some time. A personal vision is not like a strategy document, already existing and waiting for you to brush off the cobwebs and read it again. It is something you create and continue to re-create, throughout your life.

- Sometimes people are afraid of what their vision will tell them. This is especially true of those people who have gamely soldiered on through adversity, crawling up the ladder of their organization to a position of tolerable mediocrity. At least they can do the job reasonably well; at least they know what's expected of them, and what the future holds in store. But going back to the drawing board may upset this equilibrium.

Since this is *your* vision, it can't tell you anything which, deep down, you don't already know about yourself; it can only increase that self-awareness we described in the previous chapter. It is a key element in achieving emotional intelligence that you are honest about who you are and what you want from life.

You may, therefore, be right to be a little afraid of your vision. In some cases, a person's vision is in clear contradiction to their lifestyle, especially with regard to their work. You always have a choice. You can choose to carry on because this is the easy option. Or you can take this opportunity to start thinking about alternatives. For sure, unless your vision contains elements compatible with the stresses and strains (as well as the excitements and rewards) of the streetwise senior manager, you may find it easier to use the advice in this book in helping to plan out an alternative strategy.

Before you do so, however, consider whether the key element of your vision is a 'moving towards' or a 'moving away'. Visions which are 'moving towards' are constructive and developmental; those which are 'moving away' are retreats from intolerable reality. Moving towards one vision implies moving away from another. The key question is whether the 'towards' is as clear and focused as the 'away from'. If you can see what you are trying to get away from more clearly than what you are moving towards, then please revisit the vision – it needs to be sufficiently clear and focused to be a foundation for big decisions.

By now, your vision may be a collection of wants and desires which may or may not hang together as a composite whole. Some elements may feel stronger than others, and you may feel that there's something missing. Put your visions to the test by taking each item and 'chunking it up'.

This means asking, for each item, 'What would that get me?'. For example, you may have included in your vision personal wealth. When you ask the 'chunking up' question, you may find that it is simply the means to achieving something else, such as material goods, a nice home, or recognition by others. If an element of your vision is simply a means to an end, consider alternative routes to that end.

If, on the other hand, it is an end in itself – it is valuable in its own right – then add this to your completed vision. When you are happy with all the elements, step back, re-articulate the whole picture, and then ask yourself, 'To what extent is what I am doing now, and what I plan to do in the next few years, likely to contribute to achieving that vision?'.

Reaffirming your values

Our visions are often pictures of an end-goal which is 'orchestrated' by our personal values. As with so many aspects of our lives, there is a distinction between our 'espoused' values – which we profess to believe in – and our deeper values, sometimes referred to as our 'values in action' which actually guide our behaviour. These deeper values are coded into our brains at such a fundamental level that we are unable to easily see them. For many of us, they are rarely brought to the surface and questioned. They simply underpin many of our beliefs and decisions.

As with a vision, values will inform the degree to which we actually want the things we say we are aiming for. Before moving on, it may be helpful for you to explore you own core values, and ask, 'Do these values sit comfortably with my vision, and are they in line with the aspirations with which I approached reading this book?'. In order to help you do this we will introduce you to the concept of the archetypes.

Archetypes we live by

Our values are partly a reflection of our upbringing. But it is often the case that our deeper values – those that drive us – are 'hard-wired'. Just as some of us are tall, some short, some blond some dark, and so on, we are different in how our brains are wired up. These differences are relatively minor. We are able to accommodate the differences, learning to live with the diversity of character which the subtle differences produce. But they do affect us in ways which we may otherwise overlook.

In Chapter 21 we explored one aspect of these differences, when we looked at such characteristics as extraversion and introversion, and so on. But even deeper than these typological differences are differences in the ways in which 'archetypal drivers' influence us.

By 'archetypal drivers' (or 'archetypes' for short), we mean those influences on our behaviour which evolution has built into us as humans over the millions of years. They are often ignored, overlooked in the haste to demonstrate how clever we human beings are to have language and self-awareness. But they are still there, working away at our unconsciousness as they have been since well before we learnt how to speak and to think with concepts.

They are similar in nature to the automatic systems which, for example, keep our heart beating. Imagine how difficult life would be if we had to concentrate, to tell our heart to beat. Imagine the enormous concentration we'd need if we had to breathe consciously. And imagine how long we'd survive as a species if each newborn baby had to learn to suckle. Suckling classes would be fully subscribed, but I guess few would survive long enough to pass the exam.

Luckily for us, vast numbers of hard-wired systems look after vast aspects of our lives. It would be naïve to suggest that they had no impact on our characters, our behaviours and how we think and feel. They do. And what is more, they have different levels of impact on each of us as individuals. Not vast differences, but enough to differentiate the fun-loving profligate from the deeply responsible father figure. Often lying below the level of consciousness, these archetypes are 'inclinations to behave' in certain ways, rather than predictable paths.

One helpful way in which to see the concept of archetype is as a 'story'. Every human society in the world tells stories. Many such stories have powerful similarities from New Guinea to Greenland, and from the Amazon basin to Japan. The regularity of stories is matched by the regularity of cultural models and transitions. In almost all societies, young boys rebel and seek adventure; young male adults fight against the antagonist; parents bring up, educate and nurture children; and older, wise, insightful people are respected for their learning and powers of intuition.

Even in our own 'sophisticated', technological society, our deep-rooted tendency to act out these stories persists strongly through our archetypes. Literature is full of evidence for the ways in which archetypes shape our lives and our characters.

Recent history, steeped in an individualist tradition of free will has tended to make us unwilling to contemplate such drivers. Yet more and more we are finding that simple explanatory models such as those provided by the archetypes help managers we work with break through rationality and into areas which are important at a lower level of consciousness.

So, archetypes are, in one sense, the stories we are acting out in our own unique ways in our lives. They can become quite visible to other people, especially to those whose 'dominant' archetypes are different from one's own.

There are an almost infinite number of such archetypes. However, eight seem particularly influential in shaping life choices and character. Four of these archetypes are associated with the 'masculine' character, and they are more likely to be the driving forces for males. Four of these archetypes are associated with the ‘feminine’ character, and they are more likely to be the driving forces for females. However, each gender can be strongly influenced by any of the eight archetypes (Guzie, T. and Guzie, N.M. (1984) ‘Masculine and Feminine Archetypes: A complement to the psychological types’, *Journal of Psychological Type*, vol. 7, pp. 3–11).

A ‘dominant’ archetype is one which seems to inform much of what makes us who we are and what we want from life. According to this model, most of us can identify one (or at most two) dominant archetypes from the set. This enables us to ‘plot’ on the model where people ‘fit’ (see Figure 26.1).

The four ‘masculine’ archetypes are potential influences on everyone’s lives, as are the four ‘feminine’ archetypes. In practice, most males identify more strongly with the masculine set, and most females with the feminine set. But there are exceptions.

The masculine archetypes follow a notional sequence, which approximates to the development of an overall life story. It starts with the *eternal boy*, that set of tendencies towards play, irresponsibility, fun, adventure and the gratification of personal desires. Those acting primarily within this archetype rarely hold

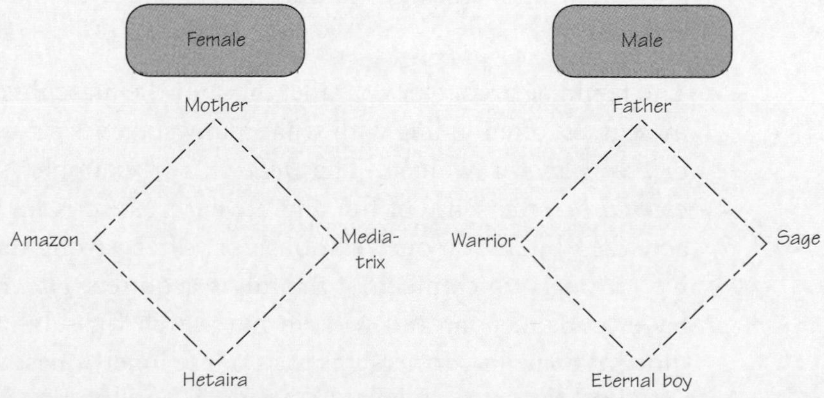

Figure 26.1 Where people ‘fit’

down careers or jobs for long periods; often have a series of failed personal relationships and marriages; but maintain a youthfulness of approach to life, and an enthusiasm for the new.

In the normal pattern of most cultures, *warrior* takes over at some point. The *warrior* is driven by ambition to win, often at all costs. Epitomized by the sporting greats, those who act out of this archetype drive themselves towards ambitious goals, have an energy and will to succeed, and a dislike of weakness or failure. Politicians, business tycoons and military personnel are others who are often following the lure of the *warrior* archetype.

The borders having been secured, *father* takes over. This archetype seeks to develop in the next generation the competencies and skills needed for the culture. *Father* nurtures to some extent (although most nurture comes from the *mother* archetype, which can be active in men as well as women), but is more the authority figure, laying down the law and rules, and providing the discipline to those who step out of line.

In maturity, *sage* shares with the world the accumulated wisdom of the years. However, the archetype can become influential well before physical maturity sets in. It manifests itself in a thirst for knowledge or understanding. It drives people to reading, research, and often into teaching, letting others share in the knowledge acquired.

The feminine archetypes parallel those of the masculine, but differ in degrees, often in line with what many societies set up as appropriate roles for women. The *hetaira*, for example, shares with *eternal boy* the sense of fun and adventure, but is far more characterized by one-to-one relationships, often strong and supportive, through which much of the fun is acquired. *Hetaira* does not have to wander far and wide in her search for fulfilment, and is more at home in partnerships than in the lonely quest which characterizes the *eternal boy*. Once again, males can be *hetairas*, females can be *eternal boys*.

Amazon differs from warrior in that her battles are more defensive than acquisitive. *Warrior* seeks to conquer, *Amazon* defends aggressively. This makes *Amazon* even more fearsome an opponent since she fights on her own territory, knows her own ground, and will not outsmart herself by trying to go beyond her locus of control.

Mother is the nurturing, caring half of the parenting set. Blind to any defects of her charges, she is devoted love incarnate. She provides a powerful sense of safety and protectedness.

Mediatrix contrasts with sage by being more focused upon the 'spiritual' side of wisdom; sage is about rationality and knowledge gleaned from 'out there'. *Mediatrix*, however, knows without finding out; can read minds and feelings through what seems like extrasensory perception. She knows the universal truths which transcend the specific, contingent world of the merely human.

This 'progression' from *eternal boy* to sage is an 'idealized' picture, largely based on what has been observed as taking place in many societies throughout human evolution. Although anthropologists argue that 'patterns' we see in other cultures may be conditioned by what we see in our own culture, there is a fair amount of evidence in the study of myths and rituals which suggest that similar kinds of 'stories' make sense in most cultures. In practice, it may be social pressure more than archetypes which tend to make many people 'follow the sequence' from *eternal boy* to sage, or from *hetaira* to *mediatrix*.

The work we have done with many managers seems to suggest that for each individual, the strengths of these archetypal drivers is different. One or two of the drivers are strong, while the others are relatively weak. For many people, the relative strength of their personal drivers only becomes clear later in life, when they step back and ask themselves the big questions about who they are and what they truly believe in. Until then, the relative strength of the 'push' of each driver remains mostly unconscious.

However, these drivers do seem to have a clear influence on making each of us the 'kind of person' we are. Some of us are keen achievers, others studious. Some of us are keen to create a central role for ourselves in a 'family'; others are contented to wander. Although everyone's 'life story' is unique, many of them have strong elements which appear and reappear in stories from almost every human culture.

Some of the key characteristics of the archetypes are explored in Table 26.1 and Table 26.2.

Some people look at these characteristics and say that they are a mix of all eight. Clearly this is true. But for most people, one, or, more often, two of these archetypes exercise stronger influence over them than the others.

One reason for this is that there are in-built contradictions between the archetypes. The pull of the *eternal boy*, for example, is in the opposite direction from that of *father*. The *eternal boy* archetype stems from the evolutionary root (which we share with most higher animals) which encourages us to experiment, or to play. Baby animals and children do not have to learn how to play – they just do it, encouraged by the archetypal driver. It is in the nature of play that it is fun, and that it is irresponsible. 'Someone else will take care of us', it seems to say, and so we can concen-

Archetypes we live by

Table 26.1 Masculine archetypes

Masculine archetype	*Characteristics*	*Dark side*	*Development needs*	*Life choices*	*Examples*
Father	Providing Protecting Directing Natural leader	Dictatorial Authoritarian Condescending Rigid and one-sided Cold and inflexible	Celebrating uniqueness Wisdom Flexibility Sensitivity to other's needs	Managerial/Directorial Parenthood Medicine School teaching Youth leadership	Albert Schweitzer Nelson Mandela John Major
Eternal boy	Open to new things Seeks individuality Looks for new opportunities Seeks new adventure and new relationships Seeks one-to-one peer relationships Does his own thing Not concerned with performance	Lacks stability Never finds personal identity 'Love them and leave them' Undependable Poor provider Fickle	Maturity and responsibility Perseverance	Adventure Chequered career Experimenting	Peter Pan Adonis The Knight Errant
Warrior	Accomplishment in the outer world Good competitor Go-getter Likes to manage power Likes to be the 'hero' Needs to win …	Misuse of power 'Cut-throat' Uses people for own ends Finds it hard to listen and empathise … at all costs	Wisdom Caring Compassion Humility	Big business Sports Sales Politics Military Medical consultant/specialist	Seigfreid Achilles Margaret Thatcher
Sage	Drawing forth meaning for self and others In touch with logos, mind, thought and spirit Focus on conscious meaning and ideas Helps others understand the significance of their experiences Idea oriented rather than people oriented Not motivated by competition Sharing of visions and ideas	Never gets things done Can't translate ideas into reality 'Absent-minded professor' Pretending at wisdom he does not possess – believing his own pretensions	Worldliness Practically Intellectual humility Common sense	Philosophy Teaching (university) Research IT Engineering Technical	Socrates The Prophet Confucius

Table 26.2 Feminine archetypes

Feminine archetype	*Characteristics*	*Dark side*	*Development needs*	*Life choices*	*Examples*
Mother	Cherishing Nurturing Protecting Need for social position and financial security	Anxious nursing Smothering mother Lack of trust in other's strengths	Authority Letting go Objectivity Criticality	Marriage Teaching Nursing Social work	Mother Theresa Earth Mother Queen Mother
Hetaira	Companion to others – intellectually, spiritually, sexually Awaken the individual psyche (often in the male) Helps male get in touch with self, or …	Set aside own interests or even personal values in the name of relationship and for the sake of companionship … lead a man astray	Self worth Faithfulness Perseverance	Personal assistant Air hostess Writing Beauty therapy Companion	Simone de Beauvoir Prince Albert Princess Diana
Amazon	Independent Self-contained Accomplishment in the outer world Achievement	Impatience Lack of attention to her own values and feelings, and those of others	Broader vision Patience Wisdom	Sports Public office Pursuit of causes Military	Tessa Sanderson Anita Ruddock Mo Mowlem
Mediatrix	Influence over others Mediating the world of the unconscious, the psyche	Vague Unfocused Confused Not knowing what thoughts and feelings are her own Weak ego	Strong and healthy ego Common sense Wordliness	Counselling Creative writing Painting Astrology Graphology Herbal medicine	Elizabeth Frink Germaine Greer The Buddha

trate on trying things out, with no consideration for the consequences.

From an evolutionary point of view, this driver to play is of enormous value, delivering motor skills, new learning about the environment, and so on. It is not surprising, then, that, especially among mammals, where there is almost always a *mother* to take care of the young adventurers, play has become a universal means of having fun while ignoring danger.

Archetypes do not die. The signals they send out to us remain. However, the respective strengths of the signals varies from person to person. In the case of the *eternal boy* archetype, one reason why it may seem to fade away is its innate conflict with the *father* archetype.

The *father* is fully responsible. It takes life seriously, and always considers the consequences. It encourages us to use what we know for the benefit of our family, our clan, or our business. It cares for others, while the *eternal boy* doesn't. In other words, almost everything the *eternal boy* is contrasts with what the *father* represents. For most people, personal integrity demands that one of these conflicting drivers takes precedent. Those who live the *eternal boy* life tend to be less concerned about responsibility, developing a legacy, taking charge, and so on; those for whom the *father* archetype wins the internal struggle become dependable, reliable, and strong authority figures.

The 'conflicts' between the opposing archetypes often show themselves in relationships between people – in what is sometimes referred to as 'chemistry'. Most of the time we are unaware of the many unconscious signals people are sending out about their archetypes. The few hundred thousand years of human history during which we have developed language are a miniscule part of our overall evolutionary growth. Language (both what we say and what we 'think to ourselves') has enormous benefits, but it does tend to overshadow our former capability to 'read' situations without words.

Non-verbal communication, therefore, is often very poorly perceived. And among those communications are the ways in

which we unconsciously present our archetypes to the world.

Martin 'scares' the marketing director not because he is an overtly serious person, but because there is something about Martin (being 'driven' by *father/sage*) that the marketing director (who is *warrior/eternal boy*) is uncomfortable with. It's more like the feeling you get in a haunted house than anything 'tangible'. But it is strong enough to create a vague sense of unease when people with opposing archetypes get together.

This 'struggle' between *eternal boy* and *father* is matched by a similar struggle between *hetaira* and *mother*. The loyalty and constancy of the mother is in contrast with the flightiness and disregard for convention of the *hetaira*.

There's yet more inner conflict. The *warrior* and the *sage* are also pulling in opposite directions. For the *warrior*, winning, achievement and success are the goals. These are 'outer world' experiences, built from the implicit recognition that, for every victor there is a vanquished. The *warrior* encourages strength and wariness; it creates a psychic suit of armour against the competition. It allows in only those things which will strengthen and aid achievement of the goal.

The *sage*, in contrast, remains totally open and vulnerable. In its 'pure' form it appears to the *warrior* as weak and feeble, because it does not fight. Rather it absorbs – new knowledge, new insights and new wisdom. Socrates is the embodiment of the *sage*, never claiming to know more than others, always seeking answers, and accepting his fate at the hands of his executioners without a murmur of protest. It is hard to live the life of both *warrior* and *sage* at the same time.

The struggle between *amazon* and *mediatrix* runs along very similar lines, with the largely defensive *amazon* contrasting with the ever-open *mediatrix*.

The eight archetypes are separated simply because the masculine and feminine form two distinct contrasting sets. The *father* opposed the *eternal boy*, while the *mother* opposes the *hetaira*, and so on.

Each 'point' on the model informs different aspects of our lives. The archetypes 'drive' us in contrasting ways, and these 'drivers' can often be very similar for the masculine and feminine 'points' on the model. Take what motivates us most, see Figure 26.2.

People who are primarily following the influence of the *father* or *mother* archetypes will be highly motivated to take responsibility for others, a motivator which will not appeal strongly to people influenced by the *eternal boy* or *hetaira* archetypes, who will be strongly motivated by adventure and freedom. The *warriors* and *amazons* will be strongly motivated to achieve, while the *sages* and *mediatrixes* will be strongly motivated to learn and understand.

People will often have reputations based upon their archetypal drivers. Those clearly influenced by the *father* or *mother* will be known for their maturity and sense of responsibility. *Warriors* and *amazons* will be noted for their drive towards achievement. The *sage* and *mediatrix* types will be known for their wisdom and intellect; while the *eternal boys* and *hetairas* will be renowned for their playfulness and sense of adventure.

Using the models as 'maps'

Most people seem to be influenced by more than one archetype –

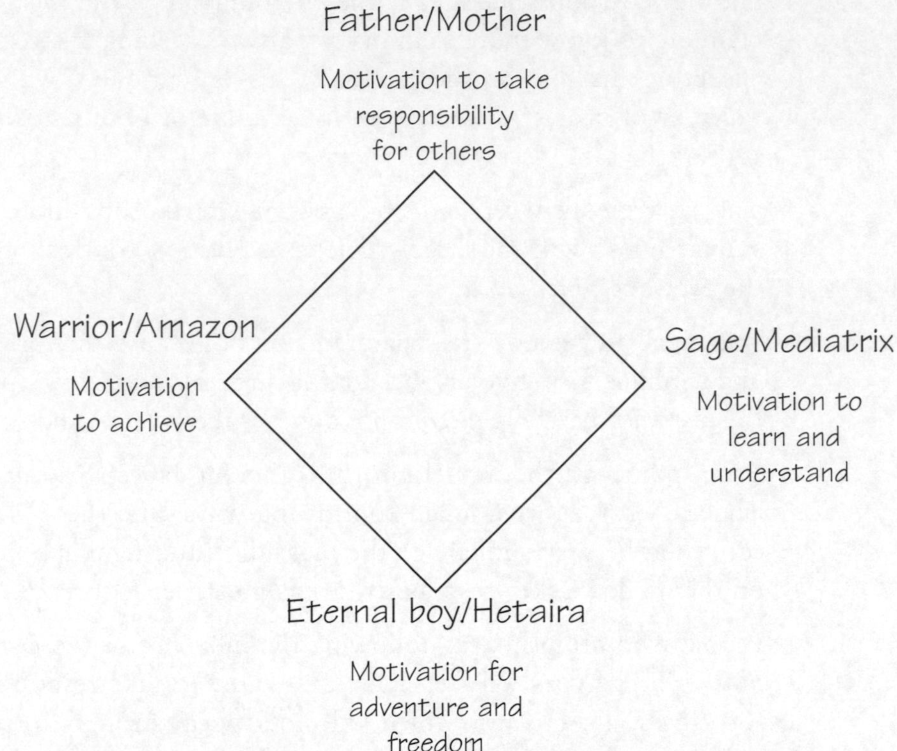

Figure 26.2 Effect of archetype on motivation

usually a primary driver and an 'auxiliary'. The two archetypes most people are driven by are adjacent on the models. This is because of the inner conflicts between the poles.

The lines round the edges of the models form 'places' on which you can 'plot' people. For example, Figure 26.3 shows where someone who is characterized by a wanton playfulness in the search for knowledge 'lives' on the model.

This is the *eternal boy/sage*. He is unlikely to feel comfortable in a job demanding high degrees of responsibility, and will almost certainly have had a number of different jobs (careers, even) by his mid-thirties. He may have difficulty remaining loyal, and will feel

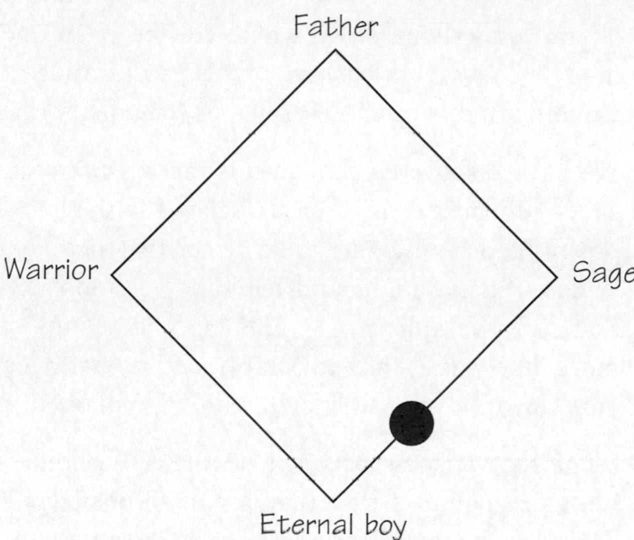

Figure 26.3 Archetypal 'home base'

restless to the point of frustration if he cannot redefine himself every few years at least. He could become streetwise, but may have difficulty in establishing and maintaining strong networks – his restlessness will reduce his patience with nurturing relationships, and will appear to his *father/warrior* colleagues as untrustworthiness and lacking in responsibility. He will not be seen as taking his job seriously enough.

The model can provide for at least thirty-two different 'stories', since one's 'home' depends both upon the relative strength of the two strongest influencers (*eternal boy/sage* and *sage/eternal boy* are different stories) and the possibility of crossing from the masculine model to the feminine. For example, a woman we know 'lives' as a *sage/hetaira*, transcending the gender-associations of the models. Another man we have worked with 'lives' largely as a *hetaira/amazon*. Some people live somewhere between the masculine and feminine domains.

Because of the 'pull' of one or two of these archetypes, each of us has an underlying story which can be positioned on one of the model's 'axes'. One aspect of this positioning is how it helps to explain what is often described as 'chemistry' between people.

We have discovered that this attraction between people which is called 'chemistry' is often associated with their being in 'similar' positions on these axes. The closer two people are on the model (where the masculine and feminine versions are superimposed so that, for example, *father* and *mother* occupy similar space) the more likely they are to simply get on with each other. A fair amount of 'love at first sight' can be explained in this way.

Similarly, wariness between people often comes from an unconscious recognition that they are at opposite poles on the model. This deep sense of difference can cause people to have to work very hard to see positive attributes in each other. When things go wrong, they can easily fall out.

It is not surprising that much of this archetypal 'chemistry' operates unconsciously. Until very recently in human history, we had no language, and consequently, very low levels of self-consciousness. Like other animals, our survival depended upon our being able to respond to threats and opportunities without conscious reflection on the pros and cons of each option. This capacity for 'unthinking' judgement remains with us, despite our veneer of civilization and culture.

Checking your 'home' on the model

Many people at this point can position themselves on the archetype model. For others there remain too many conflicting thoughts and contradictions. If you fall into this latter category, try asking a few friends or members of your family that know you well. Often they will have no difficulty placing you at all.

Alternatively, book yourself on our course, Organizational Politics and IT Management, at Cranfield, which we describe in Chapter 30. Or wait for our next book, which will contain an instrument for checking your position.

Why bother with all this?

The point of the model is that it helps explain some of the consistencies in our lives. If career decisions have not worked; if at times you have felt a little alienated from your work experience; and if you are unclear about where to go from here, consider the 'story' you are living. What will the next chapter of your story look like?

Becoming streetwise means different things to different people. For some, it is an irrelevance; for others, it is central to the achievement of their most precious goals. As you work you way through the final few chapters of this book, it may be helpful if you can be as clear as possible about your road to Damascus.

27 You lead; I'll follow

Becoming streetwise implies, amongst other things, a leadership role. A new publication in the English language on the subject of leadership is published every six hours – morning and night, including weekends. It's clearly a topic of great interest, and one on which many writers have opinions. Our own 'leadership questionnaire' in Chapter 11 is just one of hundreds or even thousands of ways of thinking about leadership.

Are leaders born or made?

This debate will run and run. We're going to sit on the fence and say that, although we believe anyone can learn the skills of leadership, the desire to lead is inherent. In other words, if you really don't want to lead, the chances are, no matter how much 'leadership development' you go though, you'll never be a great leader. On the other hand, if the urge to lead is strong enough, you'll learn the skills by hook or by crook.

How do you know if you really want to lead? The answer to this comes partly from reflection. The exercises in the previous chapter will have started that process. But it may also be helpful to know a bit more about what is entailed in this thing called 'leadership'.

Going beyond the simple contrasts

In Chapter 11 we wrote about leadership as contrasted with what we called '*laissez-faire*' and '*traditional management*'. The characteristics of what we called '*leadership*' remain valid. But in this chapter we'd like to put some flesh on those dry bones. After all, if you have got this far, it seems likely that you have decided to move away from '*laissez-faire*' and '*traditional management*'.

What leadership might feel like

In the previous chapter, we talked about our archetypal drivers, and how these may influence many of the ways in which we see the world. How we feel about leadership is likely to be similarly influenced.

Because, like so many other aspects of human behaviour, 'leadership' has no 'objective' reality, what might look like leadership to one person may look like bullying to another; what might be a perfectly valid way of leading by teaching, for one person, may look like abdication for another. Figure 27.1 shows a few of the key ways in which each archetypal driver may make us think and feel about leadership.

What leadership might feel like

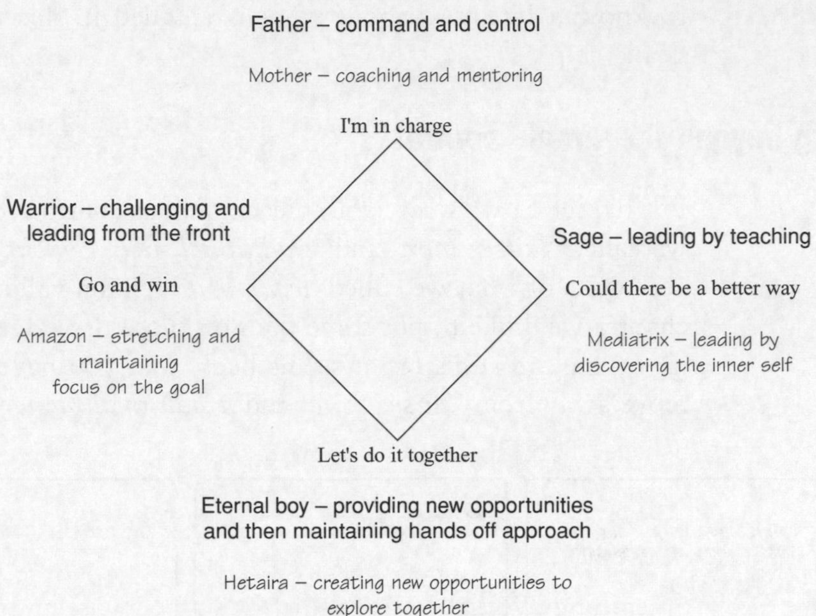

Figure 27.1 Effect of archetype on leadership style

Each of the 'leadership' styles in Figure 27.1 is a valid (if, perhaps, restricted) way of seeing leadership. The 'command and control' style of the *father* has a long and respected history in studies of leadership, but there are also many examples of the starkly contrasting 'let's do it together' style of the *eternal boy/hetaira*.

It is probable that, if you have explored your own archetypal drivers, you will recognize a pull towards one style of leadership (or two) over the others. This is only natural. But in the complex world of becoming streetwise, you may recognize that leadership is as much about followers as it is about you. And at senior levels, your followers will be numerous. They too will see different styles of leadership in different ways. You may need a portfolio of styles to enable you to appeal, in turn, to the whole range of potential followers. The *sages* will value your 'let's learn together' approach; but to get *warriors* to follow you, you will need to deliver the 'go and win' style as well.

Leadership – an example

There are many specific themes for which a 'textbook' may be useful; themes such as IT project management. These are not part of the human condition; they are peculiar to the organizational realities which, for just a few years, we are living through. On the other hand, there are a number of 'universal' themes which have exercised human hearts and minds since we became human. Leadership is one of these 'universal' themes.

Despite the huge volume of current writing on the subject of leadership, we are going to explore the theme through a story. We believe that these essentially human themes are best explored through literature (or the arts in general). There is nothing very new to say on the subject, and rigorous research seems only to leech the richness from the topic. Stories are a poorly used source of learning in organizational life today; people seem to think that textbooks are a better source of learning.

This book is a textbook. Our excuse is that it addresses a theme which is not universal – senior IT managers have not, for thousands of years, been trying to become streetwise. However, we have tried to maintain some elements of storytelling through the exploits of Martin and Terminal One.

If we are to use storytelling to tease out the key lessons of leadership, what better source could we go to than Shakespeare? We are indebted to Richard Olivier for drawing to our attention the aptness of *Henry V* to the theme of leadership. He now runs workshops for managers wanting to experience leadership through *Henry V*. These have significantly enriched the portfolio of approaches to leadership development.

The story in brief

So why the story of Henry V? Because, despite it being tainted in parts by the social mores and realities of Shakespeare's times, it is almost an essay on the complex richness of character required for effective leadership. Henry V is not, in the play, the historical figure, but the quintessential leader. This is not a story about England and France, or about specific battles and negotiations. It is a story about how great leadership makes a difference.

The story is essentially simple. At its simplest level, it concerns how Henry V, having been convinced of England's legitimate claim to certain lands in what is now northern France, demands their return. When insulted by the response, Henry gathers his army and sails across to France and fights successfully to regain those lands. To cement the deal, he marries the French king's daughter.

However, life is more complex than that for a great leader, and, during this period, Henry has to deal with a reputation which he established in his youth for drinking, gambling, and making merry instead of being serious and studious. He also has to deal with treachery, difficult decisions, motivating a depleted army and doubts about the path he has chosen to take.

In other words, Henry has to deal with many of the problems of leadership, not all of which are glamorous or exciting.

The emerging leader

One of the most fascinating elements of the story of Henry V as a leader is how his leadership qualities emerged from what to some people were unpromising beginnings. In his youth, Henry consorted with rogues such as Falstaff, spending his time in ale houses, and getting up to all sorts of mischief. It is true that some of his leadership qualities were already apparent in earlier years, but, in general, he gained a reputation for dissolute behaviour and a lack of responsibility. As the Archbishop of Canterbury says in the opening scene of the play:

His addiction was to courses vain,
His companies unlettr'd rude and shallow,
His hours fill'd up with riots, banquets, sports,
And never noted in him any study,
Any retirement, any sequestration
From open haunts and popularity.

In other words, he was habitually seen spending his time with the common people, and failing to settle down to any scholarly activities. Henry was making himself popular with the common people, if not with the nobility. Despite his noble birth, like many leaders he emerged into leadership from (in his case self-imposed) 'humble' beginnings.

This is important to the lessons of leadership, since it is all too easy for those who turn away from leadership positions to blame their backgrounds for preventing them from making progress. Henry effectively starts his story by operating in the '*laissez-faire*' mode we described in Chapter 11. Like many IT managers, he starts in the rank and file, only to emerge later.

In the play, the Bishop of Ely gives us a clue as to how Henry (and anyone who starts from the bottom) could emerge from *laissez-faire* to leadership, when he draws an analogy with nature:

The strawberry grows underneath the nettle,
And wholesome berries thrive and ripen best,
Neighbour'd by fruit of baser quality;
And so the prince obscur'd his contemplation
Under the veil of wildness; which, no doubt,
Grew like the summer grass, fastest by night,
Unseen...

Despite spending time in apparent wastefulness, Henry, like many emerging leaders, was learning during this time of play. He was learning what it is like on the shop-floor, understanding the concerns and issues of those he was going to lead in later life, and establishing the ability to communicate effectively with the 'common folk'. As we shall see later in the chapter, this was time well spent, since, when the chips were down, he was able to talk to them in language they could understand and relate to.

But reputations go before us, and Henry's reputation as a playboy has a significant bearing on how the story unfolds. Because his leadership qualities were underestimated by many people (including the French) people felt that they were still dealing with a disorganized and irresolute character. When the French Ambassador comes to talk to Henry about his claim to the French lands, he says:

The prince our master
Says that you savour too much of your youth,
And bids you be advised that there's nought in France
That can be with a nimble galliard won;
You cannot revel into dukedoms there.

In other words, the French prince scoffs at Henry's claim by saying that you can't win lands by dancing and revelling, which is all they think Henry is good at. Like so many people whose past goes before them, Henry is seen still as the ineffective '*laissez-faire*' character of his past. Like many an aspiring IT manager, Henry has a stereotype to deal with.

One of the themes of the story, then, is how Henry capitalized on his poor reputation. The 'enemy' underestimated his leadership abilities, and allowed Henry to succeed. However, in order to capitalize on this underestimation, Henry did have to call upon some significant strengths and qualities.

These strengths and qualities are in stark contrast to the elements of the reputation others had of him. Leadership is often acquired only by breaking out of the straightjacket of our former personae.

Henry V and the key qualities of leadership

The following eight characteristics which Henry demonstrate are simply one way of 'mapping' the territory called leadership. This is not a definitive or even a better list than many others in the literature on leadership. But we believe it is as good as any other in helping the aspiring streetwise IT manager to consider their own talents in comparison to a surviving role model.

Ambition

Many writers argue that one of the most significant common factors in successful leaders is ambition. People of all styles, backgrounds and temperaments become successful leaders. Some are intelligent, some relatively slow. Some are charming, others, ruthless. The common factor seems to be their strong desire to be a leader. The key lesson seems to be that, if you really want to be a leader, then you can be so; but if you are half-hearted about it, no amount of skill or training will compensate for this lack of drive and ambition.

Successful leaders share a hunger – for leadership itself, for power, or for some other goal. For Henry V:

...if it is a sin to covet honour,
I am the most offending soul alive,

Henry's ambition was for honour; but, like many leaders, he wanted people to remember what he does:

Either our history shall with full mouth
Speak fully of our acts, or else our grave,
Like Turkish mute, shall have a tongueless mouth,
Not worshipp'd with a waxen epitaph.

You can't be a leader in secret. Leadership means having the ambition to be seen, recognized, and visible enough to be shot at. And because high visibility does seem to bring with it the potential for jealousy and enmity, the second attribute or quality of leadership is almost a catch-all; you need to be multi-talented.

Multi-talented

Henry's apparently misspent youth was a 'cover' for some surreptitious learning. Somehow or other, Henry acquired at the same time, as the Archbishop of Canterbury tells us early in the play, excellence in the arts of divinity, politics, the theory of warfare, the law and rhetoric. In other words, he can hold his own in debates on most subjects.

Becoming streetwise depends upon building a reputation for such multi-faceted competence. You'll have to build networks, comprising people from a whole range of disciplines and backgrounds. You won't have to engage with the finance director in the minute details of finance, but you will be expected to talk broadly about financial affairs. Your fellow senior business leaders will debate widely on politics, on economics and on international affairs. Like Henry, you'll have to pitch in with them and appear to be very well versed in each of these subjects. You cannot become streetwise on IT stories and expertise alone.

Breaking with the past

Leadership is about changing things. If most of the play of Henry V is about re-establishing the 'rightful' order of things, Henry's later activities speak of change. This is symbolized in his courtship of Princess Katherine. In itself, the courtship is a political act, designed to bring together the warring houses of England and France. But there is a personal touch to it, too. When Katherine shies away from Henry's attempt at a kiss, because it is not the done thing for French girls to accept kisses before marriage, he responds:

> *O Kate, nice customs curtsy to great kings. Dear Kate, you and I cannot be confined within the weak list of a country's fashion: we are the makers of manners.*

The phrases, 'customs curtsy to great kings' and 'we are the makers of manners' are typically succinct Shakespearean ways of explaining that leadership is about challenging existing ways of doing things rather than simply following the traditions; and that one of the roles of a leader is to create the 'manners' (or culture) which their countries or organizations will follow.

As you take on more and more of the mantle of leadership, you'll find yourself questioning not only the obvious – the systems and processes – but also the very fabric of your organization. 'Culture change', so often a glib term for the introduction of a few new rules or practices, is all about changing deeply embedded 'customs' and 'manners'. Such changes will threaten many people, including and especially those who feel that these changes are bring imposed upon them – the 'common people' or the rank and file staff of your organization.

Empathy

Having banged on so much about empathy in Chapter 25, it's not surprising that we'd bring it into the list of critical success factors for effective leadership. Henry demonstrates his empathy in part by going among the troops incognito, and talking to them as equals. Before the major battle of the play, Henry meets up with the troops and hears what they have to say about their king. It's an early form of 360° feedback in action.

Truly effective empathy implies humility. Good leaders recognize the need to maintain their links with the people at the grass roots. Like many modern leaders, Henry chose to seek opinions from the troops. His earlier life among the 'common people' would have given him the ability to mingle with them unnoticed on the eve of the battle. And he listened to their very real concerns.

One of the main reasons for needing this aspect of leadership is that, as we shall show later, one of the key jobs of a leader is to lead. To be successful, people have to follow. But people will have concerns, they will be nervous, they may fear change and the threats it implies. Good leaders get to know these concerns directly from those who have them. When the time comes to get people to follow, being well-versed in their concerns will give you at least a fighting chance of knowing how to deal with them.

This is not just about fact gathering. Personal involvement means giving you the opportunity to know, to understand, to feel and to share their concerns. It also shows a commitment to your people as people. And it lays the foundations for the trust in you that they will need if they are to let go and follow.

Reflection and self-awareness

One of the things that Henry V does in the play is to take himself off somewhere quiet and reflect on what he has heard from the troops. He needed time to weigh up what he had heard against his own perceptions, fears, aspirations and ambitions. Before drawing up his plan or his vision, he needed to be sure of his ground. And this means being sure about strategy, about tactics, and about values and beliefs.

It also means being sure about motivation, the third element of emotional intelligence. As Henry notes in his self-reflecting before the battle of Agincourt, the responsibilities of leadership are significant, compared to the relatively trouble-free existence of the foot soldier.

If you like the style of Shakespeare, you might like, every now and again, to read through this part of Henry's soliloquy:

And what have kings, that privates have not too,
Save ceremony, save general ceremony?
And what art thou, thou idol ceremony?
What kind of god art thou, that suffer'st more
Of mortal griefs than do thy worshippers?
What are thy rents? What are thy comings in?

O ceremony, show me but thy worth!
What is thy soul of adoration?
Art thou aught else but place, degree, and form,
Creating awe and fear in other men?
Wherein thou art less happy being fear'd,
Than they in fearing.
What drink'st thou oft, instead of homage sweet,
But poison'd flattery? O, be sick, great greatness,
And bid thy ceremony give thee cure!
Think'st thou the fiery fever will go out
With titles blown from adulation?
Will it give place to flexure and low bending?
Can'st thou, when thou command'st the beggar's knee,
Command the health of it? No, thou proud dream,
That play'd so subtly with a king's repose.

As Henry says, leadership is not about glamour. It can be about ceremony, flattery, fear and the constant realization that leaders are mortal and limited in their power. The speech helps maintain a sense of perspective and humility.

Vision

Many writers on leadership start their lists of leadership qualities with vision, and we can see why, because it is so important. But Henry V helps us to remember that, for a vision to have a chance of becoming reality, it needs to be grounded.

We have built towards vision via ambition, capability, breaking with the past, empathy and self-awareness. A good leader needs to want to lead, and have the basic skills of networking with potential allies. They also need to recognize what needs to change, and what such change may mean to those upon whom change will impinge the most. And they need to be able to step back and reflect and review before creating a vision which may be flawed.

Henry's vision was born of what he saw was an injustice – the annexation of what were legitimately English lands by the French king. With the benefit of hindsight, and a more liberal culture, we may find Henry's willingness to wage war with France over what, on our maps, is clearly France, unnecessarily barbarous. But the sensitivities of our age are recently acquired, and were not part of the spirit either of Henry's age, nor of Shakespeare's.

Despite this, the early part of the play does focus on Henry's apparent desire to validate his legal claim to the lands before he sets out to press that claim. His vision was, in the terms of the England of the time, 'squeaky clean'.

The legitimacy of the vision carried with it the need for steely determination on his own part:

Now we are well resolved: and by God's help,
And yours, the noble sinews of our power,
France being ours, we'll bend it to our awe.

Your own vision is likely to be very different from this. But it may well contain some strong similarities to Henry's. Your vision for your organization may well consist of a strong competitive element, especially in these times of outsourcing and volatile markets. Your equivalent of Henry's enemy may be organizations seeking to take over your IT services; they may be competitors of your parent company; or they may be internal competitors seeking to turn back the tide of IT, against what you see as being in the best interests of your organization.

Like Henry, however, before you commit yourself to your vision, and before you, therefore, ask any of your staff to follow you, be very sure that this is what you believe in.

Courage

Organizational politics and the competitive market-place both ensure that leaders will not get an easy ride. You will not overcome politics by becoming streetwise, but you may be able to be clearer how to deal with them. You will always have enemies, no matter how compelling your vision.

Sometimes you will have to take difficult decisions. In Henry V, we see the need for some very uncomfortable decisions. Sometimes, if the vision is compelling enough, and the resistance sufficiently threatening, you may, similarly, have to be apparently ruthless.

In the play, for example, Henry finds out that there is a plot against him. His concern is not for himself:

Touching our person, seek we no revenge:
But we our kingdom's safety must so tender
Whose ruin you have sought, that to her laws
We do deliver you.

But he recognizes the threat posed by the conspirators to a greater good – that of the country. He 'delivers them' to the laws of that kingdom – laws which impose the death penalty on traitors.

Henry has to take a similar act with prisoners at the battle of Agincourt, fired on by the risks these prisoners pose to the safety of his men when there is a chance that the enemy will catch Henry's army by surprise. Such acts of 'downsizing' in the interests of the many are among the most difficult acts a leader has to undertake. What makes them more difficult is that it is the leader's decision, not a decision imposed from above, or from the HR department. It is an act of complete responsibility. That takes courage.

Inspiration

There are no right answers. Henry's cause, and Henry's methods are all questionable; indeed, he had plenty of moments of self-doubt, as all leaders do. But he kept those moments to himself. Whether he was 'right' or 'wrong' is as debatable as the decisions and actions of any leader. Leaders are no more right than anyone else. They succeed because they inspire enough people to believe they are right.

The final, but probably most important quality is inspiration. And this is the quality for which Henry V (the character in Shakespeare's play, at least) will be remembered. When he rallies the troops at the first battle in the play with the lines:

Once more unto the breach, dear friends, once more;
Or close the wall up with our English dead.

He utters lines which will be repeated time and again by leaders in hundreds of different contexts.

During the play, Henry has two major issues to deal with which require inspirational responses, both of them battles.

The first battle is the siege of Harfleur. The crisis is one which is analogous to one faced by many an IT manager – his troops were weary of the battle and wished themselves to be elsewhere:

Would I were in an ale-house in London!
I would give all my fame for a pot of ale and safety!

So Henry's challenge is to make the troops want to press on, to inspire them with a cause which will replace visions of the pub with other, more focused and helpful visions. In his speech, he alludes to the need to change behaviour when there is work to be done:

In peace there's nothing so becomes a man
As modest stillness, and humility;
But when the blast of war blows in our ears,
Then imitate the action of the tiger;
Stiffen the sinews, summon up the blood...

The analogy continues for many more lines. In their mind's eye, the troops are transformed, and have strength and spirit to press on. So they have the strength, now they need the cause. Henry reminds them of past English successes, won by their fathers (bringing family and pride into the equation). He then suggests that these troops can become role models, and 'teach them how to war'.

Finally, he creates a sense of collective and shared brotherhood and responsibility in defence of those icons which stand for the troops' deepest values:

> *For there is none of you so mean and base,*
> *That hath not noble lustre in your eyes.*
> *I see you stand like greyhounds in the slips,*
> *Straining upon the start. The game's afoot:*
> *Follow you spirit, and upon this charge*
> *Cry 'God for Harry! England! And St. George!'*

This frequent use of analogy is a key to the inspirational success of good leaders. By painting these impassioned word-pictures, leaders tap into the emotional, right-brained aspects of the personalities of their people. This is where followers will be harnessed, not in dry, logical, well-reasoned and statistically accurate 'business cases'.

To make the point even more strongly, let's look in more detail at the apex of Henry's inspirational work with his troops, before the battle of Agincourt.

The situation here is even more critical than at Harfleur: the English forces are heavily outnumbered, and it looks likely that the battle will be lost. As with many IT projects, the main complaint from the troops and 'managers' is that they have not enough resources. One of the 'project leaders' (the Earl of Westmoreland) says he wishes that they had even one more of the thousands of English men who were back at home, echoing a sentiment felt, no doubt, by most if not all of those involved.

So here is Henry facing an almost certain failure, but with a project which is of absolutely top priority. Some IT projects are called 'strategic', some 'mission critical'. This is the kind of project which Henry was leading at Agincourt. A project soon to be completed, and one for which there was absolutely no chance of getting more resources than the woefully inadequate numbers that they already had.

This is where inspiration takes over. Henry realizes that morale is in need of a major boost, but this cannot be achieved by the promise of more people. Far from it, his inspiration is to call for *fewer* people!

No, my fair cousin:
If we are mark'd to die, we are enow
To do our country loss; and if to live,
The fewer men, the greater the share of honour.
God's will! I pray thee, wish not one man more.

This is the start of the famous St Crispin's Day speech, in which Henry's successful aim is to make the people around him proud to be a part of what's taking place. He suggests that anyone in their number who does not want to stay should be helped on their way home, because, although the risks may be great, Henry's genius is not to dwell on them, but to focus on the rewards.

Let's look at his speech in six separate sections:

This day is call'd the feast of Crispian:
He that outlives this day, and comes safe home,
Will stand a tip-toe when this day is named,
And rouse him at the name of Crispian,

He starts by focusing on the name of the day – the feast of St Crispian. This gives him a reference point, because he is going to make this day the centrepiece of the inspirational idea. St Crispian's day may, up to now, be a relatively insignificant feast day. Henry is going to suggest elevating it to a major day to remember.

He that shall live this day, and sees old age,
Will yearly on the vigil feast his neighbours,
And say, 'Tomorrow is Saint Crispian':
Then he will strip his sleeve, and show his scars,
And say 'These wounds I had on Crispin's day.'

Henry now looks way beyond the battle and to the long-term. He that sees old age, he says, will have something proud to show – his scars, and he will look forward, each year, to the chance to roll up his sleeve to show them off.

Old men forget; yet all shall be forgot,
But he'll remember with advantages
What feats he did that day; then shall our names,
Familiar in his mouth as household words,
Harry the King, Bedford and Exeter,
Warwick and Talbot, Salisbury and Gloucester,
Be in their flowing cups freshly remember'd.

Whereas most things fade from memory, anyone who looks back on his involvement in this project will remember *with advantages;* in other words, he will be able, without contradiction, to elaborate as much as he likes how well he performed. His name will be associated with the other famous names. Over a few drinks, he'll be able to recall the glory, and equate himself with kings and lords.

This story shall the good man teach his son;
And Crispin Crispian shall ne'er go by,
From this day to the ending of the world,
But we in it shall be remembered:

So memorable will the story be that, as each generation retells it to the next, each family will make their own ancestor 'immortal'. Rather than being likely to die in the battle, each soldier is now being encouraged to think about his own future, and that of his proud children and grandchildren for generations to come. And now the greatest stroke of genius:

We few, we happy few, we band of brothers;
For he to-day that sheds his blood with me,
Shall be my brother; be he ne'er so vile,
This day shall gentle his condition;

Henry turns the small numbers to advantage. There are so few people who will be able to make these claims – a 'happy few'. This select band of people are to be Henry's 'brothers', and, through their involvement in the project, become ennobled ('gentle his condition'). The options are clear – whatever the personal outcome, you'll be remembered as a hero, and as the 'brother' of the king.

And what is more, anyone not here to share in this experience will be the losers:

And gentlemen in England now a-bed
Shall think themselves accursed they were not here,
And hold their manhoods cheap, whiles any speaks
That fought with us upon Saint Crispin's day.

This final piece of the jigsaw turns the entire situation on its head. We're the lucky ones; those who are not here to share in the glory will be kicking themselves for not being part of the team, year after year.

Try achieving this level of passion and commitment through an e-mail!

Becoming streetwise, and taking on the mantle of leadership will not involve you in having to inspire soldiers to go into battle. IT projects, change projects and strategy implementation are all 'mundane' compared to the 'glory' of the battle of Agincourt. But for the soldiers of the time, the threats were far more dangerous than those faced by those who you would lead. At least none of your people is likely to emerge from a major project as a headless corpse.

The principles and practice of inspiration as practised by Henry V through Shakespeare's words are as pertinent to you as they were to Henry centuries ago. Vision, passion, commitment, and the imaginative use of analogy, turning disadvantage to advantage are all still firmly in use by good leaders of today.

Breaking through

One of the most fascinating features of this story of leadership is the way in which an unpromising beginning led to supreme success. No matter how far a journey towards successful leadership you may see before you, it can be achieved. If you discover through the self-examinations of the previous chapter and the next two, that this is where you truly want to be, that leadership is what you truly aspire to, then, like Henry,

Be assured, you'll find a difference
As we his subjects have in wonder found,
Between the promise of his greener days
And these he masters now.

28 The front row of the grid

For a senior IT manager, becoming streetwise is a question of balance. From the point of view of the technical service which your department delivers to the business, you have issues around excellence in technical competence and problem solving. But, as we have suggested many times throughout this book, people's perceptions of the quality of that service are going to be coloured by how they feel about you and your staff.

And that is why you need, at the same time, to focus on the human interactions between you (and your staff) and the business. In Chapter 14 we referred to a balance between a more traditional 'technical' orientation and one which focused in addition upon managing people's perceptions of your reputation as well. This balance is summarized in Figure 28.1.

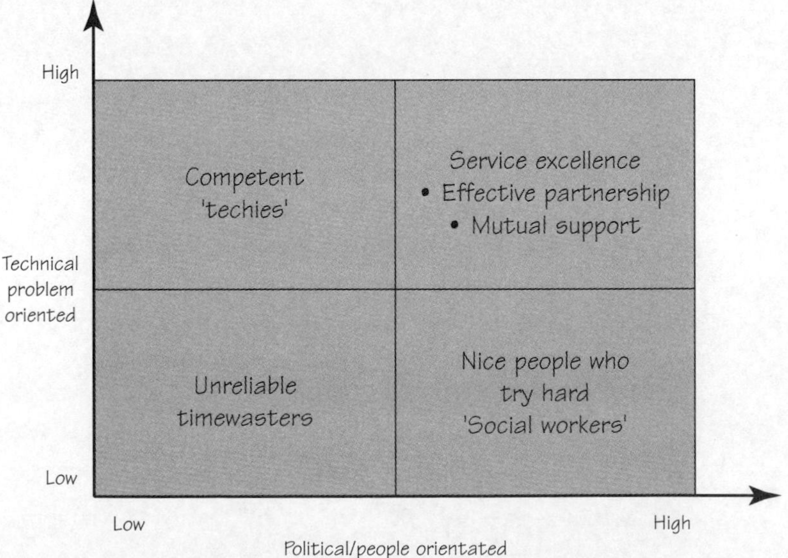

Figure 28.1 Technical excellence is not enough

The demands placed upon you are both technical and personal. The job of the senior IT manager is not easy.

Balancing is not easy

For many failed senior IT managers, whether called CIO or IT director, there remains a bitterness and bewilderment. One is quoted as saying, 'The perception of the function's performance, as opposed to the reality, was a problem'. By now, we hope that you can see the flaw in that view: there is no 'reality' concerning the function's performance, apart from the perception. This failed CIO continued to believe in the 'reality' of performance figures instead of the 'reality' of the business's perceptions. He was not streetwise.

Another failed CIO is quoted as saying: 'I do not like politics. I'm intolerant of slow people…if only things had been more rational'. Another senior IT manager failing to even attempt to become streetwise.

There is a fair amount of research evidence to suggest that the most senior IT person is more likely to lose their job than most of their business peers. Throughout this book, we have been suggesting ways of avoiding a similar fate, and focusing upon the arts of being streetwise – of being business as well as technically oriented, and of confronting organizational politics head on, as a necessary feature of organizational life, and of the responsibilities of a senior manager.

Achieving the balance is not easy. Some writers suggest that the job of the most senior IT person is the most difficult job on the board. However true this may be, it is certain that the demands are greater than they may be on other positions.

This is why you have to sort out in your own mind how much you can do by yourself, and how much you need to get from your staff, your colleagues and from others.

Winning Formula 1 races (often only achieved if you start at the front row of the grid) depends a great deal on the individual skills and qualities of the driver. But behind every Formula 1 world champion there lies a large and complex team of supporters to create for you the right 'machinery' and support you during an event. Think of yourself as the driver, and consider how you are going to ensure that your (hidden) team are going to get you to the front row of the grid.

What it takes

When a Formula 1 driver comes into the pits, he doesn't leap out of the driving seat and refuel the car himself. He trusts the team to do their job. It's this kind of trust in others, letting go of direct action and focusing on your own job, that many senior IT people find so hard. Letting go is a positive act, which send out signals to those your are delegating to, 'I trust you and respect your capabilities, without my having to lean over your shoulder and check you're doing things my way'.

Mutual trust, publicly demonstrated, can have enormous benefits. In their book on *corporate cultures*, (*The Rites and Rituals of Corporate Life*, Penguin, 1982), authors Deal and Kennedy tell of the power of mutual trust. Two junior officers in the Dutch Navy made an agreement that, on every social occasion they found themselves at, each would sing the praises of the other. They appeared to have no ulterior motive for speaking well of the other, and this had a significant effect, revealed only when they were both made admirals – the two youngest admirals ever appointed in the Dutch Navy.

This is a good illustration of how reputations are formed. Although what we do and how competently we do it is enormously important, these only contribute to our reputation when people 'evaluate' them. Our own evaluations may not count for much, as we have a vested interest in positive self-evaluation; but if someone else, especially someone with no 'axe to grind' praises highly what we do, our reputation is enhanced.

One reason for this is that most people have an unconscious respect for those who see good in others. Superficially we may want to dismiss their opinions, especially if those opinions conflict with our own. But these people's apparent selflessness, as manifested in their willingness to praise others for no return, makes us suspect that they may do the same for us when we're not around. We'll trust such selfless people more than those who we suspect will say bad things about us behind our backs. This, in itself, is 'reputation enhancing' for the people who praise others, as the Dutch Admirals discovered. Their promotions were the fruits not only of the good things each said about each other, but also of the positive impressions they created for themselves.

For some purists, this may even now seem a little suspect. You may still be wondering if these two people 'really were' good at the job, or weren't they cheating just a bit?

In the eyes of everyone whose opinion counts, these two people were suitable material for promotion and seniority. There is no 'objective' reality 'out there' against which to measure 'the truth'. In all things human, the truth is what people make it. These two Admirals demonstrated the power of perceptions, reputation and the value of letting go – of having faith and trust in others.

The role of other people

You can't build your own reputation, others have to do that for you. Your part in this process is to provide them with both the motivation to develop a positive image of you, and the evidence to support that view.

The first part is new for many IT people. In their naïve view, how people see them is unimportant (I don't care what other people think of me', they say, proudly, demonstrating their independence). But for the streetwise IT manager, how other people see you is vital. And one sure way of helping yourself be viewed positively by others is to do what the Dutch Admirals did – be positive about others.

Celebrating the positive attributes of others, and proactively seeking opportunities to talk about those positive attributes may not come easily. For some, it is difficult because they unconsciously compete the whole time – saying something good about another feels like losing because it's not about 'me'. For others, it seems suspicious – what's the payback being looked for here? The implication is that there must be a quid pro quo here. Indeed, maybe there is – as with the Dutch Admirals.

The payback, however, does not have to be a venal like-for-like barter. The payback is more likely to come in the form of a growing tendency on the part of people who know you to see the positive side of you, just as you are seeing the positive sides of others.

This is the long-term payback from networking. Your visibility is enhanced, and the reputation which goes with it has a tendency towards the positive, because it is coloured by the ways in which you deal with the reputations of others. By giving something back at the personal level, you are feeding and nurturing the network of support which everyone at the most senior levels needs.

The final hurdle

There's just one more hurdle to get over. But it's the hardest of them all. If you are going to break through to becoming fully streetwise, and capitalize on the ideas we have presented in this book, you'll have to undertake the hardest job of all. And that is to stop being an IT manager, surrounded by staff, peers, colleagues and bosses, and start to rethink all this as a person, surrounded by people not roles.

And that's what the last chapter in this part of the book is all about – real people, not managers.

29 Where am I going?

For many IT managers, organizational life is a bizarre game. Normal, healthy, well-rounded human beings leave their personalities at the door as they enter their offices, and start to act out the role of 'manager'. It is not uncommon for many IT managers to openly admit that they are 'very different' at home and at work. It is part of the fabric of modern corporate life, it seems, that a managerial 'role' at work can be almost diametrically opposed to the 'self' at home.

So deeply ingrained has this managerial role-playing become for some people that they do not even notice they are doing it. The behaviours associated with the role at work can become embedded so far that they bring the role home with them, causing stress and anxiety at home. Managers can become 'defined' by their work role, and lose the ability to gain self-esteem and a sense of identity from anywhere else than their work, performing their role. People 'become' managers.

Embedded within the mindset which this attitude creates is the assumption that the only right way to be within an organization is committed to the rational goals of that organization. Every manager's primary response to being part of the organization needs to be a repression of personal needs for the greater good of the organization.

Hence the split between role and person. For the naïve IT manager, it is 'wrong' to have personal agendas; it is 'right' to devote body and soul to the organization. Working long hours, seeking at all times the 'best' technical solution for the organization, the stereotypical IT manager is the epitome of the manager who leaves their self at the door when entering work. This is often confused with 'professionalism'.

Personal agendas/hidden agendas

If you completed the exercise we provided for you in Chapter 26, or if you already have a clear picture of your personal vision and values, then you have a personal agenda. You may have already started to reflect on how closely your role as a senior IT manager helps or hinders the pursuit of your personal agenda. It may well be that, like many others, there is a gap. You will rationalize that gap by saying that circumstances force you to compromise, that, in time, you will be free to pursue your agenda – but not yet.

We'll come back to that soon. But first, let's consider that personal agenda.

Although you may feel that your job does not fully support what you want from life, there's a strong chance that your personal agenda is influencing what you do. For example, one of your key values may be fairness – this will no doubt be a key influence on how you deal with your staff. It may be so clear an influence that everyone around you knows about your belief in fairness.

But not all these influences will be so obvious. For many IT managers, the visions and values exercises are a revelation to themselves even. In other words their personal agendas were so personal that they did not even realize themselves what they were. Even those for whom the exercises simply confirm what they supposed, they had not previously articulated their personal agendas in this way.

For these people, then, these personal agendas are (at least in part) 'hidden', especially from other people. Indeed, we believe that almost everyone's personal agendas are hidden from their colleagues. This is not a deliberate act of secrecy or dishonesty. It's simply the nature of the kinds of relationships which we have at work. In some senses, it would be inefficient to try to make each and every element of our personal agendas available to everyone with whom we work. It is almost impossible to imagine organizational life in which there were no hidden agendas (or parts of agendas).

So you, like everyone else at work, have a hidden agenda. It is not sinister. It is just a fact of organizational life.

Hidden agendas – suppressed or unnoticed?

How much we hide our personal agendas from others at work depends upon a whole lot of factors. Some people, for example, feel strongly that work should not intrude on any aspect of their 'private' life or time.

Like Martin's member of staff, they draw up boundaries around their 'work time' and their 'personal time'.

In the dark days of the industrial revolution, survival and some semblance of mental well-being legitimated this kind of response. Life in the 'dark satanic mills' was inhuman, people had few (if any) choices, and any means of staving off the predations of greedy mill-owners was seized by workers with understandable alacrity.

However, for most knowledge workers in most of today's organizations, such self-protection should not be necessary. In fact, it can be self-defeating.

IT people are often clever, intelligent folk who get a great deal of their self-image from their work. Yet some of them seem to resent the idea that work plays such a significant part in their self-identity. In consequence, they build artificial barriers, like Martin's staff member, between role and person. In effect they say to the organization, 'You own me in my role as worker during working hours, but not when I have the right to eat lunch or drink coffee'. During these times, the role is cast off, and the 'person' re-emerges.

The converse is just as dangerous. This is the 'workaholic' IT manager, who gradually loses their sense of identity beyond the work role. More and more of their time and energy are devoted to the job, as though nothing else in life mattered. In times of economic uncertainty and 'downsizing' this phenomenon may be rationalized as protecting a person's job. But more importantly, we believe, it is a willingness on the part of some IT managers to take the 'easier' route, and let 'organizations' take the blame for burn-out, rather than face the responsibility of taking charge of their own lives.

One of the key problems with this 'person versus role' model is that a role is significantly less complex than each of us is as a person. A role is a shallow, hollow one-dimensional caricature of a person. It has no aspirations, few complexities, little subtlety, and its 'values' (if such they be) are a simplified version of the 'values' of the organization. There is little humanity in roles. (Nor in the 'competencies' which many organizations are now using to define those roles.)

Roles dehumanize us. The military have known this for centuries, and have deliberately used a whole range of reinforcements to create the separation: uniforms, hierarchies, drill and salutes all serve to turn a human being into a 'soldier'. This may have some validity in times of war; it is a questionable practice for organizations which provide the place in which many of us spend the majority of our waking lives.

So how far have you colluded in turning yourself into a 'soldier' within your organization, suppressing your personal agenda, and becoming your role instead of preserving your identity? Your personal agenda must drive your life, not be suppressed (however temporarily) while you turn up on parade and lose sight of who you are and what you want.

The 'rational organization' is a falsehood

Successful people pursue their personal agendas. They do not suppress them for the sake of the organization. Clearly, the most successful people are those who can create an environment in which their own agendas and those of their organizations are in alignment. But for most of these successful people, their personal agendas come first. There is nothing sinister or wrong with this. It is naïve to believe that you will be taken seriously as a senior manager (to be seen as streetwise) if you continue to operate as though there were some kind of merit in denying your identity for the sake of the 'rational goals' of the organization.

Organizations do not have goals; people do. The 'goals' of organizations are shorthand, edited versions of the overt and covert agendas of the powerful people within them. One way to test this out on your own organization is to ask yourself how much you 'buy into' its 'goals'. If you do, ask yourself why; and keep doing it, just like in the 'visions' exercise in Chapter 26. If, for example, one of the 'goals' of your organization is to become market leader in their industry, ask yourself how much you *personally* (not as an employee of the organization) support and buy into this 'goal'. If you were employed by a competitor organization, would you similarly buy into this 'goal'?

The gregarious nature of human beings enables us to 'pretend' that we are driven by the 'goals' of the groups we belong to. This has been of great evolutionary value to the growth and development of human societies. But it does have the disadvantage that it makes us forget, sometimes, that few of us were born into our lives with the destiny of committing ourselves, heart and soul, to 'XYZ Corporation'. To the extent that XYZ Corporation is a good place to pursue our personal goals, then stay with it. But if XYZ Corporation overshadows your personal agenda, you may have strayed across the boundary from person to role.

People's goals are all about what they want from life – their visions and values. While you put the organization first, you operate as a middle manager. To become streetwise, you need to share in the responsibility for defining and setting the agenda for the organization. And to do this well, you need to be able to be clear about what you want, where you want to go, and the extent to which your current organization is the right stage upon which to act out this story. It is a personal story, but, like all personal stories, there are other players, too.

Your story has many players

Your life story is unique. It has many parallels with other stories. Your archetypal drivers will significantly influence the kind of story it is. It may be an adventure, full of discovery; it may be a story of struggle against adversity; it may be a story of the creation of something lasting and worthwhile. But it will be different from anyone else's story because the players will be unique.

You are not the only player in your story. From your point of view, you remain the central character, so knowing who you are and what you want are crucial. But there are so many other characters, all acting out their own stories at the same time, that you can never 'write the script'.

Make plans, by all means; be clear about what you want and believe in, of course. But, above all, be prepared to have both the courage to lead (by using your organization as a vehicle for the pursuit of your personal vision), and the humility to play a supporting role in the dramas of others.

And what is more, these players are people, not roles. And, no matter how important technology may appear to become, it should always be subservient to people, not the other way round.

So what are you – senior IT manager or person who happens to work in IT?

Becoming streetwise, in the end, is not so much about learning techniques, new ways of working, or any of those things. It is about learning what to let go of, and what to rediscover. It is about being firm in your commitments to what you want to become, while at the same time recognizing your place in a myriad of social networks.

The work you need to do to become streetwise is different from the kind of work you have had to do so far in developing your role as an IT manager. That work was technical, it allowed for 'right answers' and 'best practice'. This work is emotional work, it is about developing approaches which go against the grain of what has led to your success so far. It is dangerous, because, unless you are sure you want to go this way, you might end up weakening those skills which have got you this far, while failing to develop adequately the new skills to take you further.

If you want to stop being a senior IT manager and become a successful person who happens to have grown up through IT, then you have some serious choices to make.

Crossing the Rubicon of seniority

Being streetwise can have at least two different purposes. The first is to learn how to survive in a political context. Much of what we have written about in this book will help you do this. However, you may have decided to get streetwise because you want to get in there with the leaders, to take your 'rightful' place at the most senior levels possible.

If this is the case, and before you go ahead, stop, once more, and for the last time in this book, to ask yourself if this is really what you want. Your 'answers' from the visions and values exercise in Chapter 26 should help. But so should the following model, which we have adapted from the work of our colleagues, Andrew and Nada Kakabadse (*Essence of Leadership*, International Thomson Business Press, 1999, p. 292). The model illustrates the boundary between management and true corporate governance – what you need to transcend in order to become streetwise.

Crossing the wavy line means crossing into very different territory.

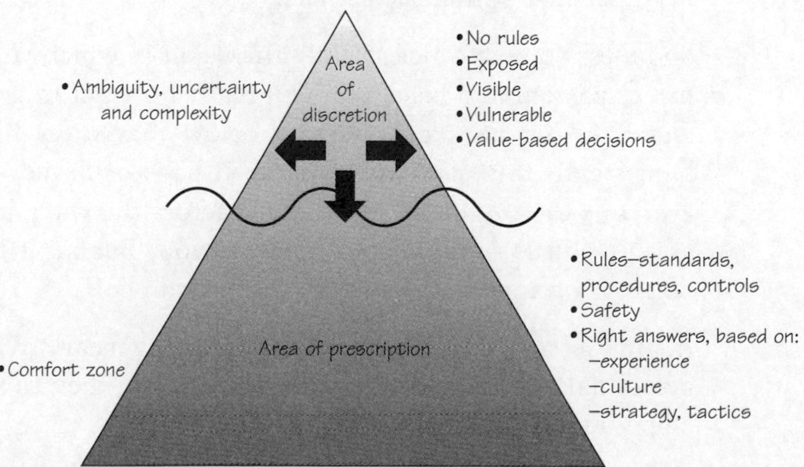

Figure 29.1 Prescription v. discretion (reproduced by kind permission of International Thomson Press)

Below the line is where *traditional management* takes place. Here, a great deal of what you do is decided for you by the rules of the organization, the culture and the instructions from the top. It is where most IT management takes place, firmly constrained by technological capabilities, budgets, 'best practice', the 'strategy' and so on. It is constrained but relatively comfortable.

Taking on the most senior roles requires moving above the wavy line into territory where you have a great deal of discretion. The world up here is ambiguous, uncertain and multi-faceted; there are few, if any rules. There are no 'right answers'. People up here are very exposed. Everyone is watching you. And all you have to go on is what you want and what you believe in. What kind of certainty can you get from that? None.

Becoming streetwise is not just about having power and authority. It is about having the courage to follow your convictions, often in the face of massive opposition and resistance. Politics is all about pitting one set of values and beliefs against another. And, unlike pitting technologies against each other, there are no benchmarks and no objective tests. There is only your ability to convince, to persuade and to influence others.

So unless you have a clear and firm vision in which you have sufficient passion and belief that you really do want to get out there and fight for, back off and stay below that wavy line, and be happy and contented with what you have achieved so far. Not everyone can or should try to move across the wavy line. We are all individuals – do what is right for you. But do it because it's what you want, not because it's all you can get.

If, after all this, you still want to get onto the mean streets of organizational politics and corporate governance, then this book will help you get started. The rest is up to you.

Part Five
Riding off into the sunset

30 You are not alone

Some of the challenges we have been writing about in this book are faced by lots of managers, not just those in IT. But others are uniquely linked to the novelties and complexities of IT management. Because IT introduces a fundamentally new dimension into organizational life, it makes it hard to be sure whether to turn for help to specialists or generalists.

Books and courses on general management often gloss over the specific challenges of managing IT. This makes it hard for IT managers to gain full benefit from them; the application of the learning requires too big an intuitive leap with no opportunity to practise in a relevant context.

But books and courses on IT management often fail to recognize the broader implications of managing at senior level, irrespective of the function or discipline you are managing. They can be very specific (and often highly prescriptive) about such areas as project management, but usually fall down on their lack of focus on the political and ambiguous nature of senior management.

We have tried in this book to unravel these intertwined themes of specialism and generalism. IT managers have a particular stereotype to confront, a set of technical challenges to sort out, and a growing potential impact on business success. We also have a particular affinity for IT managers, and have therefore deliberately restricted ourselves to writing about these issues for IT managers in particular.

A book is not the answer

It may seem a bit cheeky to leave it to the last chapter to say this, but we believe that a book is not the answer – not even this book.

In fact, this is 'the book of a course' which we run at Cranfield School of Management, that course being 'Organizational Politics and IT Management' (or OPIT for short), a one week programme which, at the time of writing, we have run ten times as a public event, and a similar number of times (in variations designed to suit local circumstances) for IT teams in individual companies. The course has been even more successful than we could have hoped.

This chapter is not an advertisement for OPIT as such, although we are aware, at present, of very few alternative sources of help for the beleaguered IT manager. Until now, the IT manager has had little alternative but to pick their way through a minefield of courses designed to solve other problems, or to go it alone. Now, you are not alone. This book, and those IT managers who have worked with us through the OPIT programmes we have run, are a force for change. The IT manager fights back.

So if a book is not enough, what's missing? The answer to that lies in our understanding of how managers learn. It is this understanding of how managers learn that we have applied to OPIT, and which, in part, has made OPIT so helpful to those who have attended it.

The learning diamond

The learning diamond is shown in Figure 30.1 and is a design tool for learning. It has its roots in the same model of the human mind we introduced in Chapter 21.

New knowledge

The left-hand quadrant deals with that part of learning which is about acquiring new knowledge. It uses the data-oriented and logical aspects of the mind which combine to focus on down-to-earth, matter-of-fact issues. If you wanted to learn about coaching, for example, you might want to start by finding out what

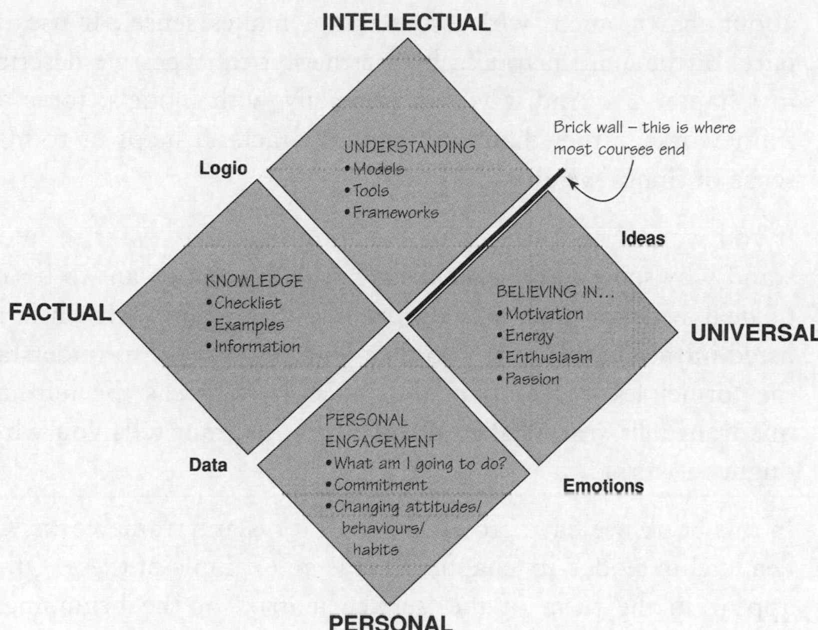

Figure 30.1 Learning diamond

coaching means, who does it, what the key steps to coaching might be, and so on.

For the IT manager who wants to become streetwise, this part of the learning process might consist of finding out what kinds of behaviour constitute 'streetwise' behaviours. It might provide checklists of what to do to be successful. We have provided some of this kind of learning throughout the book, in descriptions of leadership, for example, and in 'how to' approaches to project management.

Knowing something does not mean being able to do anything about it, so, although new knowledge may be an important part of the learning process, it is not enough by itself.

New understanding

The top quadrant of the diamond refers to the ways in which our intuition works with our logical capabilities to 'get it'. This is all about that moment which something 'makes sense'. It uses the parts of the mind favoured by the theoretical types we described in Chapter 21. And it works primarily with models, tools and frameworks, rather than with any new facts. It helps us to make sense of things we already 'know'.

If you wanted to learn about coaching, you may want to understand why some of the checklists work. You may want to be able to deal with the unexpected coaching opportunity which is not listed in the checklists. To do this, you might want to understand the 'principles' rather than the practice. Whereas the left-hand quadrant tells you what to do, the top quadrant tells you why it ought to work.

In this book, we have provided lots of tools and frameworks. Our 'leadership model' in Chapter 11 was an example of these. Others appear in the form of the 'service matrix' at the beginning of Chapter 28, and in the form of the learning diamond itself.

But even if you know what to do and why it makes sense, you may still not do anything differently.

Believing in

The right-hand quadrant represents your motivation. It asks, 'Do you really want to do anything differently?'. It doesn't tell you anything new, and doesn't explain. If it works, it enthuses you to go and do something with the learning.

If you wanted to learn about coaching, this would be the part of the learning which explores whether you deeply believe in people enough to empower them, or whether you want to become a coach rather than remain in control. Often unexplored on traditional courses because it can seem intrusive, this aspect of learning can be the most crucial. If you don't really want to be a coach, then all the knowledge and understanding in the world will not make you one. You've got to want it badly enough.

Books are not always good vehicles for this aspect of learning. When they work, they often do so through less conventional means, such as literature. In this book, we have touched on this aspect of learning, which uses the parts of the mind favoured by the idealistic types, through the Terminal One cartoons, the visions and values exercise on Chapter 26, and through our shameless borrowing of Shakespeare's *Henry V*, especially Henry's motivational speeches.

Personal engagement

The fourth stage in learning gets even more personal. It involves practical application of the knowledge, understanding and 'wanting to', and gets to grips with the habits of the past and the skills needed for the future. If you wanted to learn about coaching, this would be the part of the learning where you tried it out, and practised your skills in a relevant but safe environment.

This is hard to replicate in a book. And that's why OPIT has been so successful, because we work our way right round the learning diamond, and help people to try out the arts of being streetwise, providing developmental feedback as a key part of the learning.

Learning is interactive

Learning to become streetwise, therefore, requires more than simply reading this book. Even if you do not attend OPIT, you will need to take yourself round the diamond, and be sure that:

- You know what it means for you to be streetwise.
- You understand why some behaviours are more effective than others.
- You really want to get out there on the 'streets' with the other guys.

- You have tried out the skills and got constructive feedback which helps you do it better next time.

But be sure that you persevere.

Go and do it

If you have worked you way through the book this far, you probably know if you believe in what we have said. If you do, go and try it. The book is not enough, and we know that we have left out hundreds of ideas, models, facts and suggestions which may also have been useful.

Go and do it

In the end, it's not what's in the book, or even in your reading and interpretation of the book that will make the difference. It's what's in you. Your own route to becoming streetwise will be unique. In our experience of working with the many IT managers who have attended OPIT, or whom we know through other connections, each of us treads their own uncharted path.

If encouragement is what you seek, then take heart from the feedback we have received from OPIT 'graduates'. Each has a different story to tell.

One went back to his organization and confronted his boss straight away. He challenged his boss to admit that he had been dealing with a stereotype and not him as a person. Despite the fact that this IT manager was anything but like the stereotype, his boss had to admit that he had not seen through this mask. Six months later, our friend had been promoted to commercial director with a seat on the board.

Another went back to a problem with the help desk. Instead of trying to fix the problem, he fixed the people, and spent time listening to and understanding the concerns of the key users. His personal interest in them was enough for the news to spread throughout the organization that he had 'radically improved' the help desk service, and he was given a strategic role alongside the chief executive in the next road show across the organization.

Another returned with her completed visions and values exercise and promptly resigned from her job, realizing she had been pursuing the wrong goal. She is now much happier as a consultant.

A fourth realized during the interactions that he was his own worst enemy. Being talented and hard working, he had climbed the ladder of success relatively easily. But each promotion created more frustrations. He thought his ambitions must be outstripping his rapid rise to seniority. He realized, however, that, as an *eternal boy*, the more responsibility he got, the unhappier he became. He went back and took a sideways shift which enabled him to add value whilst remaining free from administrative concerns.

The list of stories is almost endless. Even when people come to an OPIT programme, they are often very unsure about what they want, except that they have problems and issues they would like to resolve. The key message from this book, and from OPIT, is to be sure, by going through the processes we have outlined here, and which we use interactively on OPIT, that you do address the 'right' problem. Time and again, the problems people bring with them are symptoms of a much bigger issue which will nag away at them until it is surfaced and confronted.

So as you go back to the office to deal with tomorrow's frustrations and challenges, ask yourself if you are clear about where you are going and how you are going to get there. Are the problems and issues you are facing real, or are they symptoms of a deeper challenge you have been avoiding through being very, very busy?

The streetwise IT manager

There are streetwise IT managers out there. You may be one already – or well on the way to becoming one. What characterizes the streetwise IT manager is a calmness in a storm, a certainty about their own destiny, and a thirst to learn from others. They may be busy, but not stressed and pressured. And they can always find the time to work alongside senior colleagues on an even footing, trading ideas rather than blows, and gaining respect for being a model human being first, a great senior manager second, and (if appropriate) a good IT person third.

If you started reading this book as an IT manager with a problem, and end up as a person (who happens to be in IT) with some ideas for the future, then we have done what we set out to do.

We'd love to hear from you.

Appendix: Leadership questionnaire

1a	It is important to have clear plans	☐
1b	I have provided my staff with a clear vision for the future	☐
1c	We work on tasks as they arise, rather than try to foresee the future	☐
2a	We take things on an ad hoc basis, preferring to deal with matters as they arise	☐
2b	In order to get the work done, I allocate clear areas of responsibility to each of my staff	☐
2c	I spend time with my staff ensuring that we all have a common vision for the future	☐
3a	By pulling together, we all ensure that the work gets done	☐
3b	One of my most important tasks is to motivate and energize my people	☐
3c	It is my job to 'steer the ship' and maintain control	☐
4a	In this changing world, I encourage creativity and create change within my function to anticipate the future	☐
4b	We learn by experience, and use that experience to remove the necessity for rules or routines	☐
4c	I take a systematic approach to the ongoing tasks of my function, creating routines which ensure efficient service and project delivery	☐
5a	The buck stops with me	☐
5b	Problems should be resolved or dealt with by those who create them	☐
5c	I give authority and responsibility to my staff, but always remain accountable	☐
6a	Before embarking upon activities, I spend time ensuring that my staff are committed to our chosen course of action	☐
6b	I insist on my people conforming to established standards	☐
6c	Everyone has their own best approach, with which I do not interfere	☐
7a	My people are all familiar with the terms of our SLAs, so that they can work within the appropriate contractual obligations	☐
7b	My people are so motivated that they naturally go that extra mile for the customer	☐
7c	Work patterns are relatively fluid around here; non-urgent problems rarely get to the top of the list	☐
8a	I take an interest in my people as individuals and understand what makes each of them tick	☐
8b	We tend to get on with our own work, and help each other out as and when necessary	☐

8c	My people look to me for impartiality and fair judgement in any differences of view	☐
9a	Even when we are busy, I encourage my people to consider the long-term implications of their actions	☐
9b	People work best on what interests them, so our work patterns tend to centre upon each individual's expertise	☐
9c	We are good at responding to the needs of our customers and resolving problems quickly	☐
10a	Plans and mission statements are not suitable for the way we do things around here	☐
10b	People in my function are all aware of our mission	☐
10c	Activities do not take place here without a clear plan of action	☐
11a	Everyone in my function knows their distinct area of responsibility	☐
11b	All my staff have the opportunity to contribute to our vision of the future	☐
11c	I believe in being one of the team; we all take our share of the workload	☐
12a	People often come to me with problems because they know I can solve them	☐
12b	I lead by example and am respected by my staff for my technical expertise	☐
12c	People describe me as an inspiring person	☐
13a	My staff and I get on with our jobs, and let the business get on with its work	☐
13b	Innovation is one of my most important areas of focus – and not just technological innovation!	☐
13c	It is a key part of my job to maintain equilibrium within the function	☐
14a	I help people to grow by empowering them	☐
14b	I may involve others in reviewing options, but decisions are ultimately mine to make	☐
14c	Decisions are best taken by people who are working on the relevant job; I try not to get involved	☐
15a	There's always a best way to do things, and I ensure that my people follow the rules which ensure such best practice	☐
15b	So long as my people are committed to the vision and aims of the function, I do not worry about exactly how they achieve them	☐
15c	My people are all experts in their own right; I trust them to take a professional approach at all times	☐

Question	TM-score	LS-score	LF-score
1	1a	1b	1c
2	2c	2b	2a
3	3c	3b	3a
4	4c	4a	4b
5	5a	5c	5b
6	6b	6a	6c
7	7a	7b	7c
8	8c	8a	8b
9	9c	9a	9b
10	10c	10b	10a
11	11a	11b	11c
12	12a	12c	12b
13	13c	13b	13a
14	14b	14a	14c
15	15a	15b	15c
Total			
	TM-score	LS-score	LF-score

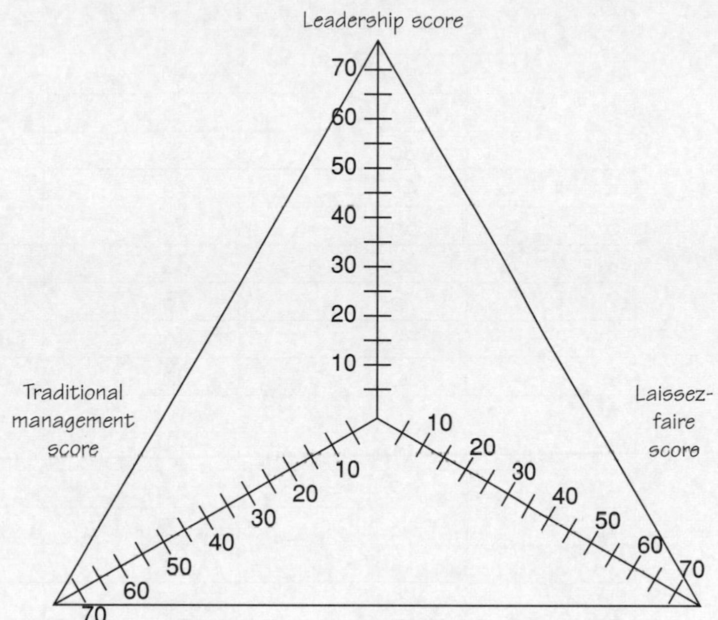

Leadership profile scoring chart

Index

Advantages, selling, 155
Advertising, image creation, 157
Agenda setting, 70–2
Amazon archetype, 247
Ambiguity, dealing with, 184–5, 209–10, 221
Ambition, in leadership style, 265
American Airlines, Sabre system, 79, 82
Applications:
  classifying, 85
  funding, 82–4
Applications portfolio, 81, 82
Archetypal drivers/archetypes, 243–56
  checking position on model, 256–7
  'chemistry', 256
  conflicts, 248, 251–3, 253–6
  key characteristics, 249, 250
  leadership and, 259–60
  masculine/feminine, 244–8, 249, 250
  sequences, 245–8
Attitudes, 134

'Being liked' personality, 222–3
Belief (learning diamond), 298–9
Benefits, selling, 155–6
Body language, use in communication, 124–5, 233
Brainstorming, 68–9
Business changes, coping with, 19
Business drivers, 148

Caring types, 193–4, 235
Cartoons:
  characters, xix–xxv
  using, 220
Chunking up, 159
Client-server technology, 47–9
Communication process, 144, 161–2
  need for human contacts, 216
Competencies required, 113–17
Competition strategy in conflict, 36
Competitive advantage, gaining, 79–80
Complaints handling, 213–14
Complexity, working with, 184–5
Compromise strategy in conflict, 36
Conflict, Between Development/ Operations, 45–8
Conflict avoidance strategy, 36
Consensus approach, Japanese, 126–7
Consultants and services, 165–6
  value propositions, 167
Consultation and stress, 211
Convergent thinking, 68, 69
Core business, defining, 84
Core values, reaffirming, 242
Corporate governance, 291
Courage, leadership style, 270–1
Cranfield School of Management, 296
Creative visualization, 230
Creativity and stress, 211–12
Critical success factors, leadership style, 264–5
Culture, organizational, *see* Organizational culture

Decision-making, right/left-brained, 191–2
Decisive lifestyle, 199–200
Definitive document, strategy, 18–19

Delegation skills, 232, 280
Department credibility, establishing, 160
Discretion, limitations, 182
Divergence approach, 210
Divergent thinking, 67–8, 69
Down-to-earth types, 193, 194, 196, 197

E-mail, 122
  defensiveness, 123
  problems, 123–4
Emotional intelligence, 224–36
Emotions:
  blocking out, 226
  following, 227
  managing, 228–9
Empathy:
  in leadership style, 267–8
  towards others, 231–4
End-user computing, 49–51
Estimating process, 26–8
  guidelines, 28–30
Eternal boy archetype, 245, 246
Expectations:
  vicious cycle, 136–7
  virtuous circle, 137–8
Extraverts, 198–9

Father archetype, 246
Features, selling, 155
Flexibility, 46–7, 49
Fuzzy thinking, 194–5

Goals, 288–9
  pursuit of, 237

Habits and stress, 211
Help desk:
  service improvements, 131–2
  stresses, 128–30
  work measurement, 87
Hetaira archetype, 246
Hidden agendas, 143–5, 285–6
Human element, importance, 128, 130

Idealistic types, 193, 196
Ideas timeline, 68
Inference:
  different levels, 140
  human ability, 179, 183
Influencing styles, 195–6
Innovation, technical, 17
Inspiration, in leadership style, 271–7
Integrity, need for, 229
Intellectual skills, 225
Internal conflict, 45–6
Interpersonal skills, 116–17
Introverts, 198–9
Intuitive leaps, 193, 220–1
Involvement, need for early, 43
Isolation, dangers, 216

Japanese, consensus approach, 126–7
Jargon, usage, 147
Judgement and stress, 211

Knowledge (learning diamond), 296–7

Laissez faire management style, 107–8
Laughter:
  benefits, 218–20
  use of cartoons, 220
Leadership profile scoring chart, 104
Leadership questionnaire, 100–3
Leadership style, 109–10, 258, 277, 280–1
  ambition factor, 265
  courage, 270–1
  critical success factors, 264–5
  culture change, 266–7
  effect of archetype, 259–60
  empathy, 267–8
  example, 261–4
  inspiration, 271–7
  multi-talented, 266
  reflection, 268
  role of others, 282
  self-awareness, 268
  vision, 269–70

Learning diamond, 296–300
Left-brained styles, 188–90, 193, 197

Marketing services, 153–4
  as manipulation, 156
  mindset approach, 154–6
  user education, 156–8
Mediatrix archetype, 247
Meeting-speak, 72
Meetings:
  achievements, 73–4, 76
  agenda setting, 70–2
  handling, 65–7
  improving, 77–8
  minutes, 74
  planning, 67
  structure, 72–3
Minutes of meetings, 74
Mission, 237–8
Mother archetype, 247
Multi-talented approach, in leadership style, 266
Mutual trust, benefits, 280

Negotiation interplay, 125–6
Non-verbal communication, 179, 233, 251

Organizational culture, 145–8
  promoting, 150
  understanding, 151
  variations, 150–1
Organizational goals, 288
Organizational politics, 4–8
  handling problems, 227
  role of meetings, 75–6
  subtleties, 210
Organizational Politics and IT Management (OPIT) programme, 296, 303
Outsourcing, 172
  partnering forms, 175–6
  planning, 173–4
  selection exercise, 174–5

Package solutions, using, 83, 84, 86
Partnering approach, 163–4
People manager role, 38
People's goals, 288–9
Perceptions:
  managing, 135–7
  right/left-brained, 190–1
Personal agendas, 285, 288
Personal engagement (learning diamond), 299
Personal goals, 289–90
Political:
  decisions, 196–7
  opinions, 134
Positive thinking, 229–30
Prescription/discretion model, 291
Price of non conformance (PONC), 89, 91
Priorities, cultural, 149–50
Problem handling, 40–1, 88–9
Profit centre, 170–1
Project failures, 42, 43
Project 'iceberg' diagram, 35
Project management, 22–3
  development, 30–3, 36–7
  estimating, 26–30
  handling problems, 35–6, 40–1
  handling uncertainty, 38–40
  planning, 24–5
  whistle-blowing, 204–7
Project plan, 24–5

Quality measurement, 133–4
Quality of service, 164–5

Recruitment, 111–12
  'cloning' process, 112–13
Relationships, suppliers and consultants, 168–9
Report writing, 55–60
  basic premises, 62–4
  purposes, 61
  for readers, 60–1
  use of jargon, 58
Right-brain, cartoon appeal, 220

Right-brained styles, 188–91, 193
Role playing, 72–3, 284, 287–8

Sage archetype, 246
SCREAM (acronym), 91
Self awareness, 225–8
  in leadership style, 268
Self management, 228–9
Senior management:
  aspirations to, 181, 181–3, 185, 186, 291–2
  effect of lopsidedness, 189
  hierarchy of needs, 131
  job advertisements, 119
  recruiting, 120–1
  self-critical ability, 221
  sense of humour, 222
  skills requirements, 117–18
Service delivery, quality perceptions, 132–3
Service level agreements (SLAs), 51–3, 87
Service orientation, 135
Service quality, 164–5
Sharing responsibilities, 33–4
Short-term horizons, 210
Single-minded approach, 210
Situation assessment, 136
Social skills, 234–5
Spontaneous lifestyle, 199–200
Stereotypes, 8–10, 13–15
  challenging, 182
  project management principles, 203–4
  rebuilding, 44
  stress levels, 212
Strategy:
  definitive document, 18–19
  developing, 16, 17
  need for, 20–1
Streetwise, becoming, 46, 290, 292, 297, 299, 303
Stress, 208–9
  indicators, 209–12
  situational causes, 214–16
Suppliers services, 165–6
  value propositions, 167
Support applications, cost-benefit analyses, 82, 84
Support function, 91

Task manager role, 38
Technical orientation/people's perceptions:
  balance, 279–80
  matrix, 278
Technical skills, 116–17
Terms of reference, 71
Theoretical types, 193
Thompsons Holidays, TOPS system, 80
Time log, weekly, 33
Traditional management style, 104–7, 292
Twin-triangles model, 53, 54

Uncertainties, handling, 38–40
Understanding (learning diamond), 297–8
User requirements, 30–1
  changing, 90, 156–8

Value measurement, 133–4
Value proposition, 166, 172, 173
  different types, 166–8
Value sets, 186–7
Values, reaffirming, 242
Values and attitudes, 134
Vicious cycle, expectations, 136–7
Virtuous circle, expectations, 137–8
Vision, 237–8
  creating, 238–42
  leadership style, 269–70

Wants and needs theory, 158
Warrior archetype, 246
Whistle-blowing, project management, 204–7
Win-win situations, 125–6, 141–2
  finding, 234
Workaholics, 287